"Alan Wilson has produced a book that focuses on solving problems based on his extensive experience in research, as a civil servant, a Vice-Chancellor and in industry. His framework provides a useful way to solve problems that commonly occur in many types of organizations."

Catherine Burke, *University of Southern California, USA*

"A timely and insightful synthesis of systems thinking and real-world leadership practice. This is a book that bridges the academic and professional divide with rare authority."

Susan Kinnear, *University of Dundee, UK*

"A fascinating reflection of a personal journey in research, education, administration, public service, and entrepreneurship. It aptly shows Wilson's managerial skill and leadership in the wide spectrum of his professional engagements throughout the years. An impactful reference for many years to come."

Professor Yee Leung, ***The University of Hong Kong*****, Hong Kong**

"Fascinating. A well-structured argument which makes the book both readable and easy to navigate."

Polly MacKenzie, ***Writer, Journalist, and Broadcaster***

Leadership and Management

Spanning a stellar career as the leader of large organisations across government, industry, and education, Sir Alan Wilson has developed a deep insight into what 'actually' works in practice through the lens of systems analysis.

Leaders and managers face daily challenges but need to articulate and communicate their objectives and plans for the longer term in a complex and rapidly changing environment. First, five key elements of the framework are demonstrated in successive chapters: systems and the 'big picture'; strategy; finance; structures; and integrating through 'making things work'. Second, the urgent challenges that translate from the global and international through to national and local scales: climate change and sustainability, security, pandemics, and social inclusion, are discussed The evolution of technology, artificial intelligence, and data science demand stronger strategies, leadership, and management across all organisations at all scales. This book responds to this need by providing international case studies, a unique framework, and references to out-of-the-box thinking that can be applied to a variety of circumstances.

Leadership and Management is a valuable resource for leaders and managers at all levels in any kind of organisation, particularly in universities, local authorities, government departments, industry, and those responsible for managing research.

Alan Wilson has had leadership and management responsibilities in universities as a Vice-Chancellor, in the civil service as Director-General for Higher Education, as CEO of the Alan Turing Institute, and in industry as a director in spin-out companies.

Leadership and Management

Learning from Experience

Alan Wilson

Routledge
Taylor & Francis Group
LONDON AND NEW YORK

First published 2026
by Routledge
4 Park Square, Milton Park, Abingdon, Oxon OX14 4RN

and by Routledge
605 Third Avenue, New York, NY 10158

Routledge is an imprint of the Taylor & Francis Group, an informa business

British Library Cataloguing-in-Publication Data
A catalogue record for this book is available from the British Library

Library of Congress Cataloging-in-Publication Data
A catalog record has been requested for this book

ISBN: 978-1-041-14159-4 (hbk)
ISBN: 978-1-041-14157-0 (pbk)
ISBN: 978-1-003-67314-9 (ebk)

DOI: 10.4324/9781003673149

Typeset in Sabon
by Taylor & Francis Books

Contents

Preface xii
Abbreviations xv

1 Core concepts 1

1.1 Into the woods 1
1.1.1 Experience 1
1.1.2 What do leaders and managers do? 2
1.1.3 The structure of the book 2
1.2 Foundations 3
1.2.1 Superconcepts 3
1.2.2 The four pillars: SSFS 3
1.3 Two new sets of building blocks: PAD and STM 5
1.4 Lessons learned: thinking things through 5

2 Pillar 1: systems and the big picture 8

2.1 Context: systems and ecosystems 8
2.2 Education 8
2.2.1 Fixing ideas: four examples 8
2.2.2 Clarity of purpose 10
2.2.3 The PAD and STM frameworks for universities 10
2.3 Government: the delivery of effective and efficient public services 11
2.3.1 Experience 11
2.3.2 Local government 11
2.3.3 Central government 1: transport 12
2.3.4 Research 13
2.3.5 Health 13

2.3.6 Central government 2: higher education 14
2.3.7 Security and defence 14
2.3.8 Central government 3: the future of cities 15
2.4 Industry: managing for profit, and beyond 16
2.4.1 Introduction 16
2.4.2 Analytics for transport engineering 16
2.4.3 Retail 17
2.4.4 Biotech 17
2.5 Research: what do we need to know? 18
2.5.1 Basic science 18
2.5.2 'Managing' research 19
2.5.3 Government funding of research 19
2.6 New challenges 23
2.6.1 Introduction 23
2.6.2 Sustainability 23
2.6.3 Health: pandemics 24
2.6.4 Security and defence 24
2.6.5 Social inclusion 24
2.6.6 Cross-cutting: technology 25
2.7 Lessons learned 25

3 Pillar 2: strategy 29

3.1 Clear thinking: stability and innovation in a volatile environment 29
3.2 Education: two examples 31
3.2.1 Universities 31
3.2.2 The Cisco formula: a 'schools' challenge and the future of HE 32
3.3 Government: education, cities, health, IT, and defence 33
3.3.1 The Department for Education and Skills (DfES) 33
3.3.2 Other government departments: the beginnings of 'joining up' 35
3.4 Industry: towards a framework 36
3.5 Research 37
3.5.1 Experience 37
3.5.2 Education research: seeking wider insights 38
3.6 Lessons learned 38

4 Pillar 3: turn every page 41

4.1 Turn every page 41
4.1.1 Following Robert Caro 41
4.1.2 Preliminaries: some principles 42
4.1.3 Where does the money come from? 43
4.1.4 Some bonuses: gifts 43
4.2 Education: how financial management can change the 'culture' 45
4.3 Government: never enough money? 46
4.4 Industry 47
4.5 Research 48
4.6 Lessons learned 49

5 Pillar 4: structures for delivery 51

5.1 Delivery principles 51
5.1.1 Structures for delivery 51
5.1.2 Basics 52
5.1.3 A note on (un)accountability 53
5.2 Education: restructuring for delivery 53
5.2.1 University 53
5.2.2 JISC 54
5.3 Government: how to be agile 55
5.3.1 Introduction 55
5.3.2 DfES 56
5.3.3 The NHS 57
5.3.4 Defence 57
5.4 Industry 58
5.4.1 What do we need to know? 58
5.4.2 GMAP Ltd 58
5.5 Research 59
5.6 Lessons learned 59

6 Integration: what works? 61

6.1 Making things work 61
6.2 Education 62
6.3 Government: ministers, civil servants, practitioners, and users 66
6.4 Industry and research 67
6.5 Lessons learned 67

7 Future challenges: radical change 70

7.1 Introduction 70

7.2 Education: building the knowledge base – universities as a key system 71

7.2.1 Universities 71

7.2.2 Education and the knowledge base 74

7.3 Joined-up government 75

7.3.1 Introduction 75

7.3.2 An example: 'levelling-up' 75

7.3.3 How to join up 79

7.4 Industry 83

7.5 Research 83

7.6 Making it work: meeting the grand challenges 85

Annex 1: Analytics 87

Annex 2: Employment and key publications 102

Annex 3: Working life: A personal memoir 105

Bibliography 158

Index 163

Preface

Les espèces qui survivent ne sont pas les plus fortes, ni les plus intelligentes, mais celles qui s'adaptent le mieux au changement.

(Christmas card from the head of a French university; translates of course to its source: Charles Darwin, *The origin of species*)

The aim of what follows is to extract from experience some principles of leadership and management deployed in a range of challenging situations: tackling complex problems. As a manager, I have been largely self-taught, but absorbing the literature. There is some *post-hoc* rationalisation in what follows as the literature has caught up with experience! I have built my argument on four pillars: systems and the big picture, strategy, finance, and structures. I hope that I have avoided the dense jargon of the management literature and that this facilitates the transfer of what has proved valuable in climbing my own learning curve.

I have been rooted in academia with research anchored in the science of cities; I have enjoyed teaching and lecturing at all levels; and I have been drawn into management. This experience has been complemented by excursions into government and industry and a broader set of management challenges. In my first ten years, I was mainly research-driven, first identifying elementary particles in bubble chamber events (Rutherford Lab, CERN); then working on mathematical and computer models of cities (Oxford); then applying the methods in the Ministry of Transport (MoT); and more broadly in the Centre for Environmental Studies (CES). These represented more or less single-focus jobs though two of them involved the beginnings of management – building the Mathematical Advisory Unit in the MoT, and as Assistant Director in CES. Early in this period, I was an active member of the Labour Party in Oxford, stood in two local elections, and in the second, I was elected as a City Councillor. That was good 'staff development' of a different kind.[1]

For the next 30 years, I was employed by the University of Leeds. Initially, as a Professor of Geography, I was very research-focused and built a substantial group, funded by research councils. After my first three years, I became Head of Department in a situation where I had to bring about a serious change in culture. I became slowly involved in university management leading to my becoming Chair of the Joint Board of the Faculties of Arts, Economic and

Social Studies and Law – about a third of the university in student number terms, always known as 'The Board of Arts', given its unwieldy title. This culminated in two years as Pro-Vice Chancellor and 13 years as Vice-Chancellor. In those 15 years, it was necessary to bring about a major restructuring and I learned a lot, sometimes in a rather hard way, about implementing significant change. Before taking on the Vice-Chancellorship, I co-founded what became a successful university spin-out company, GMAP Ltd., and that gave me some 'industrial' experience in its own terms but also brought me involvement with a range of major UK and international companies, developing their retail networks.

On leaving Leeds, I became Director-General for Higher Education in the then Department of Education and Skills (DfES). This was an opportunity to function as a senior civil servant in the heart of government – creating what was essentially a new directorate and involving wide engagement across the university sector. I left DfES to become Master of a Cambridge college, a career misjudgement on my part, and I left after a short time to return to academic life as a professor in University College London (UCL), in the Centre for Advanced Spatial Analysis (CASA). This gave me the opportunity to continue my research and to take on various non-executive roles: as Chair of the Arts and Humanities Research Council (AHRC), for example, Chair of the Home Office Science Advisory Council, and Chair of a Government Office for Science Foresight study on the future of cities.

Just over ten years after leaving Leeds, after continuing in research on cities at UCL with new research grants, I took on various roles largely involving setting up, or contributing to, new or newish organisations: the Alan Turing Institute (CEO for two years and then a Programme Director), the Ada Lovelace Institute (Executive Chair), the Institute of Finance and Technology in UCL (Director of Research), and the London Interdisciplinary School (also Director of Research).

As I have approached new challenges, I have evolved a set of key concepts which have helped me to devise strategies and ways of implementing them. These have become core elements of my intellectual toolkit and I offer these in the hope that others might find them valuable supplements to theirs. This is written in the spirit of my earlier books – *Knowledge Power* (Wilson, 2010a) and *Being Interdisciplinary* (Wilson, 2023): seeking to draw out useful insights from personal experience. I hope I can assemble the elements of this toolkit into a core framework that can be widely applied. This framework is sketched in Chapter 1 through the four 'pillars': systems and the big picture, strategy, finance, and structures. These are explored in turn in the following four chapters, each illustrated from my experience in education, government, industry, and research. Chapter 6 integrates the pillars through 'making things work'.

In Chapter 7, I look ahead, seeking to apply the framework to the future. I am conscious as I write now, that there are urgent challenges that translate from the global and international through to national and local scales: climate change and sustainability, security, pandemics, and social inclusion, are primary examples. A cross-cutting theme that impacts all of these and more is the evolution of technology which has determined much of historical change and is now accelerating, not least with the impact of AI and data science. I have touched on all of these in my own work, notably on cities and social inclusion. I am aware that cities, for example, are not meeting either the sustainability or the social inclusion challenges at a desirable speed. These provide the wider context for thinking through plans and strategies, leadership and management, in all organisations at all scales. For me, this means translating what I have learned from my earlier experience into contemporary challenges. Responding to change will be a priority, ever present, but which now has a new urgency. It brings back to my mind a famous quote from *The Origin of Species*, paraphrased here: 'The species that survive are not the most brave or the most intelligent, but those that adapt most effectively to change' – brought to my attention in a French translation by a Parisian university head.

I should conclude with some acknowledgements. First, to the staff of Routledge, who have all been very helpful and excellent to work with: Rebecca Marsh for her initial enthusiasm and support; Isabel Voice and Grace Collier, who steered the book through its crucial early stages, recruited reviewers, and handled my responses; Reanna Young who took over at the production stage; Susan Dunsmore, a brilliant co-editor, always helpful and a delight to work with. And, of course, the two anonymous reviewers for their support and helpful comments. In my research career, I have had over a hundred collaborators and co-authors, and in 'management', this number increases by an order of magnitude! This makes it impossible to name everyone, but friends and colleagues will recognise where they have helped me to 'learn from experience'! The responsibilities for errors and weak arguments are mine alone, of course. One name does stand out: I thank my wife, Sarah, for love, wisdom, and support over the almost 50 years spanned by this book – including much direct help, from 'thinking things through' to speech writing! There have been very difficult work challenges at times and there were periods when we were carried along by a theme tune: Irvine Berlin's (1936), 'There may be troubles ahead … let's face the music and dance …'!!

Note

1 I had five good mentors in that period: Bill Walkinshaw and John Burren (Rutherford Lab), Christopher Foster (Oxford and MoT), Henry Chilver (CES) and Harry Cole, the Constituency Secretary of Oxford City Labour Party, who taught me a lot about basic organisational skills!

Abbreviations

AHRC	Arts and Humanities Research Council
AI	Artificial Intelligence
ASG	AI for Science and Government
BBSRC	Biology and Biochemical Sciences Research Council
BCW	Baghai, Coley, and White
BEIS	Department for Business, Energy & Industrial Strategy
BIS	Business, Innovation and Skills
BSQs	big strategic questions
CASA	Centre for Advanced Spatial Analysis
CAST	Centre for Applied Science and Technology
CBA	cost-benefit analysis
CEO	Chief Executive Officer
CERN	European Organization for Nuclear Research
CES	Centre for Environmental Studies
CoI	co-investigator
COO	Chief Operating Officer
CPD	continuing professional development
CSA	Chief Scientific Adviser
CVCP	Committee of Vice-Chancellors and Principals
DEFRA	Department for Environment, Food and Rural Affairs
DfES	Department for Education and Skills
DSAC	Defence Science Advisory Council
DSEC	Defence Science Expert Committee
DSTL	Defence Science and Technology Lab
DV	developed vetting
DWP	Department for Work and Pensions
EPSRC	Engineering and Physical Sciences Research Council
ESG	environmental, social and governance
ESRC	Economic and Social Research Council
FE	Further Education
GCHQ	Government Communications Headquarters
GCSA	Government Chief Scientific Adviser
GDP	gross domestic product

GMAP	Geographical Modelling and Planning Ltd
GMC	General Management Committee
HE	Higher Education
HEFCE	Higher Education Funding Council for England
HOSAC	Home Office Science Advisory Council
IIASA	International Institute for Applied Systems Analysis
IMD	Index of multiple deprivation
ISCF	Industrial Strategy Challenge Fund
ISTA	independent science and technology advisers
JANET	Joint Academic Network
JISC	Joint Information Systems Committee
JVA	joint venture agreement
JVU	Joint Ventures Universities
LIS	London Interdisciplinary School
LMS	London Mathematical Society
LP	Labour Party
LRF	Lloyds Register Foundation
LTUoR	Leeds Teaching Unit of Resource
LWM	Living with machines
MAU	Mathematical Advisory Unit
MHLG	Ministry of Housing and Local Government
MIT	Massachusetts Institute of Technology
MK:U	Milton Keynes University
MoD	Ministry of Defence
MoT	Ministry of Transport
MRC	Medical Research Council
MVA	Martin Voorhees Associates
NDPB	non-departmental government body
NEDC	National Economic Development Council
NERC	Natural Environment Research Council
ONS	Office for National Statistics
OR	operational research
OSCT	Office for Security and Counter-Terrorism
OU	Open University
PDA	policy, design, analysis
PQA	post-qualification admission
PS	Permanent Secretary
PVC	Pro-Vice-Chancellor
QR	Quality-related Research
RAE	Research Assessment Exercise
RSS	Royal Statistical Society
s and t	science and technology
SCORE	Science Community Representing Education
SDGs	Sustainable Development Goals
SELNEC	South East Lancashire and North East Cheshire

SIS	Science and Innovation Strategy
SLC	Student Loans Company
SMT	Senior Management Team
SPF	Strategic Priorities Fund
SRC	Science Research Council
SSFS	systems, strategy, finance, and structures
SSRC	Social Science Research Council
STEM	Science, Technology, Engineering, and Mathematics
STFC	Science and Technology Facilities Council
STM	systems, theory, method
TF	Turing Fellowship
TIL	Turing Innovations Ltd
TRC	Traffic Research Corporation
UCH	University College Hospital
UCL	University College London
UKRI	UK Research and Innovation
ULD	University Liaison Director
VC	Vice-Chancellor
VFM	value for money
WUN	World-Wide Universities Network

1 Core concepts

1.1 Into the woods

1.1.1 Experience

I have learned from experience while continually absorbing the management literature. This is reflected through the key authors who figure in my intellectual toolkit. In the jobs I have taken on, all have had major challenges at the outset: an important large university that was none-the-less rather tired and drifting; setting up a new directorate in a government department; chairing a research council; and building start-ups more or less from scratch: GMAP Ltd,[1] the Alan Turing Institute, and the Ada Lovelace Institute, are examples. This has led me to be invited to review challenges in a variety of areas: education more broadly – schools and universities – NHS complaints procedures,[2] JISC,[3] the Home Office,[4] defence,[5] and finance.[6] Throughout all this, I have been a researcher, building mathematical and computer models of cities with applications in policy and planning – both public services and commercial. Indeed, I see research as 'problem solving', and more broadly as 'tackling complex problems'; the associated skills are transferable to leadership and management.

This experience will provide my illustrations. In retrospect, they all have one thing in common: as in the title of a famous Sondheim show, I was thrown 'into the woods'. Seeing both wood and trees always demanded answers to the question: what are we for? And to seek to respond to this comprehensively. What is the big picture? What are the system's elements and their interrelationships? Very quickly, part of understanding the challenges is to recognise interdependence. Siloed thinking must be avoided: intervention in one area will usually have impacts, often unintended, in others. This led me to propose four pillars to support my argument: (1) The idea of a 'system' and 'the big picture' becomes a key starting point. Above all, if we can build that picture in the context of answering the question 'What are we for?', this provides a foundation and a focus. We can then think more conventionally of (2) building a strategy, (3) finance, and (4) organisational structures to complete the four pillars. These combine in the myriad of elements which 'make things work'.

DOI: 10.4324/9781003673149-1

1.1.2 What do leaders and managers do?

There is leadership and management at all levels: Chief Executive Officer (CEO), Division Head, or Group Leader, for example. I would also argue that each of us as individuals, anywhere in an organisation, has to manage ourselves, and so the principles of leadership and management apply here as well. If there is a distinction – there is certainly an overlap, as every manager has leadership functions – the leader has the final responsibility, and the manager implements. To make the leader's job feasible, he or she not only has to have in-depth knowledge of each of the four pillars, leading on each, but must be able to delegate to members of the team.[7] Indeed, if this is done effectively, it brings to mind an old joke: 'Question: What do leaders do? Answer: what no one else is doing!' However, perhaps what is distinctive of a good leader is inventiveness, meeting challenges, planning, and problem-solving. (If the structure is working, only the most difficult problems should be passed upward to the leader.)

An overall responsibility is 'making things work'. This demands good access to information flows, some formal, many informal. It means having a good sense of what has to be done to maintain the workings, but also to have a view of future challenges and to begin to plan to invest in a development agenda. This is a sketch of a broad agenda which will be expanded and developed more formally as the book proceeds.

1.1.3 The structure of the book

In the rest of this chapter, I begin by laying the foundations of the argument: first, an introduction to interdisciplinary thinking through superconcepts; second, the 'four pillars' – systems, strategy, finance, and structures (SSFS), integrated through 'making things work'; third, the 'systems' focus in more depth through the system of interest and its ecosystem, theory, and methods (STM) framework; fourth, policy, analysis, and design (PAD). There are five further chapters, one for each of the four pillars, one integrating through 'making things work'. Chapter 7 is future-focused, through examples which become the main foci, each explored through the four pillars working in combination.

Each chapter is illustrated through case studies which are drawn principally from education, government, research, and industry. The examples will include working in the University of Leeds, the Department for Education and Skills, GMAP Ltd, and the Alan Turing Institute. A wide range of non-executive roles will be added, along with commissioned reviews of a variety of challenges within organisations. The aim is to provide examples of where the applications of the ideas represented in the 'pillars' have made a difference. The case studies are specific, but the intention is that they illustrate the general principles and provide the basis for wider applicability and for meeting new challenges and handling change through a continually developing agenda.

1.2 Foundations

1.2.1 Superconcepts

Interdisciplinary thinking and practice are critical for leaders and managers for problem solving. The argument to be developed will be a continual drip-feed towards building the four-pillars toolkit to facilitate this thinking. The starting point is the idea of a superconcept, one that has usually been established in a particular discipline but turns out to have a much wider range of applications. As we identify these, we can add them to the toolkit. In my early research, I was able to transfer the idea of 'entropy' from physics into the social sciences as a route to building computer models of cities. The range of application of this kind of transfer has been enormously expanded and it has alerted me to look out for other examples for my own toolkit for future use. Around 15 years ago, I began to formalise this and it led to my book, *Knowledge Power* (Wilson, 2010). Some are more useful and powerful than others, of course. It is potentially invaluable for everyone in building their intellectual toolkit, to include a set of personalised-to-needs superconcepts. A first range will be introduced here through the 'four pillars' in Section 1.2.2. This is expanded in Section A1.3 of Annex 1.

1.2.2 The four pillars: SSFS

It should go without saying that a leader is expected to know the basics of management.[8] The aim here is to highlight and illustrate the distinctive nature of the leader's deployment of these by adding a problem-solving interdisciplinary toolkit. Some basic principles that have worked for me can be summarised through the four pillars – all superconcepts themselves, integrated through 'making things work'.

We consider in turn, the *system* of interest – understanding the big picture – providing focus. What are we for? What are our challenges? A clear long-term *strategy* that can be maintained in a volatile financial and policy environment. Build on this with tactics to optimise achievement in the short term. For *finance*, follow the money; understand the past, plan future budgets. Implement *structures* that deliver, both formal and informal, capable of supporting devolution, and the integration of these through making things work, being ambitious.

The foundational four pillars can be supplemented by additional superconcepts to be developed fully later.[9]

The big picture

- Define your *system of interest*; recognise *interdependence*; think about *system models*.
- Provide *requisite variety* (from Ashby,[10] developed by Beer) – what do you need to know to be effective? – in technical jargon, the levers of 'control', though that is a dangerous word for managers! Outline an *information system* (Beer[11]); start to build analytics through STM.

Strategy

- Everything under the 'big picture' is relevant and provides a starting point for strategy: what we need to know, systematically organised.
- *Markets* and clients – part of 'what are we for', that is 'who are we serving?' But handled more formally.
- Writing a *strategic plan* involves working through all the core headings; used the PAD framework.

Finance

- 'Read every line'[12] – rewriting the Robert Caro maxim.
- *Budgets.*
- *Investment, cost-benefit analysis.*
- *Management vs financial accounts.*
- *'Open' accounts.*
- Implementation of '*devolution*'.
- *Maintenance vs development.*
- *Top-down and bottom-up*: bidding mechanisms.
- *Underspends.*
- Sources of income: *philanthropy.*

Structures

- Effective structures are needed: 'strategy is 5% of the challenge, implementation is 95%.'[13]
- *Devolution* again.
- Mintzberg:[14] *front-line professionals* in management.
- Christensen:[15] handling *disruptive technologies.*
- *Maintenance vs development.*
- Michael Barber:[16] focus on *delivery.*

Integrating: making things work

- *Implementation* – responding to all the challenges.
- *Integration, interdependency.*
- Create a good workplace *culture*; have great people; a place of life-long learning, continuing professional development (CPD).
- Devolve responsibility where possible.
- Build in *accountability*; commit to openness; solve problems.
- *Teams*, SMT; leadership and management at all levels; project groups, agile deployment.
- *Experiments*: innovating and handling (technological) change, disruptive technologies.
- *Estates*, as an integrator.
- Above all, be ambitious, take on the big challenges.

The 'four pillars', with their associated superconcepts, provide the basis for the following chapters. As a preliminary in the next section, we offer a complementary approach with further superconcepts: policy, analysis and design (PAD); systems, theory and methods (SMT).

1.3 Two new sets of building blocks: PAD and STM

Building the big picture involves working to specify at least a first draft of our objectives, challenges and problems (*P*-policy), what do we need to know, what data do we need (*A*-analysis), and how to invent 'solutions' (*D*-design, in a broad sense). We can then add STM to provide a framework for the analysis: *S*-systems thinking; what is known, summarised as *T*-theory; and what is in our toolkit of *M*-methods.

It has been remarked that the three different kinds of thinking in the PAD framework are rarely found in the same room together![17] That poses a challenge which we will take up under a number of headings. In particular, analysis itself won't solve problems; design – invention and creativity – is needed, possibly along with bold out-of-the box thinking. In particular, we need all three kinds of thinking to support each of the four pillars.

The PAD/STM steps can be worked through iteratively. The starting point in articulating the big picture is a preliminary run through the P – what are we for?, what are our functions?, what are our challenges? This can then be followed by a first shot at defining the system of interest – the entities that make up the system and the relationships between them. The system of interest narrowly defined will be the organisation on which we are focused, but it is clearly vital to articulate the system's environment, including, for example, its stakeholders ('owners', customers/clients, employees, suppliers). This expanded version can usefully be thought of as an analogue of an ecosystem. This is a crucial foundation for analysis. Once this starting point has been established, it is possible to cycle through the six steps – PAD/STM, iteratively, progressively adding understanding and detail, the end point of which will be the big picture![18]

1.4 Lessons learned: thinking things through

This framework will provide the foundations for 'thinking things through'.[19] A key feature emerges very quickly: there will be a high degree of *interdependence*: an intervention in one area to meet a challenge will have impacts, some unintended and often unforeseen, in other areas. In my own field, the development of new housing policies should be related to access to services and employment – but this seemingly obvious point is not taken up as work is typically organised in silos. An understanding of the big picture, through systems thinking, is vital.

The frameworks in combination (SSFS, PAD, STM) in Sections 1.2 and 1.3 offer a starting point and, perhaps more importantly, an iterative process. Each element in the framework is vital: the big picture followed by thinking through strategy, finance, and structures, integrated through what is usually the very large task of implementation – making things work.

Stage 1 of the iteration, when starting from scratch, is essentially a sketching process: from 'What are we for?' through to 'How are we doing' and listing problems and challenges. The big picture can be further elaborated in iteration 2 and beyond, perhaps as discussions with stakeholders come into play. In subsequent iterations, possible 'solutions' – ways forward – will emerge, albeit constrained by finance and budgets. It is obviously different when not starting from scratch: an old strategy may be in place, budgets exist at least for the short run, there is a structure; but, essentially, the same iterative process works.

Notes

1 GMAP: Geographical Modelling and Planning Ltd.
2 See Department of Health, *Being heard: The report of a review committee on NHS complaints procedures* (London: Department of Health, 1994).
3 The Joint Information Systems Committee, financed by the Funding Council to support HE IT and library services.
4 As Chair of the Home Office Science Advisory Committee.
5 Conducting a review of the Defence Science Advisory Committee.
6 As a non-executive director of the Banking Standards Board.
7 Devolution will be a key concept here, to be developed below.
8 Whatever the organisation, you need to be business-like; do you need an MBA? See (Wilson, 2023), pp. 110–114. For management basics, see Wilson (2010), pp. 84–88; Glass (1996); Cisco (2007).
9 There is a glossary in *Knowledge Power* (Wilson, 2010) with over 100 superconcepts.
10 See Ashby (1956).
11 See Beer (1972; 1994).
12 Paraphrased from *Work*, by Robert Caro (2021). His original line as an investigative journalist was 'Turn every page.'
13 An old adage, source unknown. Related to another: 'At the first sight of the enemy, the plan is abandoned!'
14 See Mintzberg (1989).
15 See Christensen (1997).
16 See Barber (2015).
17 Britton Harris, private communication.
18 The PDA/STM framework is elaborated in Wilson (2010; 2021).
19 'Thinking things through': Lord Boyle, when Vice-Chancellor of Leeds, defining 'research' and the wider purpose of a university, but clearly it is more widely applicable.

Bibliography

Ashby, W. R. (1956) *An introduction to cybernetics*, Chapman and Hall, London.
Barber, M. (2015) *How to run a government*, Penguin, Harmondsworth.
Beer, S. (1972) *Brain of the firm*, John Wiley, Chichester.
Beer, S. (1994) *Designing freedom*, John Wiley, Chichester.
Caro, R. (2021) *Working*, Vintage, London.
Christensen, C. M. (1997) *The innovator's dilemma*, Harper Business, New York.
Cisco (2007) *Equipping every learner for the 21st Century*, Cisco Systems Inc, San Jose, CA.

Clarke, M. (2020) *How geography changed the world, and my small part in it*, Sweet Design Ltd, Bristol.

Department of Health (1994) *Being heard: The report of a review committee on NHS complaints procedures*, Department of Health, London.

Department of Health (1995) *Acting on complaints*, Department of Health, London.

Glass, N. M. (1996) *Management masterclass: A practical guide to the new realities of business*, Nicholas Brealey, London.

Mintzberg, H. (1989) *Structure in fives: Designing effective organisations*, Prentice-Hall, Englewood Cliffs, NJ.

Wilson, A. G. (2010) *Knowledge power: Interdisciplinary education for a complex world*, Routledge, Abingdon.

Wilson, A. G. (2021) Entropy in urban and regional modelling, in Aura Reggiani, Laurie A. Schintler, Daniel Czamanski and Roberto Patuelli (eds), *Handbook on entropy, complexity and spatial dynamics: A rebirth of theory?*, Elgar, Cheltenham, pp. 20–31.

Wilson, A. G. (2023) *Being interdisciplinary*, UCL Press, London.

2 Pillar 1: systems and the big picture

2.1 Context: systems and ecosystems

As we start the process of building the big picture for our system of interest – our organisation, or 'our part' of an organisation – we need to bear in mind that our particular system will be part of a wider ecosystem with many interdependent strands. This context must be part of the picture building as it will contribute to understanding the drivers of change. We can also seek to account for the global challenges we sketched in the Preface: sustainability and climate change, pandemics, security, and social exclusion, along with technological change. All will almost certainly have implications when translated to a particular system. These challenges, translated into those of government agencies, will demand transformations. The big picture framework, fully connected in 'ecosystems', will recur in later chapters as we seek to articulate the strategy, finance, structures, and new ways of working that transformation demands. As our work begins, and we define our organisation as a system of interest within a wider ecosystem, a recurring starting point is the question: what are we for? Followed by: what do we need to know?

2.2 Education

2.2.1 Fixing ideas: four examples

Most of my working life has been in education, mainly in universities but also, from varying perspectives, with schools. I use this experience in broad terms to provide a first illustration. For universities, the outline of the big picture is clear: the elements are concerned with teaching, research, and outreach (T, R and O), and with supporting services (S) and administration (A) and hence the package can be labelled as (T, R, O, S, A); who teaches, who researches, who learns – multiple foci – staff and students, and their mix of work. This can look obvious but clarity is not always achieved. As Vice-Chancellor of a large university, I inherited an administration which was supposed to serve as the core of 'central management'. In fact, it was focused on running a very large committee system – with over 100 committees listed in the University

DOI: 10.4324/9781003673149-2

Calendar – rather than on supporting teaching, research, and outreach. The big picture was not connected to the structure and one challenge was to refocus and restructure – see Chapter 5.

A second example is provided by a review I carried out of the Joint Information Systems Committee (JISC),[1] for the universities funding council, the Higher Education Funding Council for England (HEFCE). As an organisation, JISC, possibly misled by its name, saw itself as supporting IT and Library services in universities and not directly as supporting the whole of T, R, O, S and A. Into the bargain, it was divided into non-interacting silos which did not help in finding the big picture focus. It was necessary to switch from (IT, Libraries) to (T, R, O, S and A). Establishing this provided a framework for the review. The necessity for refocussing allowed the review group to articulate the main headings of what became its final report in the first meeting! The recommendations were implemented.

A third example comes from my involvement with schools. I chaired a group in DfES[2] on schools' science with the objective of improving the delivery of STEM[3] students to universities. Big picture thinking led to a preliminary analysis. It emerged from the Department's own statistics, that (more or less) only students who had taken three separate science subjects at GCSE level (as distinct from a single-subject 'General Science') went on to A-levels, and hence to university science, engineering, and mathematics courses. There was, therefore, a need for a requirement on schools to provide this route – many didn't, possibly due to science teacher shortages.[4] A solution had to be invented: a D-challenge within the policy, analysis, and design (PAD) framework.

A fourth example also relates to schools but offered a very different challenge. I supported Cisco's $40M grant to New Orleans after Hurricant Katrina – which involved building a schools' system from scratch, facilitated by hi-tech – a different kind of 'big picture' starting point. This led to the development of the Cisco formula:[5]

$$C[(T, C, A, L), S, P, Tech]$$

which will be explained and deployed in Chapter 3! Essentially, a system to provide good teachers (T), an effective curriculum (C), with accountability (A) and Leadership (L), all in the context of skills (S), the best pedagogy (P), and making the best use of technology (Tech). This provides a succinct system description which then provides the basis for moving forward through strategy, finance, and structure, being inventive where necessary.

We follow through the university example in more detail, beyond the administration, by applying the PAD/STM framework (Sections 2.2.2 and 2.2.3), and then present examples from government (Section 2.4), research (Section 2.5) and industry (Section 2.6) with 'lessons learned' summarised in Section 2.7. As a preliminary, we tackle the first big picture question: what are we for?

2.2.2 Clarity of purpose

'What are universities for?', a first shot might be: 'the delivery of knowledge through teaching and learning'. We can elaborate by noting as components of 'purpose', the *curation* of knowledge ('scholarship'!), along with the *creation* of knowledge (research). There is a constant tension between 'knowledge for its own sake' and 'knowledge for instrumental purposes', notably to support employment. This sometimes manifests itself as the distinction between 'education' and 'training'. For present purposes, we seek to have it both ways: to devise a curriculum which provides a core framework for learning on a broad basis while at the same time being aware of what is valuable in employment. It can be argued that training is typically short-run and may have a short half-life while the core framework is both valuable in its own right and provides challenges which are the basis for future-proofing. In Section 2.2.1, we began to characterise the elements of an education system through the 'Cisco formula'.

2.2.3 The PAD and STM frameworks for universities

In Section 2.2.1, I established the main elements of the university system, codified as T, R, O, S, and A. There are deeper questions that need to be articulated as part of building the big picture: the curriculum for teaching, the optimum pedagogy and support for learners, how to assess students' work; research areas; and the role of the university in outreach. If we can get this into good order, then we can review the supporting services and the administration. These questions are raised at two scales: (1) the (usually subject-based) department, and (2) the university as a whole. And perhaps also at an intermediate layer: the faculties.

We can apply the PAD/STM (system of interest, theory, and methods) framework to universities as a first example of how to use it. The policy question, implicitly opened up in the preceding subsection, has to be tackled initially on a very broad basis: is the universities' role to 'educate'; or is it more instrumental, providing the foundations for employment? These are not necessarily incompatible (but can be made so!). A good education can and will be a good foundation for employment: some grounding in philosophy facilitates clear thinking, some mathematical skills are widely applicable; language and writing skills are much in demand. As noted, education provides the basis for future-proofing, whereas a narrow training-based course may be quickly out of date. There is a related question: how to educate to lay the foundations for tackling difficult problems? In many areas, this involves in-depth knowledge in a particular discipline. How do we construct a curriculum which marries breadth and depth and provides a variety of pathways for a student population? How do we combine disciplinary depth with interdisciplinary breadth?[6] There are no easy answers to these questions and most universities will seek to meet these demands by providing alternative pathways.[7]

Once these questions have been tackled, at least in broad terms, we can begin to use the big picture framework as the basis for later chapters: possible academic structures – disciplines, interdisciplinarity – and relate these to the student market and to local and national economies. We can examine the present disposition of student numbers – in relation to the national environment on access to higher education (HE) – alongside instrumental objectives relating to direct benefits for the economy, public and private; and as a primary source of income for the university. This kind of core analysis provides the basis for the 'design' of key elements in the strategic plan: future student numbers, how they are distributed across departments and interdisciplinary 'units', implications for research and outreach. It is a time to begin to review the current budgets and the split between 'maintenance and development', ensuring effectiveness for the first but making resources available for the second. We are assembling the big picture as the basis for thinking through strategy, finance, structures, and making things work, to be explored in the following chapters.

2.3 Government: the delivery of effective and efficient public services

2.3.1 Experience

We need to build the big picture for each of a variety of services to be delivered by government at both local and national levels. I illustrate the process through the elements of my own career.[8] My experience has been in a variety of roles: local government as a City Councillor; providing the computer-model base for cost-benefit analysis in transport planning in the then Ministry of Transport (MoT); urban analytics in the Centre for Environmental Studies, part-funded by the then Ministry of Housing and Local Government; Director-General for Higher Education in the then Department of Education and Skills (DfES); as a member of health authorities; science advisory roles in the Home Office and the Ministry of Defence; and chairing a Government Office for Science Foresight review on the future of cities. All involved establishing the big- picture base, or in my early years, failing to do so! At least ten years' experience was needed in my case to recognise the importance of the big picture perspective.

2.3.2 Local government

I represented Labour for East Ward on Oxford City Council and I was as much involved with Labour Party business as with the Council.[9] This meant that my view of the big picture was determined more by national Labour policy than a deeper self-generated understanding. There were the beginnings of using the 'maintenance vs development' framework (though not consciously): some things simply had to be kept going efficiently – Water, Libraries, Childrens were some of my committees; others were major development areas – notably education and the introduction of comprehensive schools. As a young and junior councillor, I was not involved in setting the agenda, though in my three years, I managed to introduce two innovations: the first to remove the stipulation that the Town Clerk had to be a lawyer, the second that the council should have a five-year budgeting process. A big picture view was to come much later. However, I did learn much about structures and how they worked, both in the Council and, particularly, working on elections – local and general – in various roles for the Labour Party. This enabled me to build a big picture understanding of how organisations worked, and I guess the moral of this is to be aware of the structures you are working in, even if you are not in a position to organise or change them. It also gave me good experience of talking to a wide range of people – knocking on doors, street by street, while electioneering; and taking part in a wide range of meetings – both Party and Council. I think this was the beginnings of one skill which was much deployed in later years: how to find a route to bringing disagreements to some kind of compromise, not least between the then right and left wings of the Labour Party. (I always came top in the elections to the Executive Committee of the Constituency Labour Party because I was on the 'slates' of both left and right!) This is an interesting part of developing and understanding the big picture: it does not typically represent a neat system: there will be many perspectives and disagreements and one management challenge is to handle these, largely in informal meetings, outside the formal structures, and possibly leading to careful agenda setting for the formal meetings.

2.3.3 Central government 1: transport

I moved to the Ministry of Transport from Oxford when Christopher Foster[10] was appointed as Director-General for Economic Planning. I was appointed as Mathematical Adviser with the role of introducing model-based analytics as a crucial part of the big picture that underpins government policy making for both inter-city and intra-city transport systems. One issue that emerged early on was that it could be applied to ports. There was a proposal to build a large new port, Portbury, in Bristol, with the investment cost to be borne by central government. My big picture contribution to this policy decision was to model the expected throughput of the new port. The analysis showed that it was not viable, and the decision was made not to support the proposal. This was announced in a government White Paper, which may be unique in that it had a mathematical annex, which included all the data used in the model, and the equations, as a demonstration of the basis of the decision, so that this could be both attacked and defended, and indeed opponents were free to rework it.[11]

I was encouraged to set up the Mathematical Advisory Unit, the MAU, to help build the capacity for the model building that would underpin the cost-benefit analysis of future transport investment – making the department an 'intelligent customer'. The aim was to facilitate the introduction of these techniques at scale by introducing the US-developed skills of the American Wilbur Smith company with the British engineering consultants, Freeman Fox. The in-house MoT basis for this would be a study led by the MAU which carried out a model-based analysis of South East Lancashire and North East Cheshire – the SELNEC study – a different element of the big picture.[12] My experience here was valuable but far too narrow to provide a comprehensive big picture. I was rooted in analytics, I mistakenly believed that my computer models were more capable of forecasting for planning purposes than was the case.

2.3.4 Research

The transport and MAU work reported in the previous subsection was a kind of research. It was applying university research in government which had been transferred from Oxford University through the move of Christopher Foster and myself to London. I left MoT to be Assistant Director of the newly-established research centre, the Centre for Environmental Studies (CES) and this enabled me to broaden my own research base. It was part-funded by the Ford Foundation in the USA, and part by the Ministry of Housing and Local Government (MHLG) – and hence there was potentially serious government interest. In this case, I was so concerned with setting up the computer model-based analytics for what I saw as a new future for town and city planning, that I pretty well wholly neglected the more broadly-based CES Trustees, including MHLG representatives – and therefore the policy elements of the big picture. We were successful in terms of model development, but much less so on the broader front. This was a big mistake on my part and I learned a number of lessons from this: with hindsight, essentially, the importance of remaining connected to the wider ecosystem. This was certainly a failure on my part to establish an appropriate big picture. Of course, I was heavily involved in research in my Leeds days, and this is reviewed in Section 2.5.

2.3.5 Health

In the NHS, I was a member of a District Health Authority and then Vice-Chair of an Area Health Authority, which was created when two districts were merged. This experience coincided with a change in structure with the authorities to be run by professional generalist 'managers' rather than clinicians. At the time, I was unaware of the Mintzberg argument that there would be problems for a professional organisation if the front-line professionals – in this case, the hospital consultants, for example – were not involved in the higher levels of management. I think that, for several decades now, this has been a contrast with universities' management, and we pursue this in Chapter 5. At a later time, I was a member of a Regional Health Authority and a member of its Audit Committee. In retrospect, I did not have the experience to understand the need for a big picture starting point and this meant that, as a member of an authority, I accepted the management's agenda meeting by meeting and didn't ask the fundamental questions. Later, I chaired a review of NHS complaints procedures for the then Secretary of State, Virginia Bottomley. I was better equipped to articulate a big picture starting point and to establish some principles for independence in complaints procedures which led to a battle with consultants who wanted to retain overall control![13]

2.3.6 Central government 2: higher education

Many years later, in the DfES, my role was developing a new Directorate of Higher Education in a large government department. By this time, I had a reasonably developed big picture from my Leeds experience. The objectives were as in a university, but with a focus on government policy and delivery. The big picture repeats itself but on a bigger scale. The agenda covered the national ecosystem: fair admissions; 'top' universities;[14] tensions between academics and 'uses' (instrumentalism); how research-led innovation can be supported. Challenges included: how to meet the 50% student recruitment target;[15] inadequate investment and maintenance of infrastructure, how to handle intervention without invading university autonomy, focused grants (to be bid for); quite a lot of micro-management. There were also cross-cutting issues – notably 'progression', tracking policy impacts across 'ages' – from the Children's Directorate through Schools, onto further education (FE) and HE. At the outset, I identified what I called 'strategy clutter' and the refocus was in terms of not a strategic plan as such, at least initially, but a formulation of the BSQs – the big strategic questions – and a focus on these – see Section 3.3.1 in Chapter 3.

2.3.7 Security and defence

I took on the chairmanship of the Home Office Science Advisory Council (HOSAC) in 2013. It had become more or less defunct and needed a reset. Bernard Silverman was the Chief Scientific Adviser (CSA) in the Home Office and he was keen on drawing in a good range of expertise that would support him and the Home Office more broadly on its science and technology agenda. It had its own S and T research unit, the Centre for Applied Science and Technology (CAST) – the Home Office's version of MoD's DSTL.[16] CAST and DSTL were very different in scale, and size inhibited the range of projects that CAST could undertake and, almost inevitably, this generated a programme that was more of the 'shopping list' than something based on a clear strategy. The big picture was clearly needed, both at the Home Office scale and also for CAST. The framework for this was provided by the Home Office's own policy programme which at least in broad terms was well defined. Connecting this to an S and T support programme was challenging.

My HOSAC role also made me an ex-officio member of the Ministry of Defence (MoD) in the Defence Science Advisory Council (DSAC). Later, after I had left DSAC, I was asked to carry out a review of it as part of a government review of all NDPBs.[17] An interesting feature of my final report[18] was the emphasis on the need for a big picture – a map of science and technology across the MoD – which could then become the basis for DSAC strategy. There was a telling comment in one of my interviews: 'There are problems in not having a broad map of MoD S and T when deciding priorities.' This led to the first two recommendations:

> Recommendation 1. DSAC, working through the CSA, should generate a 'map' of MoD S &T capability – in Head Office, and across Dstl, DE&S, the Commands and other linked agencies and suppliers. Particular attention should be paid to MoD objectives – strategy, capability and delivery by commands – so that the S&T map can be explicitly related to these. Indeed, the 'map' could be structured in these terms.

There is a corollary which in turn leads to: 'Recommendation 2: the map should be used to generate an "assurance and risk" map to establish a year by year work plan on an audit of quality assurance.' (See Recommendations 8 and 9.) Along with 'Recommendation 8: DSAC should, as noted in cross-cutting recommendation 1, use its 'map' of MoD S and T activity and plan its quality assurance functions – audit and deep-dive – against priority requirements on that framework' and 'Recommendation 9: DSAC should audit MoD's current quality assurance processes, make recommendations for any improvements, and possibly take on some quality assurance roles itself where there are gaps.'

2.3.8 Central government 3: the future of cities

In the Government Office for Science's *Foresight for Cities: Future of Cities* review (https://www.gov.uk/government/uploads/system/uploads/attachment_data/file/516443/gs-16-5-future-cities-foresight-for-cities.pdf) – establishing the importance of handling interdependence in developing future plans and policies – starting with a big picture perspective was vital. In this case, it worked very well through the three years of the project. At the outset, we defined six elements which made up an outline of the big picture:

- people, and how they live in cities
- the economy and employment
- the environment and sustainability
- infrastructure
- governance.

Rather than publish one substantial report, we published four reports[19] and a series of commissioned working papers. The summary report embraced the PAD framework, expanding it from three elements to five with some renaming: visioning (P), analysing (A), designing (D), and adding testing and assembling (https://www.gov.uk/government/uploads/system/uploads/attachment_data/file/520963/GS-16-6-future-of-cities-an-overview-of-the-evidence.pdf). The second report was on the science of cities and research priorities (https://www.gov.uk/government/uploads/system/uploads/attachment_data/file/516407/gs-16-6-future-cities-science-of-cities.pdf), and this included a recommendation that links to the generation of big pictures: the need for further research on the architecture of information systems on cities – an area which is still underdeveloped. The third was, in effect, a manual for cities considering developing their own foresight project with a focus on the building of alternative long-term future scenarios as a basis for policy exploration (https://www.gov.uk/government/uploads/system/uploads/attachment_data/file/516443/gs-16-5-future-cities-foresight-for-cities.pdf). The fourth was a more specialised report on graduate retention in cities as support for economic development (https://www.gov.uk/government/uploads/system/uploads/attachment_data/file/510421/gs-16-4-future-of-cities-graduate-mobility.pdf). As ever with these kinds of report, there is much good analysis of the challenges and insightful recommendations on how to deploy them. This has only been partially successful and bears further reading in relation to ongoing challenges!

2.4 Industry: managing for profit, and beyond

2.4.1 Introduction

The simple textbook way to look at an industrial organisation is to think of it as managing to generate profits for its shareholders. This is undoubtably core, but there are many other corporate responsibilities – from the welfare of employees and the rewards to senior staff,[20] through to contributing to the sustainability agenda.[21] As with public services, we need to build big pictures for each of a wide variety of industry sectors. We will pursue this in more detail in Chapter 7, but meanwhile, I will illustrate the process through my personal experience. This is more limited than was the case with the public sector. Nonetheless, there was at least one element of having the depth of experience along with a wider perspective that was developed through exploring the challenge of connecting university research with industry – 'exploiting our research successes' – both from within a large university and though involvement in reviews of particular sectors, notably biotechnology and IT.

2.4.2 Analytics for transport engineering

My first experience was through working with engineering consultants on large transport projects while in the Ministry of Transport. The work is presented under the earlier 'government' heading in Section 2.3.3. This involved building a computer model of flows on transport networks which can be used in cost-benefit calculations of alternative transport investment. The models were complex – recognising different person types, transport modes, and network link capacities: it provided the analytics basis of transport engineering. This was very much the analysis component of what was needed – the A-part of PAD along with STM. The models could be used to test alternative investment plans – the D-part of PAD – to meet the objectives of the day, such as shifting trips from cars to public transport – the P-part of PAD.[22] Partly to complete the big picture, and partly to experiment and build up expertise in the Department (and to learn to be an 'intelligent customer' – a useful superconcept!), we carried out a study ourselves of South East

Lancashire and North East Cheshire – the SELNEC study.[23] This was a good but unusual example of the possibility of publishing the results of government research in an academic journal.

2.4.3 Retail

The second example was a more direct involvement: with the retail sector through GMAP Ltd, a University of Leeds spin-out company.[24] In this case, 'retail' was broadly defined to include any organisation that provided a service to customers: supermarkets, retailers and retail centres, car manufacturers and their dealerships, petrol companies, and banks. The big picture had a simple foundational question: what was the optimal network of retail outlets for a particular organisation? This had to be elaborated through a computer-model-based understanding of the spatial distribution of the population, its key characteristics, and its travel behaviour, along with measures of the attractiveness of different kinds of facilities. Taking a supermarket company as an example, it was possible to model the flows of revenue into all supermarkets, say, in a region, including competitors, so that if there was a proposal to invest in a new outlet, that could be inserted into the computer model and the revenue attracted to the new centre (and what might be lost elsewhere) could be predicted. This in turn enabled a calculation of the amount that could be spent on the land which would still generate a financially successful development, generating a model-based big picture that was the basis of strategy and planning. GMAP had 'first-mover' advantage though it was not surprising that in later years, this expertise was developed internally in far-sighted companies.

2.4.4 Biotech

The biotechnology example arose from membership of a government group, led by Lord Sainsbury, then the Science Minister, to explore the development of biotech clusters in a number of British cities. My role was to be the group member who 'knew' about cities. We toured the UK, and the USA, visiting both universities and pharmaceutical industry sites. We made a number of recommendations on university-industry collaboration, fiscal initiatives, infrastructure, and the planning system.[25] One recommendation related to the importance of the big picture for future planning: 'To better understand the dynamics of clusters, the DGTI will consider developing the UK Competitiveness Index to stimulate data capture for individual clusters and conduct a mapping exercise of cluster activity across sectors in the UK.' The tour included visits to the Massachusetts Institute of Technology (MIT) and Stanford University. We were interested in whether we could learn how this kind of development, through spin-out companies, for example – could support university finances. Each university had large offices to support technology transfer. However, the Head at MIT stated baldly, 'If you want to raise money for the university, you would be better off opening a McDonald's franchise'! We visited a company in Boston, Gen Tech, I think, which had a huge piece of machinery, cathedral-like, to produce a very small quantity of a drug for a rare disease. I was told that, ironically, it could be produced naturally in cows. I raised my eyebrows. 'I have a herd of cows in Western Massachusetts' was the response! In the Stanford case, their accounts showed that their office did generate very large revenues but further investigation showed that a large proportion came from one set of patents – for recombinant DNA.

2.5 Research: what do we need to know?

2.5.1 Basic science

Understanding the big picture is a vital part of planning where to invest in research. These decisions are made at all scales – from the individual (new to research or experienced), through university departments and industry, to large organisations, and on to government. I sometimes argue to new PhD students in discussions on finding research topics that the subject must be 'interesting to you and important to someone else'. This pinpoints the challenge: these qualities are subjective and elusive but the search, the hard thinking, the explorations are all necessary.

As a researcher, I had a lot of luck in my early days – I didn't need a big picture, though I enjoyed understanding the context of what I was doing. I was given the project: identifying 'events' in bubble chamber experiments in elementary particle physics.[26] This gave me foundations in big computers, coding (with huge Fortran files on trays of punched cards!), and delivering something challenging. But I didn't have to find the topic. I then found an opportunity to work on cities – so no problem there about 'interesting and important' – and I stumbled on to a method for building mathematical and computer models of cities that turned out to be valuable.[27] Productive, but no hard choices to be made. It was the start of a large research project which has sustained me through my career.

Big picture thinking took me beyond what was essentially a methods' focus to ask wider questions about the uses of these methods and this opened up questions about where the biggest impacts could be made. It turned out that was easier to think this through in the commercial sector where 'increase in profits' was an obvious measure – and this led to the founding of GMAP Ltd, noted earlier, and discussed further in Annex 3, Section A3.3.3. The public sector in areas like health and education was ripe for the application of this kind of analytics, but this proved to be much more difficult. In the GMAP case, we had enthusiastic clients; the challenge of finding these in the public sector may have been the problem of finding 'measures' analogous to 'profits'. This was not impossible – indicators such as 'accessibilities' would provide a starting point. We had a small number of clients for pilot projects but couldn't build any enthusiasm, perhaps because of the lack of in-house skills.

2.5.2 *'Managing' research*

As I moved into management roles, the questions and choices associated with horizon scanning and research investment became much broader. As a university Head of Department, I largely followed the tradition that individual colleagues determined their own research agenda without building the big picture of my disciplinary field – a weakness on my part, probably too concerned with my own research agenda and thinking of the rest of the job as administration. This changed fundamentally by the time I was Vice-Chancellor, thinking through the research objectives of a large university. I then did seek to build a big picture, though not as systematically as I might have done. I visited industry leaders who were responsible for substantial research programmes, first, with pharmaceuticals which I wanted to connect to university biological sciences. I started with Glaxo (now Glaxo Smith Klyne, GSK) and visited the Chief Executive, Richard Sykes, in his office in Berkeley Square. He arranged for me to spend two or three days in their research labs at Greenford and I learned a tremendous amount which greatly influenced my future thinking. Another example was the BT research lab at Martlesham. I had long conversations with Bill Stewart, then the Government Chief Scientific Adviser, and George Radda, the Chief Executive of the Medical Research Council. The latter confirmed my own intuition – an amateur's big picture kind of analysis – that 'physiology' research was being neglected relative to molecular biology – though this was beginning to be rectified by the Council funding projects in 'systems biology' – something that has not been carried through on a big scale![28] All of these explorations provided pieces of a complicated jigsaw and the elements of a big picture. I pick up some of the consequences of this thinking in Chapter 3.

2.5.3 *Government funding of research*

I had an involvement over a long period with the wider government-funded system. I was a member of an ESRC[29] committee, then a member of the ESRC Council, and many years later, Chair of the AHRC[30] Council. As a Head of Department, I was involved with the first Research Assessment Exercise – the RAE – in 1985, and I was fully aware of the significance of the Quality-related Research (QR) funding that was allocated to universities as a core research budget, based on RAE outcomes.[31] At no time did I do any serious thinking through a 'big picture'. I was conscious, certainly at the AHRC, that we frequently proclaimed that the research we funded was 'world-class' without any clear idea of what this meant. In a debate at a Council away day, we managed to conclude that research that was 'world-class', rather than 'simply very good' or 'excellent', was in some sense 'transformative'. This was still subjective but provided the basis for some new thinking.[32]

I undertook a number of reviews of aspects of government-funded research, within the DFES as sole reviewer; and for the remainder as Chair of a group: AHRC, for the British Academy, and jointly for the British Academy and the

Royal Society. Comments on each follow in relation to big pictures. There are common threads which can be noted!

Government departments have their own research budgets. At my time in the DfES, the budget was around £20M a year, rising to £40–50M when indirect sources were taken into account. a significant sum, for example, relative to the ESRC budget of around £150M a year. The management of it was rather weak and I investigated it at one point and found some anomalies. The upshot of this was the Permanent Secretary asking me to review our handling of research and make some recommendations. The starting point was that the research that was funded was very fragmented. I wrote a substantial report from which I extract two main features. First, the research programme should be related to what at the time we called the big strategic questions – the BSQs. This was in effect, the big picture that was required as a foundation for research planning. The second was the need for a comprehensive management information system that would support each of the research planning functions of the policy directorates. (There is a valuable general point here: big picture thinking provides the template for the design of an information system.) It is interesting in this case to show how this thinking provided a framework for a new strategy. This was developed through Table 2.1, in effect, a 'local' representation of the PDA/STM approach.

The rows provide the user and provider foci. The columns indicate the core capabilities that have to be given to support the research agenda. Working across the first row, for users, we would first articulate the issues and BSQs, then the analysis, underpinned by an appropriate information system; finally, an account of the policies, etc. already in place. Against that background, the research agenda can be articulated and can contribute to strategy, plans, funding decisions, and problem solving more broadly. We can illustrate the argument as follows. A review of the BSQs suggests that the key issues can be combined. User issues are mainly concerned with *participation, attainment*, and *progression* (all of which involve effective tracking mechanisms); provider issues are about *systems, workforce*, and *a package around curriculum, skills, and pedagogy*.

This framework then leads us to the idea that the research agenda could be defined in terms of *programmes* of research (which may be made up of bundles of projects) underpinned by some core capabilities (which should themselves

Table 2.1 A framework for exploring research priorities

	Issues (BSQs)	*Analysis*	*Information systems*	*Policies, strategies, plans, funding (problem-solving)*
Users				
Providers				

sometimes be supported by research). The BSQs should be components of these programmes. This led to a focus on the seven issues identified as:

1. Participation, attainment and progression
2. Delivery systems
3. Workforce development
4. Curriculum, skills, pedagogy
5. Special projects
6. Evaluation
7. Core support

Participation, attainment and progression

These involve research programmes for users.

Delivery systems, workforce development, and curriculum, skills, pedagogy

These are applicable to research programmes for providers.

Special projects

Inevitably, there will be topics that do not fit into these categories, and these should be designated as special projects. These projects can underpin the core capabilities (embracing both users and providers):

- Policy directorates identifying issues and BSQs.
- A comprehensive toolkit available within the Analytical Community, for example, including, for example, geodemographic and modelling capabilities.
- Top-class integrated information systems, anchored in modelling, that would chart the route from data to information to the knowledge that is encapsulated in a management information system with good key performance indicators (KPIs) and targets.
- A management system that records policies, strategies, plans, and funding allocations and outcomes, KPIs, progress towards targets, etc., this was tackled through the specification of a new business process system. Revised BSQs could then grow out of this.

We should also note the importance of impact measures and evaluation methods and these might fit together in another research programme.

Evaluation

This should generate good KPIs and therefore the basis of an effective management information system as well as evaluations of particular initiatives.

Core support

This encompasses formulation and updating of BSQs, multidisciplinary analytical capability, data and information and management information systems – led by Strategic Analysis and the Strategy Unit with contributions from other Directorates.

This shows that it may be possible to move beyond a very fragmented bottom-up programme to one that has some strategic top-down direction through a smaller number of larger research programmes. This framework can be seen to arise directly from the BSQs – and hence the big picture.

There is a particular issue here: determining government's own research needs and their funding in relation to research councils and the autonomy of universities. Government departments, of course, have every right to 'require' appropriate research to support their work: should they 'instruct' research councils, and through them, universities? Or should they fund their own projects from their own budget? Something of both?! This was an issue that Paul Nurse sought to tackle in his review of the then relatively-new UKRI.[33]

At a time when I was Chair of the AHRC Council, there was much government-drive to link funding to impact. We produced a report immodestly titled 'Leading the world' to quantify the importance of UK arts and humanities' research on a global scale, and hence its importance for UK funding. A big picture framework, charting the role of AHRC research in the UK cultural ecosystem was crucial to the argument. It ranged from accounting for its cultural importance through to its economic impact.

Around the same time, I chaired a group for the British Academy on the importance of arts and humanities and the social sciences for public policy making. The starting point was the need for another kind of big picture: tackling the question systematically of what policy makers need. This provided a framework for a review of what was on offer and some recommendations on how the system could be made to work more effectively.

At a later time, I chaired a joint group for the British Academy and the Royal Society on education research, which was thought to be in a poor state. It emerged that while there was a lot of good research, it tended to be small-scale and in sub-disciplinary silos, with a variety of funders. In other words, very fragmented and unfocused. In this case, it was very important to establish a big picture starting point and we did this through the idea of an education research ecosystem, with three main categories: researchers, practitioners, and policy makers (the last including the funders) to form the principal nodes.[34] See Section 3.5.2 in Chapter 3.

The common thread in these reviews relates to the need to think through the strategic objectives to provide a framework for thinking through research priorities, and, again, in all cases, the need for the development of a good management information system.

The reviews in different ways tackled the challenge of translating the benefits of universities' research into industry and the public sector – a long-standing issue. One government response was to set up Innovate UK which awarded grants to university research teams for this purpose – with a condition that the grant could only be awarded to a company. In my case, I was a member of a team that won one such grant, rooted in urban modelling. We set up Prospective Labs Ltd. – we had to set up a company as a condition of receiving the grant. Our big picture was well defined but the 'market' turned out to be poor, and hence it had to be redefined and the company has achieve modest success through this new focus. It can be argued that this is a success for the Innovate UK mechanism: academics being 'forced' into a commercial environment, via a steep learning curve, to success. (See Section 5.4.2 in Chapter 5 and Annex 3, Section 3.3.3 on GMAP Ltd, where some wider issues in supporting spin-outs are explored.)

The setting up of the Alan Turing Institute – the national institute for data science and AI – demanded a big picture overview, in part to sort out whether the focus of its research should be on foundational methods as distinct from applications. At the outset, there was a preference for the former, but it quickly became clear that an applications focus was likely to be much more productive. It was, of course, possible to have it both ways with a matrix structure. The areas chosen were partly determined by available funding but hopefully, more on the areas that could be transformed by AI and data science. They included health, defence and security, finance, cities, and data-centric engineering. Many stakeholders had to be drawn in and accounted for in the discussion – Turing as a system within an ecosystem. The outcome was only partially successful, partly because of competing demands for funding with some universities seeing Turing as a mini research council.

2.6 New challenges

2.6.1 Introduction

Although this takes me somewhat beyond the big picture, this does provide a framework within which I can note my own experience relating to the new grand challenges. The challenges are so huge – examples of the so-called 'wicked' problems – a notion to be picked up later – that 'failure' is inevitable.[35] We pick up each of the illustrative grand challenges in turn along with technology in its cross-cutting role. Even this brief analysis demonstrates the interdependence involved in responding to the challenges and we conclude this section by underlining this point. Progress in each case calls for the big picture specification as a basis for analysis (A), which then feeds into policy (P) and design (D) – deploying the PAD framework. This serves as an introduction to a broader review in Chapter 7.

2.6.2 Sustainability

An important question is: how can cities contribute to the *sustainability* agenda? Urban modellers have been slow to respond, even though the models can be easily adapted to calculate indicators such as carbon outputs from transport and buildings. An exception is Michael Wegener's model-based work on the Ruhr in Germany.[36] He was able to demonstrate that even with the most stringent policies in place, the government would not be able to meet its low-carbon targets in the foreseeable future. In terms of PAD, the model base provides the analysis in terms of carbon (for example) production in cities, policy objectives relate to urban design, and there lies the biggest challenge. In the UK, the present policies of continuing low density residential development, leading to increased car usage, need to be reversed.

2.6.3 *Health: pandemics*

In analysis terms, the control of pandemics needs as a foundation a fine-scale spatial big picture: spatial interaction modelling provides this – with 'interaction' representing the probability of spread of infection. This was developed in the RAMP group convened by the Royal Society.[37] The analysis demands the integration of interaction models with epidemiological models and this leads to the possibilities of calculating R-numbers at a fine spatial scale.[38]

2.6.4 *Security and defence*

In terms of my own experience, a contribution to *security* is through another new interpretation of spatial interaction, as threat, taking us beyond the usual deployment in terms of movement of people or goods. This has applications in policing at a local scale, or defence and security at national and international scales. It has been applied to an analysis of the London riots of 2010,[39] leading to a capability of estimating the number of police needed to quell the level of rioting quickly; and to the defence of shipping in the Gulf.[40] A broader study, linking spatial interaction modelling to network analysis has been used in a study sponsored by the Ministry of Defence to predict the probabilities of conflict on an international canvass.[41]

2.6.5 *Social inclusion*

There is a long history of the spatial analysis of *social inclusion* (or its inverse, exclusion), something I have been working on myself at least since 1970. It was the theme of my inaugural lecture in Leeds in 1971.[42] We use the index of multiple deprivation later as an illustration. The comprehensive urban model provides the basis for calculating a wide range of relevant indicators, including measures of accessibility to employment, housing, and services. As with the other grand challenges, the problem is not so much in the analysis (the 'A' in 'PAD'), but in policy (P), which is heavily politicised in this case, and in inventing and designing (D) possible 'solutions', possible plans.

2.6.6 *Cross-cutting: technology*

Technology has driven many of the transformations of the economy and society at various scales and a big picture history provides an important backcloth: hunter and gatherer change to semi-mechanised agriculture, the industrial revolution, the shift from manufacturing to services, and now, possibly, the AI and data-driven 'fifth' revolution. Technology has been a major driver in all these changes. AI, whether through office processes or robotics, will transform much of employment. At the very least, it is accepted that there will be substantial 'hollowing out' with 'middle-income' categories providing most of the job losses. In previous revolutions, jobs that have been lost have been replaced in new sectors. This may happen again, but it may be a long process; and it may not happen. Fears of increasing unemployment, and that the fruits of the new economy are flowing more to capital than to workers, have led to an interest in the idea of a 'basic income', independent of employment.

We return to the core of this section and address the challenges, the thinking through, and thinking ahead, for leaders and managers. A dominant feature of this thinking is again the interdependence of all the issues. Progress can be made: possible future plans will be the subject of heated political debate. The framework of Chapter 1 and the focus here of the big picture starting point should provide the basis for clear thinking and laying out the future options. It needs a new kind of systems-based leadership! We return to this agenda in Chapter 7.

2.7 Lessons learned

Experience confirms the importance of the big picture as a starting point and that the PAD/STM framework within a systems perspective is a valuable way of articulating this. In higher education, it established the focus as 'teaching, research, and outreach' and this was carried through into strategy, finance, and structures. This also opens the 'What do we need to know?' question and in the DfES schools' case, it pointed to a failure in structure: the provision of three-subject GCSE science. In the Cisco/New Orleans case, the 'formula' – essentially the big picture – helped articulate priorities: 'teachers first', for example, but also the need to take the opportunity to revisit the curriculum and the associated pedagogy. In this particular context, there was a focus on hi-tech support. The CES case represented a complete failure on my part to establish a big picture which led to me having an overly narrow view of my role as Assistant Director; and to a new Director being appointed with my role as Assistant Director hanging by a thread for a while. Even now, I recognise that I only understood this failure in retrospect!

Experience also showed that progress is almost never straightforward. The analysis that begins with the big picture exposes disagreements about objectives, or even when the objectives are agreed, with budgets. At least it provides a framework for making the issues clear, though it is not always possible to make progress through mutual agreement. The 'What do we need to know?' question often exposes the inadequacy of what the underlying analytics in a planning process should be, and this was the case in virtually all of the examples. Budget constraints and lack of skills often made this a very difficult problem to resolve. This first stage also brings to the forefront the 'maintenance vs development' issue. What do we have to do to keep going? What do we need to invest to solve problems, meet challenges and to develop? All of this provides the basis for continuing debate and discussion which are necessary elements for achieving successful progress.

Notes

1 As noted, JISC is the Joint Information Systems Committee, funded by the HEFCE.
2 Department for Education and Skills.
3 Science, Technology, Engineering and Mathematics.
4 This was made a statutory requirement with the specification that if a school could not provide it, students could be bussed to a school that did. I am not sure to what extent this was ever implemented, if at all!
5 Cisco (2007).
6 There is an old joke: 'industry has problems, universities have departments ...'.
7 My own school experience is interesting in this respect. In contrast to the current notion that post-16 education should remain broad, I was in a stream that focused on mathematics and physics – though complemented by an hour or so a week in each of English Literature and Philosophy.
8 A different and higher-level take is provided by Michael Barber (2015) in his book, *How to run a government*.
9 I first stood in the Summertown Ward and duly became bottom of the poll; in the following year, I stood in East Ward and was elected by a majority of two votes after four recounts!
10 Foster and Beesley (1963).
11 The Secretary of State at the time was Barbara Castle and I much admired her agreeing that all the analytics should be published in the White Paper. Later, following a change of government, the port was actually built without, as far as I know, any further analysis! See Ministry of Transport (1966); and for a later review of the method, 20 years later (Clarke, Clarke, and Wilson, 1986).
12 Wilson, Hawkins, Hill, and Wagon (1969).
13 Department of Health (1994).
14 As a former Russell Group Vice-Chancellor, I knew the top universities well and so I made sure that my visits from DfES were to smaller and newer ones. This made me realise how good and inventive many of them were and I persuaded our ministers to stop talking about 'top universities', which implied superiority. When I left, 'top universities' started to appear in speeches again!
15 The Prime Minister, Tony Blair, had announced this target unexpectedly in the House of Commons. There were hurried attempts, which I inherited, to define what it meant. It was settled as 'those under 30 who had some experience of higher education'!
16 DSTL is the Defence Science and Technology Lab at Porton Down. Later, CAST and DSTL were merged.
17 An NDPB is a 'non-departmental government body'.
18 Defence Scientific Advisory Council (2014).
19 Future of Cities Project reports by the Government Office for Science (2013).

20 See Marris (1964), *The economic theory of managerial capitalism*, and many later books with similar titles.
21 For example, through the Environmental, Social and Governance (ESG) agenda in finance.
22 Thanks to Brian Martin (Voorhees), Tony Ridley, and John Wootton.
23 The SELNEC report (Wilson et al., 1969).
24 Martin Clarke and I founded the company and it was driven forward by Martin as Managing Director. Sadly, Martin died suddenly and unexpectedly on the 18th of April 2025. For a full account of GMAP, see Clarke (2020).
25 Department of Trade and Industry (1999).
26 The formal fruits were recorded in Wilson et al. (1963) – with 20+ co-authors!
27 See Annex 3, Section A3.1.3.
28 See Palsson (2006).
29 The Economic and Social Research Council, possibly at the time, still the Social Science Research Council until a Government Minister, Keith Joseph, insisted on removing the word 'science' from the title.
30 Arts and Humanities Research Council (2009).
31 In my case, my Department did well, the University much less so.
32 Arts and Humanities Research Council (2009) and British Academy (2008).
33 Paul Nurse's review of UKRI, available at: www.gov.uk/government/publications/research.
34 Royal Society (2019).
35 A term first introduced by Rittel and Webber (1973).
36 Huber et al. (2011).
37 Spooner et al. (2021).
38 Wilson (2020).
39 Davies et al. (2013).
40 Marchione et al. (2016), Marchione and Wilson (2016).
41 Guo et al. (2019).
42 I gave my inaugural lecture in Leeds in 1971 on this theme, arguing that if policies to respond were not developed and implemented, social exclusion would become worse. Fifty years later, this has improved on some fronts but worsened on others. It remains a very big challenge. See Wilson (1972).

Bibliography

Arts and Humanities Research Council (2009) *Leading the world: The economic impact of UK arts and humanities research*, AHRC, Swindon.

Barber, M. (2015) *How to run a government*, Penguin, Harmondsworth.

Clarke, G. P., Clarke, M., and Wilson, A. G. (1986) Re-examining old problems with new methods: Portbury re-visited, *Environment and Planning*, C, 4, 353–374.

Clarke, M. (2020) *How geography changed the world, and my small part in it*, Sweet Design Ltd, Bristol.

Cisco (2007) *Equipping every learner for the 21st century*, Cisco Systems Inc, San Jose, CA.

Davies, T., Fry, H., Wilson, A. G., and Bishop, S. R. (2013) A mathematical model of the London riots and their policing, *Nature Scientific Reports*, 3, 1303. doi:10.1038/srep01303.

Defence Scientific Advisory Council (2014) Triennial review report, 24 March, Ministry of Defence, London.

Department of Health (1994) *Being heard: The report of a review committee on NHS complaints procedures*, Department of Health, London.

Department of Health (1995) *Acting on complaints*, Department of Health, London.

Department of Trade and Industry (1999) *Biotechnology clusters*, HMSO, London.

Foster, C. D. and Beesley, M. E. (1963) Estimating the social benefit of constructing an underground railway in London, *Journal of the Royal Statistical Society, A*, 126, 46–92.

Guo, W., Gleditsch, K., and Wilson, A. (2019) Retool AI to forecast and limit wars, *Nature*, 562, 331–333.

Huber, H., Spiekermann, K., and Wegener, M. (2011) Cities and climate change: A simulation model of the Ruhr Area 2050, in Schrenk, M., Popovich, V. V., and Zeile, P. (eds), *Proceedings, REAL CORP 2011*, Essen. Available at: http://www.corp.

Marchione, E., Johnson, S. D., and Wilson, A. (2016) Agent-based models of piracy, in Wilson, A. (ed.), *Geo-mathematical modelling*, Wiley, Chichester, pp. 217–236.

Marchione, E. and Wilson, A. (2016) Spatial interaction as threat: Modelling maritime policy, in Wilson, A. (ed.), *Global dynamics*, Wiley, Chichester, pp. 187–194.

Marris, R. (1964) *The economic theory of managerial capitalism*, Palgrave Macmillan, London.

Ministry of Transport (1966) Portbury: Reasons for the Minister's decision not to authorise the construction of a new dock at Portbury, Bristol, HMSO, London.

Palsson, B. O. (2006) *Systems biology: Properties of reconstructed networks*, Cambridge University Press, Cambridge.

Rittel, H. W. J. and Webber, M. M. (1973) Dilemmas in a general theory of planning, *Policy Sciences*, 4, 155–169.

Royal Society (2019) *Harnessing education research*, British Academy and the Royal Society, London.

Spooner, F., Abrams, J., Morrissey, K., Shaddick, J., Matty, M., Milton, R., Dennett, A., Lomax, N., Malleson, N., Nelissen, N., Coleman, A., Nur, J., Greig, R., Shenton, C., and Birkin, M. (2021) A dynamic microsimulation model for epidemics, *Social Science and Medicine*, 291.

Tanton, R. and Edwards, K. L. (eds) (2013) *Spatial microsimulation: A reference guide for users*, Springer, Heidelberg.

Wilson, A. G. (1972) Understanding the city of the future, *University of Leeds Review*, 15, 135–166.

Wilson, A. G. (2020) Epidemic models with geography: A new perspective on r-numbers, *ArXiv*: 2005.07673 [physics.soc-ph].

Wilson, A. G., Hawkins, A. F., Hill, G. J., and Wagon, D. J. (1969) Calibrating and testing the SELENEC transport model, *Regional Studies*, 3, 337–350.

Wilson, A. G. (1963) Direct measurement of ≅− and ≅°C lifetimes, *Physical Review Letters*, March.

3 Pillar 2: strategy

3.1 Clear thinking: stability and innovation in a volatile environment

Bear in mind the old adage: 'strategy is 5% of the problem, implementation is 95%'. So this chapter can be relatively short: the hard work comes in the following chapters, Clarity of objectives is a crucial starting point and the 'big picture', built on the 'what are we for?' question, is the key foundation. Responsibility for thinking through the strategic plan rests with senior management. It is not easy to find support for exploring the broad terms needed at the starting point. Colleagues are likely to have their own areas in mind and this can inhibit bold strategic thinking. The Chief Executive Officer (CEO) role is crucial here. It is probably best to start with a project group chaired by the CEO and to site this in a framework that provides wider consultation, and indeed a conduit for ideas from the rest of the organisation. However, I mentioned my difficulties as a Vice-Chancellor in drawing colleagues into the strategic planning process to a friend. He worked for a merchant bank and had a wide variety of experience. He smiled and said: 'I have never known a CEO who didn't write his or her own strategic plan!'

Articulating the strategy is about sketching a path towards achieving objectives, indicating the challenges (and 'solutions') along the way. It is essential to think in terms of the organisation's own objectives, certainly taking fully into account those of other organisations in its environment, notably in the case of public services, those of the government. The 'environment' is likely to be volatile and with a short-term focus. The stability of the organisation year-by-year, can be rooted in its own longer-term objectives, deploying tactics to aid the best way of achieving these in the short term. Clear thinking for strategy development, even at an early stage, involves precision about aims: we should beware of 'missions' stated in terms that are so general as to be almost meaningless. Beyond this broad thinking, comes the operational element, in effect, the subject of the following chapters, but the headings are included here for completeness: finance, structures, making things work; devolution becomes the critical recurring challenge and opportunity.

DOI: 10.4324/9781003673149-3

We can recall, and begin to rephrase for strategy purposes, the 'four pillars' check list from Chapter 1. Start with the big picture and recognise as key foundations for strategic thinking:

- what are we for? System definition; recognise interdependence; use the policy, analysis, and design/system of interest, theory, and methods (PDA/STM) framework to articulate objectives and challenges.
- maintenance vs development: how do we keep going, how do we develop?
- what are our challenges? How can we invent solutions?
- what do we need to know? Requisite variety, according to Ashby; information systems, according to Beer; models ('flight simulators').[1]

Writing a strategic plan involves working through these headings. These starting points are illustrated through examples in Sections 3.2–3.5. We will then move on to finance and structures.

Finance (see Chapter 4) includes the following features:

- accounts: management versus financial; 'open'; 'read every line'[2]
- budgets
- implementation of devolution
- maintenance vs development
- top-down and bottom-up: bidding mechanisms
- investment (mainly): cost-benefit analysis
- underspends

Structures (see Chapter 5) include the following features:

- an effective structure is needed: strategy is 5% of the challenge, implementation is 95%
- devolution
- front-line professionals in management (Mintzberg 1989; Mintzberg and Quinn 1992)

Making things work (see Chapter 6) includes the following features:

- the CEO roles in different parts of the organisation, especially meeting new objectives
- handling (technological) change, AI and data science; disruptive technologies (Christensen 1997)
- changing the dynamics: the DNA
- informal meetings
- project groups – agile deployment
- culture
- ambition

We shouldn't neglect some tools of long standing: *cost-benefit analysis*, balanced scorecards etc. In deploying these tools, the *maintenance vs development* (investment) issue should always be borne in mind – particularly the challenges of innovation, new technologies, etc.; always be prepared to experiment – noting Christensen's (1997) argument on *disruptive technologies* in Chapter 5, see work-based learning in Chapter 6.

In the following sections, we draw on examples that between them, with this framework in mind, offer tools for strategy building. These are presented under the usual headings: education (Section 3.2), government (Section 3.3), industry (Section 3.4), and research (Section 3.5).

3.2 Education: two examples

3.2.1 Universities

I was able to retrieve a University of Leeds 'Corporate Plan' (aka a strategic plan!) for June 1992 – drawn up after one year in office as Vice-Chancellor. Although over 30 years old, its structure stands up very well (and it indicates that some elements of my intellectual toolkit are of long standing!). It is titled 'Teaching and research excellence' – so objectives were clear and up front. Its headings, with a brief commentary, are as follows.

- Aims and objectives: the structure of the plan.
- Planning and targets: the plan was in the context of ambitious national growth targets in student numbers. It suited us at the time to sign up to this on the basis that if a large university cannot contribute its share, the national target cannot be met. However, it also suited us as a way of resolving some financial challenges. There were five-year student number targets as required by the then funding council, the University Funding Council; and more speculative ten-year targets. In the event, all were met early and indeed exceeded.
- Finance: setting out five-year income and expenditure targets up front as a framework to express what is possible and what has to be achieved. This is further illustrated in Chapter 4.
- Teaching and learning: modularisation, which turned out to be a key element for future academic development as well as providing the foundation for 'audit' foci on facilities, methods, and audit.
- Research: plans for expansion, with increased central support and the introduction of graduate schools (which turned out to be an interim step).
- Academic development: all the big 'how to' issues here, picked up in Chapters 5 and 6.
- Student affairs: recognising the importance of supporting students, both because we ought to support the national expansion objectives, and provide increasing access to higher education; and, of course, to ensure student welfare[3] and to make the university more attractive for recruitment.

- Outreach: we established a City and Regional Unit,[4] illustrating the need to have someone responsible for something new; and similarly, a widening access unit.
- The physical estate: the necessary underpinnings and a huge capital development programme.
- Public relations: both internal and external. This involved multiple features, notably increased collaboration with the (then) Leeds Polytechnic and with the City of Leeds.
- Management: more of the 'how to'.

In some ways, all this is a statement of the obvious, but a clear one, which also recognises the interdependencies. The aims and objectives in the university context were set out in Section 2.2.1 in Chapter 2: essentially, teaching, research, and outreach. This provides a framework but then demands first an outline, and then the detail in relation to all the headings of the plan structure sketched above. The 'how to' questions are far from obvious, and we pick up these in subsequent chapters. I have also examined the corporate plan for 1996–2000 which reviewed progress on the first corporate plan and set out future plans in detail. The structure of the plan remained largely the same, which suggests that we managed to have a good starting point!

3.2.2 The Cisco formula: a 'schools' challenge and the future of HE

A different kind of strategy challenge was provided by the Cisco programme and offers an international case study. This generated, in broad terms, the development of White Papers on schools' reform and HE 3.0[5] – the latter also exploring corporate universities.[6] In parallel, specifically at the time, this also generated a response to Hurricane Katrina in New Orleans in 2005 and the task of rapidly rebuilding the schools system from scratch as outlined in Section 2.2 of Chapter 2. This programme of work, with both immediate and longer-term objectives, produced what I have referred to as the Cisco formula:

$$C[R(T, C, A, L), S, P, Tech].$$ [7]

The elements of the formula are:

T: teachers (staff)
C: curriculum (what are we here for?)
A: accountability (responsibilities, performance management)
L: leadership
S: skills
P: pedagogy (how to ...)
Tech: technological change (disruption?)

It was based on research studies that argued that for a good schools' system, the quality of the teachers must come first, and then the other elements put in place.[8] It can be generalised. It provides a tool to help to assemble the elements for a strategy and was deployed in the post-Katrina schools strategy.

More broadly, the White Papers, particularly the HE 3.0, produced some ideas that can still be brought into play for current and future strategic thinking, some with uses beyond higher education (HE). Four of these are identified here:

- First, Andersson's idea that a successful region needed three capabilities: cognitive, creative, and communications.[9] In HE terms, these obviously map onto teaching and learning (and the maintenance of a knowledge base), research, and outreach.
- The second of these emphasised the importance for the future of life-long learning, which connects to work-based learning, and the ability of universities, as repositories of knowledge, to develop their outreach through consultancy. This led to the suggestion that the university of the future should have some version of a College of Life-Long Learning, a College of Corporate Learning, and a company – University Consultants PLC. Versions of these exist, of course, but few on a big enough scale to be fully effective, inhibited by competition with traditional departments for resources.[10] This competition is short-sighted, of course: beyond the costs of the initial investment, departments are likely to benefit, offering courses to a new market, and supporting university spin-outs such as GMAP.
- A third idea was to recognise the importance of 'translational research' as a particular branch of applied research. This illustrates the need for horizon scanning for new ideas which can be applied more widely. Translational research captures these and explores how they can be applied, and the range of fields of application. This is very much a neglected area.
- Fourth, the idea that the concept of a university teaching hospital associated with a medical school was a model that might be applied in other areas.

There is much food for thought here notwithstanding that the HE3.0 paper was written around 15 years ago! Progress is slow!

3.3 Government: education, cities, health, IT, and defence

3.3.1 The Department for Education and Skills (DfES)

I begin with my experience in DfES, and then move on to other government departments, and a range of operational units on which I conducted reviews.

My DfES experience could have been included under 'education', but it represents a change of scale and it helps to illustrate the distinctive role of 'government'. We can pick up the elements of the big picture introduced in Sections 2.1–2.3 in Chapter 2, which in the university case was represented by (T, R, O, S, and A). These headings have to be translated into central policy headings, bearing in mind that the levers for implementing these policies range from an annual letter of guidance from the Department to universities, and through the actions of a number of agencies – NDPBs[11] – notably the funding council, HEFCE at the time, which allocated the central spend to universities, largely based on a formula relating to student numbers by subject, along with research funding. This core could be supplemented by central strategic 'initiatives'.

I identified a number of areas and sub-areas of policy (which, as noted earlier, at the time we called the BSQs – the 'big strategic questions'):

- learning and teaching, including:
  - a expanding student numbers to reach the 50% target
  - b lifelong learning and continuing professional development (CPD)
  - c widening access
  - d student support (including responsibility for the Student Loan Company)
- research, including:
  - a connecting the Research Assessment Exercise (RAE) and quality-related research (QR) funding
  - b links to the economy and communities
- funding: implementing, in the early days, student fees
- effective system delivery.

There were challenges on all fronts which demanded strategic thinking and problem-solving. In fact, there was no strategic plan as such until 2005 when Michael Barber,[12] who was Head of the new Prime Minister's Delivery Unit at the time (of which more in Chapter 5) demanded a strategic plan from each government department. There was more attempted micro-management rather than 'strategy plus clear devolution of responsibilities for implementation'. Indeed, the annual letter of guidance to universities at the time I arrived was 54 pages in length. We immediately managed to reduce the next one to five or six pages.[13]

The student fees' issue was highly controversial and the Bill to authorise its implementation was only carried by four votes in a House of Commons second reading debate in January 2004. There were problems with the 'fairness' of university admissions and this led to a long exploration of the possibilities of post-qualification admissions (PQA); the management of the Open University thought they were underfunded,[14] and indeed there was a continuing problem with part-time student funding and support. There was a problem with science education in schools, noted earlier, that not enough STEM – science, technology, engineering and mathematics – students were being delivered to universities.

I can add a second example which shows how elements of a strategic plan can suddenly generate a new problem which demands creative thinking. Around the time that Alan Johnson returned to the Department as Secretary of State, He asked to meet me to discuss the 50% target, i.e. that 50% of the population under 30 should have some experience of HE. The target had been announced a couple of years earlier by the Prime Minister, Tony Blair. Alan had had a meeting with the PM who had asked him when the 50% target would be achieved. The question was passed on to me. I said that I didn't know but I would find out. My analysts produced a mini model and estimated that it would be 20 years into the future. I reported back and Alan was horrified. I offered a solution: invest in part-time work-based learning, provided by universities, increase the take-up, and the 20 years could be reduced to 5. The proposal was accepted with relief, and that refined a small part of the Department's strategy! This was an example of problem-solving within the context of strategic thinking – adapting to meet a target through the addition of a good output.

A third example: JISC. I was asked to review of Joint Information Systems Committee (JISC) already mentioned as an example in Section 2.2.1 in Chapter 2. The big picture perspective was critical in the formulation of an ongoing strategy. The refocus that was needed on teaching, research, and outreach, in addition to the IT implications for management and administration, was central. The existing structure incorporated four companies, 13 regional centres and a scatter of units in different locations. There was also a range of funders, with the funding not clearly related to structures and projects. The new strategy, therefore, demanded a new funding system, part funding from government, part from users; and some serious restructuring which we record in Chapter 5. The changes that were needed were complex and so it was necessary to suggest immediate priorities for the short term. The good news was that the recommended changes were implemented!

3.3.2 Other government departments: the beginnings of 'joining up'

Shortly after I took up my post in DFES, I was given the Chief Scientific Adviser (CSA) role,[15] though I don't think I ever had the formal title! This made me a regular attender of the Wednesday morning CSAs' meeting, chaired by the Government Chief Scientific Adviser, then Sir Dave King, and so connected me to a wide range of other departments. None of this directly connected me to strategic planning as such, but it did provide opportunities to contribute to cross-departmental challenges. It emerged, for example, that many departments needed demographic forecasts for their planning and, albeit supported by the Office for National Statistics (ONS), there were teams in each department – Transport and Work and Pensions, for example, as well as within DfES – that were doing the work. It was clearly possible to have a larger and more effective joint team and I proposed this. It was accepted in the CSA community and then passed on to a cross-departmental Whitehall committee – I think whose brief was 'research' – and it was shunted into the long grass to await the next Comprehensive Spending Review, and that was the last I heard of it.

I had productive discussions with Frank Kelly, then the CSA in Transport, on urban modelling and with Sally Davies – later Chief Medical Officer – on health research. In the latter case, she formally had a large budget but most of it was not being spent on research and she wanted to redirect it.

The most interesting case came a number of years later after I had left DFES, when I chaired the Foresight Future of Cities group for Mark Walport, then GCSA, as introduced in Section 2.3.8 of Chapter 2. Our work had academic and local impacts but not in Whitehall where the silos continued to flourish. We identified 14 government departments that had urban policy interests that would be represented in their strategic plans. However, attempts to get them to work on a joined-up strategy largely failed, essentially because they wanted to run their own policy briefs without 'outside interference'. We were much more successful with examples in local government where we were able to support the setting-up of local mini foresight studies – notably in Newcastle and Milton Keynes.[16] In the latter case, we explicitly worked through the policy, analysis, and design (PAD) framework, concluding that Milton Keynes, while very successful, was 'tired' and needed half a dozen big ideas to drive it forward – the D-challenge from PAD. One of these ideas was the creation of Milton Keynes University – MK:U – which is now being implemented. Our reports, notably on scenario development for example, were intended as 'manuals' to encourage further work, both centrally and locally.

Another example is the Defence Scientific Advisory Council (DSAC). At the time of the review, the DSAC agenda was more like a shopping list of small initiatives and needed a comprehensive base on which it could prioritise. Although the remit was 'science and technology', discussions led to a recommendation that the focus of DSAC should be aligned with the Ministry of Defence (MoD) delivery focus, for example, to the four 'commands'.[17] In this case, a new CSA abolished DSAC and started again with DSEC[18] which still exists!

3.4 Industry: towards a framework

My own experience is limited, but we can think through what the strategic planning might look like, particularly looking for common elements, across industry. We can work through the categories of the standard industrial classification, starting with business-to-people organisations, supplying goods and services. These include a wide range of sectors: auto; banking, insurance, investment companies and finance; construction and property; consumer goods; leisure; media; retail; telecoms; transport; and utilities. Business-to-business organisations include (with some repetition) auto; banking, insurance, investment companies, and finance; construction and property; engineering; industrials; natural resources; professional and support services; real estate; technology; telecoms; transport; utilities. Then we can add, as another kind of 'industry' under the heading of 'government', public services to people: health; education; defence; security and, police; and many others. Each has customers or clients to whom they deliver goods and services, usually competing with other organisations in a market. We need to understand the 'production technology' of each organisation in each sector, from sourcing inputs – the supply chain – to production and on to delivery. As ever, the big picture is critical. Many case studies are available, not least because most university business schools focus on 'research on' rather than 'research for'. Large organisations will have their own 'research for' operations and may use consultants to fill gaps: we should treat consultants as important agents in the industry ecosystem.

In thinking through the research base for strategic planning in industry, we will focus on markets, part of 'what are we for?', in this case, 'who are we serving?' but postpone this discussion to Chapter 7.

As a starting point, a useful template is that provided by Baghai, Coley, and White[19] – in many ways stating the obvious, but valuable as a strategy building tool and it is useful to introduce it here and then follow through in more detail in Chapter 7. It is aimed at supporting growth and income generation and has seven elements:

- existing products to existing customers
- new customers
- the possibility of new products and services
- new geographies
- development of new technologies
- a new industry structure – that is, in the 'environment'
- new competitive arenas.

This of course, has wide applicability. University planners should work through this as part of exploring the development of a strategic plan.

3.5 Research

3.5.1 Experience

In terms of my usual range of examples, with the possible exception of the Arts and Humanities Research Council (AHRC) and the Alan Turing Institute, I was not engaged in producing a strategic plan for research as such. It was implicit in Chapter 2 that gathering intelligence to build a big picture also involved gathering intelligence on research priorities. As a process for me, in the first ten years of my working life, I took the priorities as largely given in terms of the jobs I was doing – in the CES case, failing to build a big picture as I should have done! In the Leeds case, in my later stages, as noted, I made many visits to people who were themselves involved in setting research priorities – the Government Chief Scientific Adviser (GCSA), a head of a research council and research-based industries, as in BT and pharmaceuticals – certainly intelligence gathering. In the university, departments retained the responsibility for research planning, but this was influenced from the centre in two ways: (1) having a development fund with a bidding process for projects, many of which laid foundations for new research; and (2) setting up new departments to invest in new areas which certainly had a research component, notably Environment and Communications, for example. In the AHRC case, we did have a wide range of links with the research community. There was little agreement about new priorities but as a Council, we were able to identify some new areas to prioritise. We did document some of this in the context of establishing that arts and humanities research had impacts![20]

3.5.2 Education research: seeking wider insights

The British Academy/Royal Society project on education research was interesting in terms of strategic thinking, though not producing a plan as such. We noted in Chapter 2 that the identification and articulation of the research ecosystem were crucial and this included three groups of agents: practitioners (users, teachers), researchers, and policy makers (including funders). Each of the principal agents in the ecosystem needed their own strategic plan! So, rather than attempt a plan for the whole system, an impossibility, we made a series of recommendations aimed as appropriate at each of the three groups. A summary of the recommendations follows:

1. Setting up an Office for Education Research which could have some kind of oversight of the ecosystem, perhaps achieve some coordination, but this was never implemented.[21]
2. Review the 'geography' of the distribution of researchers and seek to promote collaboration with practitioners and policy makers in local areas.
3. Focus research on the Department's 'big strategic questions', emphasising interdisciplinary approaches.
4. Build the researcher pipeline, for example, ensuring the provision of PhD training.
5. Ensure that universities use their QR funding to secure appropriate research infrastructure.
6. Ensure that research is deployed to support teaching, encouraging critical evaluation and research-informed practice.
7. Facilitate the needs of policy makers; second policy makers to research teams.
8. Support the production and use of evidence synthesis.

It can be seen that most of these recommendations are focused on connecting researchers, practitioners, and policy makers and ensuring that teaching is research-informed. These ideas could easily be transferred to other research-related ecosystems!

3.6 Lessons learned

The hard work is in articulating the big picture and associated problems and challenges, and its PDA/STM basis. Strategy can be based on the discussions and debates around the big picture. This 'thinking-through' stage will bring 'maintenance vs development' issues to the fore and will place new emphasis in the 'D' part of PDA: inventing solutions and assembling projects. This will lead into finance, structures, and 'making things work' in the following chapters.

It will pay to look ahead and perhaps aim for a five-year plan which might also include ambitions for the longer term. It is likely that there will be a need to revise it, perhaps every two years, so it becomes a rolling five-year plan. There will be a need for a precise financial plan for one year, probably called an 'operational plan' and produced well before the relevant financial year to allow time for adjustments, recruitment, and so on.

Notes

1 Ashby (1956), Beer (1972; 1994).
2 Adapted from a saying by Robert Caro (2021).
3 Elements: widening access, health support, and disabled student support.
4 An idea 'borrowed' from the neighbouring Leeds Polytechnic.
5 Cisco (2007) and see Schlecty (2005).
6 This could have been implemented in the Cisco case but failed to gain enough traction with the management. A missed opportunity!
7 Cisco's philanthropic arm donated $40M to support the rebuilding of the New Orleans schools system.
8 McKinsey and Company (2007).
9 Andersson (2005).
10 These ideas illustrate the D-role in the PAD framework.
11 NDPBs are non-departmental public bodies.
12 Michael Barber (2015).
13 The scale of micro management was borne out in a comment to me before I took up the post by Howard Newby, then Chief Executive of HEFCE, who conjectured, rightly as it turned out, that I would have more staff working for me on 'policy' than the whole staff of HEFCE.
14 Picked up in Chapter 6 and Annex 3, Section A3.4.1 where the visit to Milton Keynes is discussed.
15 Charles Clarke, the Secretary of State, was asked in the House of Commons why his Department did not have a Chief Scientific Adviser. He replied, off the cuff, I think, that 'we now have Alan Wilson as Director-General for Higher Education, and he can act as the CSA'.
16 See Government Office for Science (2013) and Dixon and Tewdwr-Jones (2021).
17 See Defence Scientific Advisory Council (2014), Ministry of Defence.
18 DSEC: Defence Science Expert Committee.
19 Baghai, Coley and White (1999).
20 See Arts and Humanities Research Council (2009).
21 Royal Society (2019).

Bibliography

Andersson, C. (2005) Urban evolution, Department of Physical Resource Theory, Chalmers University of Technology, Gothenburg.

Arts and Humanities Research Council (2009) *Leading the world: The economic impact of UK arts and humanities research*, AHRC, Swindon.

Ashby, W. R. (1956) *An introduction to cybernetics*, Chapman and Hall, London.

Baghai, M., Coley, S., and White, D. (1999) *The alchemy of growth*, Perseus Publications, Cambridge, MA.

Barber, M. (2015) *How to run a government*, Penguin, Harmondsworth.

Beer, S. (1972) *Brain of the firm*, John Wiley & Sons, Chichester.

Beer, S. (1994) *Designing freedom*, John Wiley & Sons, Chichester.

Caro, R. (2021) *Working*, Vintage, London.

Christensen, C. M. (1997) *The innovator's dilemma*, Harper Business, New York.

Cisco (2007) *Equipping every learner for the 21st century*, Cisco Systems Inc, San Jose, CA.

Dixon, T. and Tewdwr-Jones, M. (2021) *Urban futures*, University of Bristol Press, Bristol.

Defence Scientific Advisory Council (2014) Triennial review report, 24 March. Ministry of Defence, London.

Government Office for Science (2013) Future of cities project report. Available at: https://www.gov.uk/government/uploads/system/uploads/attachment.data/file/520963/GS-16-6-future-of-cities-an-overview-of-the-evidence.pdf.

McKinsey and Company (2007) *How the world's best school systems come out on top*, McKinsey and Company, London.

Mintzberg, H. (1989) *Structure in fives: Designing effective organisations*, Prentice-Hall, Englewood Cliffs, NJ.

Mintzberg, H. and Quinn, J. B. (1992) *The strategy process*, Prentice-Hall, Englewood Cliff, NJ.

Royal Society (2019) *Harnessing education research*, British Academy and the Royal Society, London.

Schlecty, P. C. (2005) *Creating great schools: Six critical systems at the heart of educational innovation*, Jossey-Bass, San Francisco, CA.

4 Pillar 3: turn every page

4.1 Turn every page

4.1.1 Following Robert Caro

In the strategy, looking at the long term, and in an associated short-run operational plan, we need to have a full understanding of the finances in order to set out provisional budgets – both overall and for our spending units (not yet defined!) – and identify the investment necessary to implement strategy.[1] This will involve evaluating investment alternatives and exploring sources of funding; cost-benefit analysis will be valuable. We need to be able to monitor spending and related achievement. If, as often happens, the starting point is that any 'budget' is showing a loss, an idea that has stuck in my mind came from a Chief Executive Officer (CEO) of a large steel company in Sheffield when we were both on a course for CEOs: 'You have two alternatives: either cut your costs or increase your income!'

A key idea here comes from my reading of Robert Caro, a journalist who became a distinguished biographer. In both professions, he argued that you had to 'turn every page' to make sure that you didn't miss any gems. It is helpful to translate this to 'accounts'. 'A full understanding' means that senior management, including the CEO, needs to be comfortable in 'reading every line' of the accounts.[2] There is no substitute for this. This also involves ensuring that the Finance Director, working with his or her financial accounts and bound by complex regulations, has also to translate the financial accounts into management accounts, presented in a way that supports management without the necessity for complicated translation, if only financial accounts are being used.[3] This also has the advantage that if, as is common, the senior manager is not an accountant, it is possible to ask apparently naïve questions which can be very fruitful in what they can uncover. Ultimately, an objective in reading accounts is to be able to relate income and expenditure to activities, and activities to objectives.

In the rest of this section, I offer some observations from my university experience but, as ever, they translate easily into other fields. In the remainder of the chapter, I work through the usual range of examples.

DOI: 10.4324/9781003673149-4

4.1.2 Preliminaries: some principles

It is worth drawing attention to a number of subsidiary principles which apply to many of the examples in following sections.

- *Open accounts*: subject to obvious areas where confidentiality and privacy are important, make the accounts as open as possible. This eases, for example, budget discussions at times when an argument about 'increasing *my* budget' can be coupled with 'show me where else in the accounts that increase could come from'! More broadly, it facilitates understanding across the organisation.
- *Budgets*: the annual 'budget' process is often about cutting vs investing. Recall: if there is a financial problem, there are two possibilities, 'increase your income or cut your costs'! We have emphasised the benefits of devolution of responsibilities. This is likely to include planning and allocating devolved budgets – both managing costs and increasing income. This can build in financial incentives to drive towards achieving objectives – a crucial management tool. Devolved budgets do demand a mechanism for integrating the organisation's budget with those of its devolved units. This can partly be achieved by ensuring that there are annual unit plans which can be made consistent with the top-level plan. Another means of integration is to ensure that at the top level, there is a 'development fund' from which units can bid.
- A perennial problem is the end-of-year *underspend*. In many organisations, this is recouped by the centre, and this of course leads to some unproductive spending in units as the year-end approaches. This can be handled if the units are allowed to retain surpluses (up to a sensible amount – perhaps as 'savings for future investment'). But in situations where there is always an underspend, budget for, say, 110% of income rather than 100%.[4]
- A related principle to be implemented through the budget process, is the maintenance of adequate *reserves*. This facilitates the management of 'surprises', on the one hand, and unexpected *opportunities* for development, on the other. One example in the first category: the double-counting of £4M in expected income in the Finance Department, meant that the already agreed budget had overestimated income by the £4M. Another surprise is related to a £20M loan from Hambros which we were expecting to renew. The renewal had been 'forgotten'. I went to London and had a traditional 'bankers lunch' with Sir Chips Keswick, then the CEO of Hambros, to discuss the problem. Lots of social chat and finally at coffee time, I did raise the £20M loan issue, the main agenda for the lunch. There was no discussion. 'That's not a problem,' said Chips, 'we'll just roll it over.' When I told this story to a friend later, he remarked, wisely, that the 'social chat' was probably an informal exploration of my, and the University's, reliability. In any case, the problem was solved.

An example of an unexpected opportunity was a request from the Funding Council for us to take over Bretton Hall, a neighbouring College of Higher Education, which was in severe financial difficulties. The financial challenge here was to estimate the cost to the University of implementing this and negotiating with the Funding Council to provide the requisite sum. A knowledge of the accounts, and the financial impact of this proposed development, was vital. It had to be large enough to satisfy the University Senate, which at best was lukewarm, and small enough to be acceptable to the Funding Council. With some difficulty, I persuaded the Funding Council to provide £12M (from an initial 'offer' of half of that). A second example, was the golden opportunity to purchase 10 acres of land adjacent to the university campus, and the buildings, to be vacated by Leeds Grammar School which had decided to move to a more spacious out-of-town site. More on that below. This means that £6M had to be found at short notice, and having reserves was crucial.

4.1.3 Where does the money come from?

To state the obvious: to understand and plan finances, an in-depth understanding of the organisation's 'business' is crucial. Which community – customers or clients – is served with goods and services? How does the 'market' work? Who competes with us? What is our 'production function'? What is our 'technology'? All the terms in inverted commas are in one sense basic economics and have to be understood as such. But they also have to be interpreted for the organisation and fitted into the management structure in a way that is understood by both management and employees. Generating and deploying this understanding build on our core pillars – notably developing the big picture and recognising that financial planning is critical to strategy, structures, and 'making things work'! We pursue these questions in relation to our examples, but, first, it is worth spending some time on a special category, philanthropy, whether as giver or receiver.

4.1.4 Some bonuses: gifts

Philanthropic donations can be valuable, often making big capital investments possible. Generating these was not one of my strengths but I did have quite of lot of luck in potential donors coming forward. Mrs Mary Keyworth approached the university and said that she would like to make a donation in memory of her husband who had graduated from the Colour Chemistry Department in 1922. We had no idea at the outset what she had in mind and two of us travelled to meet her in Jersey to explore, carrying a shopping list of possibilities. In the event, she wanted to be assured that her donation would be one of the largest we had ever received and signed a cheque for £2M – I think to the consternation of her solicitor who was in attendance! Our purchase of the Leeds Grammar School site followed shortly afterwards and her donation allowed us to achieve an excellent conversion of the main building, now named the Maurice and Mary Keyworth Building, for a new Business School. We did persuade her to visit Leeds to see the fruits of what her donation had achieved.

Another unsolicited donation came from Dame Kathleen Raven, a former Chief Nursing Officer at the Department of Health. She had been concerned that in becoming a graduate profession, nursing had lost its ability to be a caring profession. Her donation enabled us to endow a new Chair and was an important stimulus in the development of a new Faculty of Health.

A third example, which also required some creative thinking on the University's part, was from Robert Ogden (later Sir Robert). He was a donor to the University, mainly to the Medical School but he phoned me and said that he would like to make a donation that somehow supported struggling South Yorkshire mining villages where he had in early life built a profitable business moving slag heaps. He wanted to put something back into that community, now declining. I could only think of scholarships, but was aware that school pupils in these areas were mostly leaving school at 16 and were unlikely to be eligible for university scholarships. We co-invented Ogden Scholarships, but to be awarded to 16-year-olds to encourage them to stay on at school. We awarded 40 of these a year and the scheme was hugely successful. Most of the scholars went on to university and we continued their scholarships as a top-up to state funding. In this case, there was a greater success: David Blunkett, then Secretary of State for Education, was impressed by what we were achieving and Ogden Scholarships became the template for a national scheme: Education Maintenance Awards (EMAs).

A fourth example that enabled me to make a different kind of contribution, already noted in Chapters 2 and 3, was in the field of disaster recovery and innovation: Cisco's $40M grant to New Orleans to support the rebuilding of the schools system following the Hurricane Katrina devastation. At the time, I was working for Cisco's Vice President for Global Education, Michael Stevenson, as a consultant on higher education. I was diverted from HE to help with the New Orleans schools project. This led to the 'formula' (Section 3.2.2 in Chapter 3) and, in relation to higher education, the exploration of the idea of a corporate university – an exploration that failed, possibly because of internal 'politics' in Cisco management. Nonetheless, we generated some good ideas relating to the future of HE, still surprisingly relevant after almost 20 years. These are pursued in Chapter 7.

A fifth example is totally different. It illustrates the possibility of using access to generous philanthropists to solve problems which are not in themselves central to the organisation. I learned from a newspaper report over New Year of 1997 of two sisters, a 16-year-old and an 18-year-old, who lost both parents between Christmas and the New Year. The latter was a Leeds first-year student. I saw her at the beginning of term and she told me that she was going to leave, return home to look after her sister who would otherwise be taken into care. Then, to cut a long story short: I wrote to around 20 people, some known to me, some not, but very well known and thought by me to be 'charitable', and I asked for donations of between five and ten thousand pounds. We very quickly raised £100,000, set up a Trust Fund with the help of as local solicitor acting pro bono. The house where the younger sister lived was heavily mortgaged. The Trust bought it. We bought the older one a car so she could get home easily and frequently. And with a bit of luck, a teacher from the younger one's school lived next door and we managed to convince Social Services that this provided enough 'care'. Both have graduated, have good and interesting jobs, and are now married with children. It was a privilege to be able to rescue people from a tragic situation. Celeste Hicks, the older of the sisters, wrote her own account of the event, 25 years later, in *The Guardian.* [5]

These examples all illustrate how philanthropic donations can be transformative and can offer, in these cases, real pleasure to the donor.

4.2 Education: how financial management can change the 'culture'

A shift in culture achieved in the University early on in my management role provides a useful example of how policies on finance can bring about major changes in culture. I had two years as a Pro-Vice-Chancellor (PVC) before taking on the Vice-Chancellorship. In the first of these years, I attended the committee that was allocating departmental budgets for the coming year. Departments had been allowed to bid, and, of course, the total of bids far exceeded the total budget available. The argument was always about what were perceived as 'cuts'. For the following year, though the same process was followed, I suggested to the VC that I prepared a 'provisional' allocation to lead the discussion. This allocation was very largely accepted and there was no discussion about 'cuts'! The vocabulary was changed.

By the following year, I was Vice-Chancellor and a 'resource centre' system was in place. Budgets were devolved to departments along with rules that stimulated income generation. There was a cultural switch from 'cuts' to the 'opportunities for new income'.[6] Departmental budgets were largely determined by the drivers such as student numbers and of course this encouraged growth. The effect was a formula that determined income on the basis of these drivers; 40% of income earned was retained by the centre as an 'overhead' – something that was understood and accepted; but 60% of all income generated by a department stayed in the department's budget. One example of the new rules illustrates the speed of the impact. Under the old system, departments were given 6% of the international student fee, the centre keeping the rest. In the new scheme, the centre kept only the 40% overhead and 60% of the fees went to the department. Needless to say, international student numbers rose rapidly. This financial system change, along with the devolution of financial responsibilities to departments, became the driver of the growth of the university. We were lucky, of course, that national policy supported an expansion in higher education, so we could more or less freely expand student numbers. It is easier to manage challenges in that situation.

The culture changed: the debate shifted from 'cuts' to 'development'. There was a first-year driver: cuts were made that were larger than was required to balance the budget. This enabled the creation of a development fund, and departments could bid for access to this through project proposals – again helping to create a new culture.

The key change was structural – the fourth of our key pillars in play.

4.3 Government: never enough money?

Ministers decide policy, and civil servants are responsible for planning projects, even a strategy, and, indeed, sometimes implementing it directly. A common starting point is to identify the 'levers' which can be used and a major element of this is the planning of government expenditure: the money. In many cases, fiscal policies are important, essentially tax and benefits, but the immediate elements are revenue and capital spend. Implementation is usually in the hands of other autonomous agencies – local government, health and welfare services, and universities, for example. Devolution and subsidiarity principles are important here: micro-management is to be avoided, but very often was not! There are some guiding principles: i.e. is it VFM, 'value for money'? And avoiding spend on 'deadweight': 'would it have happened anyway?'

These spending decisions were, and are, set in the broader framework of spending reviews: the Treasury allocates money to departments, and departments allocate the money to broad internal budget lines. There is likely to be a 'maintenance vs development question': what do we have to spend to maintain services at a good or adequate level? What can we spend on new projects to implement new policies? Serious battles ensue between departments during the spending review which might include 'shroud waving' or 'security' threats! And there are further battles within the department. In the latter case, some expenditure is sometimes 'ring-fenced' to ensure protection of key policies. There was one such case in my own experience when the Secretary of State, who was 'reading every line', wanted to divert spend on university research to other uses. I had to explain that it had been ring-fenced as part of an earlier 'deal' with the Treasury on universities, which was then accepted with rather bad grace!

The allocation and spend system worked reasonably well though it exposed two issues: (1) there was not always the expertise in the Department to plan effective projects; and (2) it was very difficult to ensure that external agencies to whom the spend was allocated would use it appropriately, or, indeed, had the expertise to do so. The latter is a large-scale version of the challenge of managing budgets to departments in universities, something which is easier to organise on a smaller scale.

An example of my own on the benefits of 'reading every line' emerged when I undertook my own review of the Department's own research budget, introduced as an example of the importance of the 'big picture' in Section 2.5.3 in Chapter 2. The budget was about £50M per annum, half the size of one of the research council's budget – serious money. I found one line with an expenditure of £20M on one project and investigated this with as much curiosity as concern. It turned out to be an 'evaluation' of the Sure Start programme. How could we be spending £20M on this? The answer was that there was an element of evaluation for each local authority receiving Sure Start funds and market research was being commissioned to be carried out in each authority; and the costs of this soon mount up. There was no way it could be value for money, and, in any case, it was clearly too soon to do the evaluation – and inevitably, the results were inconclusive. As noted in Section 2.5.3 in Chapter 2, the Permanent Secretary did what was probably the only thing he could have done: asked me to review the whole process of allocating research funding and to make some recommendations. I left DfES shortly after I submitted the report and I am not sure they were ever implemented!

4.4 Industry

'Industry' is made up of a great variety of organisations all of which need effective financial plans. The principles introduced in Sections 4.1.2 and 4.1.3 are widely applicable and can be transferred and interpreted for any organisation (or unit within an organisation). Finance is a crucial (third) focus within the four pillars, and building up a framework – a toolkit – for financial planning has to incorporate elements of all of them. Section 4.1.3 provides the starting point: which community – customers or clients – is served with goods and services? How does the 'market' work? Who competes with us? What is our 'production function'? What is our 'technology'?

Analytics and an articulation of the big picture provide the starting point. An understanding of the relevant markets takes us to 'marketing' how to spend to attract customers and clients. Broadly, particularly to explore new markets, we can refer back to the framework introduced in Section 3.4 in Chapter 3 through the work of Baghai, Coley, and White[7] – the BCW framework, aimed at supporting growth and income generation – repeated here for convenience:

- existing products to existing customers
- new customers
- the possibility of new products and services
- new geographies
- development of new technologies
- a new industry structure – that is, in the 'environment'
- new competitive arenas.

The marketing plan is one element of a financial plan. In terms of strategic thinking, we have seen that we need to explore the challenges of both maintenance and development: how to spend to maintain the business, and how to invest to cover both depreciation and future growth; and to respond to changing technologies. In the case of investment, we can draw on cost-benefit analysis (CBA) – we gave Portbury as an example in Section 2.3.3 in Chapter 2. We can respond to technological change either as an innovator if we are fully connected to research, or as a follower if we can at least keep up-to-date with the possibilities. What we can't do is fall behind! Investment early in the game may give a short-run 'first mover'[8] advantage and what will be short-lived but potentially valuable monopoly power.

The implementation of new technologies will raise structural challenges (cf. Section 5.1 in Chapter 5 where we introduce Christensen's (1997) argument about disruptive technologies). Mintzberg's (1989) argument about structures, also presented in Section 5.1 in Chapter 5, is important for planning in specifying the financial responsibilities of different units, particularly within a devolved system.

We have focused implicitly on revenue attracted from customers and clients as the bedrock of a business. We also need to be concerned with raising investment, for example, for a start-up if that was appropriate; and how to determine dividends relative to retention of profits for investment purposes. More broadly, we need to review the sources of investment: bank loans, equity via the stock market, government, or private equity.

This can be all be illustrated by the company of which I was a co-founder and director: GMAP Ltd, which was introduced and sketched in Section 2.5.1 in Chapter 2 and to which we will return in Section 5.4.2 in Chapter 5 and Annex 3, Section A3.3.3 with a structural point. In terms of the framework of this section, GMAP illustrated how the analytics can be provided to clients to connect the production function, markets, and customers. Financial analysis is at the heart of this. If we take retail in a broad sense as an example, and then specifically a supermarket to fix ideas, then GMAP begins with a client's network of outlets which supply goods to customers at a variety of locations. Its models connect each outlet to each possible residential zone of customers – generating a large matrix of cash flows between customer locations and retail outlets. Flows from competitors can be estimated. The revenue attracted into a store can be calculated. The costs of running the store will be known to the company and so profit can be calculated for each store. This computer model can be used to test efficiencies, to modify the network to increase company profits, to estimate the capital that can be invested in a new site to produce a profitable store, and to explore the possibility of take-overs. In other words, to provide an analytics base which functions as a real-time information system rooted in finance.[9]

4.5 Research

The financial issues relating to research and industry have been largely handled, if implicitly, in earlier sections. For research budgets, once priorities are decided, and the total budget available is known, allocations can be made – though typically not without difficulty as different elements, within and between organisations, compete. There are technical issues to be handled, of course: identifying sources of income, articulating overheads and full economic costs, for example. In the case of industry and public services, this means understanding costs and revenues associated with different activities, supply chains – essentially, the production technology.

4.6 Lessons learned

All in all, the financial accounts need to be understood in detail, and be in good order well in advance of audit requirements. But the plans and implementation will be based on management accounts that link directly to objectives, performance, and targets. The CEO should 'read every line'! The management accounts will be 'open' (apart from anything which needs to be private – probably salaries and wages, for example). This will have provided the basis for discussion and debate, and be a record of final decisions and, hopefully, broad agreement. In the likely event of having financial constraints, it is necessary to bear in mind the mantra that in that situation, you have two choices: 'increase your income or cut your costs' (or both!).

As we have seen, devolution of responsibilities is likely to be key; and rules for managing budgets at different levels of the organisation will provide an important driver. This is particularly the case since the responsibility includes cost management, but, just as important, income generation.

Notes

1 There is an idea here which has stuck since my GMAP days when we had Mel Hopley as Chair of the Board. He used to say, 'Devise your strategy, and then assemble the resources to implement it.' This from a former director of ICI who in past lives would have been able to go to the market, or to shareholders, for capital for development. This was not so easy for start-ups.
2 Robert Caro (2021), 'turn every page', modified here to 'read every line'.
3 It took me several years after becoming Vice-Chancellor in Leeds, to achieve this.
4 In my university experience, there was always a substantial underspend on the estates' budget because of projects always taking longer than planned. I took advantage of this by taking back the surplus in many years, much to the consternation of my Estates Director who saw this as committed future expenditure. I explained that this was not a cut, they could continue as usual, and I took the surplus into the university development fund.
5 For her own version of this story in *The Guardian*, see Hicks (2021).
6 A complement, at the start, was to make a bigger cut than seemed necessary to create a development fund to make the 'new opportunities' real.
7 Baghai, Coley and White (1999).
8 For those who are not horse racing aficionados, the term 'first mover' comes from a strategy which is sometimes adopted on the course: as the field begins to speed up in the final furlong, the 'first mover' accelerates slightly early and establishes a lead which cannot be overtaken!
9 See Martin's GMAP book, Clarke (2020).

Bibliography

Baghai, M., Coley, S., and White, D. (1999) *The alchemy of growth*, Perseus Publications, Cambridge, MA.

Caro, R. A. (2021) *Working*, Vintage, London.

Christensen, C. M. (1997) *The innovator's dilemma*, Harper Business, New York.

Clarke, M. (2020) *How geography changed the world, and my small part in it*, Sweet Design Ltd, Bristol.

Freedman. S. (2024) *Failed state: Why nothing works and how we fix it*, Macmillan, London.

Hicks, C. (2021) Experience: I was orphaned at Christmas – and saved by kind strangers, *The Guardian*, 17 December.

Mintzberg, H. (1989) *Structure in fives: Designing effective organisations*, Prentice-Hall, Englewood Cliffs, NJ.

5 Pillar 4: structures for delivery

5.1 Delivery principles

5.1.1 Structures for delivery

We now move on to the fourth and last of our core pillars. We have the big picture (Chapter 2), we have a strategy (Chapter 3), we have, at least in broad terms, finance and budgets (Chapter 4). We now have to deliver the strategy, having already noted the old mantra that having a strategy is 5% of the challenge, implementing it is 95%. Above all, effective delivery means that we must have effective structures.

A key idea which runs throughout is that it is impossible to run an organisation of any size from the centre: there has to be effective *devolution.* [1] At the top, and for each devolved unit, there has to be effective leadership – a need for a CEO or equivalent, a management team, at all levels of the structure – to drive and to keep focused.

There are some points which we need to keep in mind at the outset, noting Mintzberg's more or less self-explanatory classification of types of organisation:[2]

- simple – early stage
- machine bureaucracies – Fordism and beyond
- professional bureaucracies – such as universities and hospitals
- divisionalised – large and subdivided, possibly conglomerate
- ad hoc – for example, management consultants, project-organised.

Mintzberg's argument that in professional bureaucracies, front-line professionals should be properly involved in the management is telling in relation to universities and hospitals in the UK.[3] In terms of the examples used here, universities, hospitals, and the civil service – and their various agencies – are professional bureaucracies; research institutes are adhocracies; much of industry is divisionalised, though start-ups, which connect to research, are 'simple'!

We need to keep in mind 'maintenance vs development' – one of the four issues for strategy building discussed in Section 3.1 in Chapter 3. The first of these will, typically, be well defined (subject to processes being updated to take

DOI: 10.4324/9781003673149-5

advantage of new technologies); the second refers to more radical innovation – 'responding to change' – and is more likely to be, in Christensen's terms, disruptive.[4] He argues that it is likely that current staff will object and make implementation of change difficult. His solution is: set up a new unit, and if it succeeds, it will absorb the old one. (My paraphrasing.) There is also a useful tip, source now forgotten, that in introducing what might be a controversial innovation, 'let someone else take the credit for it!'

A key reference here is Michael Barber's book – heavily focused on delivery.[5] This is a good place to note elements from his check list. In fact, he has 57 points – recommended reading – but here we extract a subset which complements the four pillars, adding practicalities:

- decide priorities
- consult without conceding on ambition
- set up a delivery unit
- understand the potential drivers of change
- have a plan that is good enough to get started
- anticipate the implementation dip
- diagnose problems precisely, and act
- take all excuses off the table
- invest deeply and continually in skill and capability
- periodically adopt a bold clean-slate approach to budgeting to liberate resources
- accept that big data and transparency are coming!

This can be used as part of the chair's briefing!

5.1.2 Basics

The next preliminary step is to outline the key features which will appear in some form or other in any organisation. There will be some kind of hierarchy with a Board, Trustees, or a Council, for example, at the head of it. The Board may have non-executive members, and there may be an inner executive board – the ExCo – which meets more frequently – the latter perhaps known as the 'senior management team' – or SMT – jargon builds up quickly here. There will be devolved units which may be responsible for some decisions through 'delegated authority'. For example, the wider board may be responsible for strategy, the executive board for implementing it along with devolved units, where devolution includes decision-making authority. The organisation may have some kind of committee structure with decision-making authority, possibly also with a hierarchy. Overall, there is likely to be a constitution which aims to make clear who is responsible for which decisions – which may be a board, a sub-committee, or an individual – the Chief Executive Officer (CEO) or the Finance Director, for example. Decision authority may be quite widely distributed in devolved systems.

There are size issues for (management) teams at all levels: how many 'heads/directors', for example. There are also significant issues about 'levels' and the extent to which the management structure should be 'flat'. Devolution is the critical driver here and we have already seen that this is strongly connected to financial incentives, and indeed, recognition and promotion. (Accountability is an issue in the first of these and maintenance of standards is an issue in the last two.) Even with effectively devolved systems, there is an issue of deciding on functions that should be retained at higher levels: HR, accounts or Comms, for example.[6] This depends on the sizes of the organisation and of the devolved units. There will be pressures to retain more at the centre (or higher levels) as a form of control and, unless there is an efficiency case, given the small size of devolved units, this should in general be resisted. It is possible to retain a desirable level of influence on future spend through full delegation of 'maintenance' budgets, and possibly substantial elements of 'development' funds, but the centre may retain an organisation-level development fund and use it either to launch initiatives or to set up a bidding mechanism for devolved units to offer projects, thus enabling simultaneous top-down and bottom-up approaches to development. Informal meetings will support the flow of information and intelligence on development issues.

5.1.3 A note on (un)accountability

We can note here the very important argument by Dan Davies (2024) in his book, *The Unaccountability Machine: Why Big Systems Make Terrible Decisions – And How the World Lost Its Mind*. He builds on the work of Stafford Beer (1972; 1994) on complex systems in management. To paraphrase a complicated story, the decision-making structure in a complex organisation can have many decisions that are in practice determined by 'rules', say, as part of the strategy. If the rules can't handle particular cases and there is no scope for a different kind of human intervention, perhaps to apply 'common sense', this leads to what Davies calls 'accountability sinks'. In my own experience, I have tried to avoid this in regulation-driven decision-making by always including the word 'normally', or something equivalent, in any regulation to provide wriggle room. It is of the greatest importance to take Davies' excellent exposition into account in devising structures, particularly in relation to devolution.

5.2 Education: restructuring for delivery

5.2.1 University

The trigger for restructuring in my Leeds University experience was the devolution of financial responsibilities – as noted in Chapter 4 – mainly to departments, sometimes to small groups of small departments. The devolved units were called 'resource centres' to emphasise that they were not merely cost centres but were responsible for income generation as well, through student recruitment, research grants, and outreach. We were early adopters of this kind of devolution and as it became more common, different universities have used different systems.[7] The most common is probably devolution to faculties. In the Leeds case, we judged this to be retaining an unnecessary layer of management and responsibilities were more appropriately located nearer to the front line in departments. Faculties, and their Deans, still had extensive responsibilities for overseeing academic standards, and the Deans had additional informal responsibilities, in association with Pro-Vice-Chancellors, for linking departments in their faculties to central management.

The starting point was to find, or create, departments that were both large enough to function as resource centres but also academically coherent. At the outset, for me, the University had 96 departments, 19 of these were in Medicine and 7 were in Biology. These were unified as a single School of Medicine and a School of Biological Sciences respectively. A School of Modern Languages was created by merging language departments; and a small group of more disparate small humanities departments were grouped into a Sub-Faculty (borrowing an Oxford term). The 96 were reduced to 55, named, usually, as a 'School' as a mark of something more important than a 'department'![8]

When the budgets were calculated for resource centres, based on what was agreed as a new formula, there were, of course, winners and losers. The School of Medicine was a big loser – bearing out what was thought to be the case in many universities, that Medicine was always being heavily subsidised by the rest of the university. The application of the devolution principles and the thrashing out of the detail are picked up in Chapter 6.

The University's outreach objectives were mainly associated with research but also began to spread into teaching with part-time work-based courses. In order to support this, we instituted a Faculty for Work-based Learning so that the formalities of course approval and assessment, for example, could be devised in a way that was appropriate for the new context. (With hindsight, this can be seen as a response to the Christensen challenge.) Looking ahead, there is a case for universities having a College of Corporate Learning, a College of Life-Long Learning and a company – University Consultants PLC, as argued in the Cisco HE 3.0 White Paper!

5.2.2 *JISC*

It is sometimes possible in developing a new strategy for an organisation to postpone any serious restructuring given other short-run priorities. In the Joint Information Systems Committee (JISC) case, restructuring was itself a high priority. As noted earlier, while JISC itself was not a legal entity – it was 'owned' by the Higher Education Funding Council for England (HEFCE) – it was responsible for four companies, notably the infrastructure company that ran the JANET system.[9] In all, there were around a dozen 'units', each run by a senior manager, with the whole not well coordinated. The Board did not have a clear-sighted view of operations and hence priorities. It was important, therefore, to consolidate services, to simplify the structure, and to ensure that the Board had an adequate oversight. This can be summarised by a skim of the report's recommendations:

- JISC activity should be focused on achieving a large impact:
  - a Activities need to be clearly linked to the sectors' priorities.
  - b JISC should offer sector leadership through 'routes to best practice', wherever such practice resides.
  - c Research and development activity should focus on horizon scanning and thought leadership.
  - d Services and projects should be rationalised, with a view to significantly reducing their number.
- JISC should be funded through a combination of grants and subscriptions/ user charges.
- It should become a separate legal entity and the implications of this for the four companies should be reviewed.
- Governance arrangements should be clarified, to ensure that the Board takes clear overall strategic control.
- The internal structure should be clarified and simplified, to improve efficiency and control.
- A plan for the proposed internal structure and operations should estimate the savings to be achieved.
- There should be discussions between JISC, the funders, sector representatives, and other bodies, to determine an overall funding strategy for ICT in the Higher Education and Further Education sectors.

5.3 Government: how to be agile

5.3.1 Introduction

I have chosen three areas which illustrate how structural change can be valuable. This in itself will not solve problems. It always needs to be connected to, indeed, driven by, work on the other three pillars. These areas are in turn: the Department for Education and Skills (DfES), the Health Service, and the Defence Science Advisory Council.

There is an interesting challenge lurking here: how can an organisation be agile and able to respond to new opportunities, or to implement its development agenda rapidly? I once travelled back from Kings Cross to Leeds with Roger King, the first Vice-Chancellor of the University of Lincoln. I knew he had lots of new projects under way, and I asked him how he managed this. He explained that he had a Project Management Group that could take on any of a variety of new roles at short notice. I immediately set up my own Project Management Group which turned out to be invaluable.[10]

5.3.2 DfES

When I joined the DfES as Director-General for Higher Education, I expected to have a small policy-oriented staff, say, around 20. In fact, I had of the order of 200, with many of the senior staff involved in overseeing – sometimes micro-managing – agencies like the Student Loans Company. It was a time of cuts in civil service staffing and so that provided opportunities for restructuring. One challenge, common across the civil service, I think, at least at the time, was a rigid hierarchical structure. As D-G, I had a private office of three or four which included, for example, a diary secretary. There were Directors, each with a number of Deputy Directors, each in turn with a number of Principals (Grade 7s), each with supporting executive officers and secretarial staff. It was easy to see how the staff numbers grew to 200. A serious issue was that this kind of structure produced a set of silos which were not very efficient in the distribution of workloads and did not facilitate work on new policy challenges. In general, if there was a new challenge, it was tempting to make a new appointment to oversee it. I responded to this by introducing *project groups* – sometimes called 'task and deliver' groups – with the additional rule that the chair of such a group – the 'driver' – was not necessarily the most senior person in the room! This provided more time and energy and was good for staff development. (I had learned from Roger King by this time!)

An additional structural change came from the Permanent Secretary. The Department had around 120 analysts, run as a central unit. They were devolved to Directorates and 26 were allocated to me. They were spread between DfES sites in London, Sheffield, and Darlington and it turned out that they were mostly junior staff who were doing the groundwork to prepare answers to Parliamentary questions – some good people, but not the gain I hoped for.

Perhaps the biggest structural issue was the arrangements for linking DfES and Higher Education policy to the universities. In this case, the emphasis was on having effective informal arrangements in place. This is a specific case of the general challenge in implementing the devolution of responsibilities: how do you ensure that the collective outcome from the devolved units meet the 'central' targets? This has to involve some, perhaps annual, review and coordination. In the universities' case, this was particularly sensitive as 'autonomy' – an endpoint of devolution – was rightly regarded as crucial. The formal link, already mentioned in an earlier context, was the annual letter of guidance from the DfES to the universities. This was important in terms of laying down general principles, but also in seeking to make universities, which are not government institutions, accountable for their spending of public money, and for meeting government targets. There was a large staff in DfES who were, essentially, monitoring this – almost certainly too large.[11] Of equal, and possibly greater, importance were the informal links between DfES and the universities. I was an 'observer' on the HEFCE Board, and the Chair treated me as though I was a member, free to speak as I wished. I attended dinners, more or less annually, of the different university consortia – the Russell Group, the Million

Group, and even the 'unaligned' group, in addition to more regular meetings. I made many visits to universities. In my case, I had the advantage of being a recent former Vice-Chancellor and there was mutual trust in these meetings, conducted on an 'off-the-record' basis.[12] In general, this trust has to be developed. Indeed, this is easily lost, as has happened in recent years in government-universities relationships in the UK, and is currently happening in the USA.

5.3.3 The NHS

As noted in Chapter 2, I had a range of involvement with the NHS, from membership of health authorities to being Vice-Chancellor of a university that had a large medical school. I had one opportunity in the latter role to develop strategy through an interesting structural change: to combine the NHS dental hospital in Leeds with the School of Dentistry in the university. This was challenging: to merge two institutions with their own managements and cultures, but we succeeded and this became a model for other universities to implement. There is a potential to employ this model more widely, wherever two organisations work closely together with overlapping staff.

Another kind of structural change was brought about through my chairing, as noted earlier, a review of NHS complaints procedures and this produced a set of recommendations which were, in effect a new strategy and a proposed a new structure for handling complaints.[13] We produced 62 recommendations that ranged from laying out the principles – including that essentially there should be one procedure instead of nine – to setting out detailed requirements for implementation. This included, controversially, and to the horror of the consultants, that the most serious complaints would be reviewed by a panel which had a majority of independent lay members. Virginia Bottomley, the Secretary of State, was very supportive and the recommendations were mostly implemented.

We noted in Section 5.1.1 Mintzberg's argument that front-line workers in a professional bureaucracy should be directly involved in management, and noted briefly that the changes in this respect in the NHS in the 1970s contradicted this principle. It is possible that the NHS has never recovered from this!

5.3.4 Defence

Some years after I had left the Defence Scientific Advisory Council (DSAC), I was commissioned by the Ministry of Defence to review DSAC as part of the Government's quinquennial review programme for NDGBs[14] – with terms of reference which embraced the questions of: is this something worth keeping? And, if so, what should change?

In Section 2.3.7 in Chapter 2, we emphasised the importance of the Ministry of Defence (MoD) having a big picture, and this was vital for DSAC. The structural challenge for DSAC was to find a way of covering the big picture agenda in relation to science and technology and moving beyond a 'shopping list' approach in setting meetings' agendas. There were two responses to this.

First, that each member of the Council should be allocated a part of the broader picture to 'overlook', and to be able to bring issues to the Council's attention. The second was to make better use of an advisory panel, ISTA,[15] of security-cleared academics who could be drawn on for expertise and advice. Indeed, it was also recommended that ISTA could be more widely used in some other government departments. More broadly, it was argued that the Council's strategic focus should be on three areas: advice, quality assurance, and horizon scanning. These would work on different time scales: advice was usually need quickly, and therefore was short run, and it was suggested that convening workshops (or ISTA) might be more useful than commissioning reports, which often came too late to be useful. Quality assurance demanded a rolling programme of mini-reviews, with occasional deep dives, and represented the middle-run time-scale. Horizon scanning, by its nature, related to the long run. The identification of these time scales for the Council's work represented an interesting dimension of the structural challenge.[16] The recommendations were implemented but then, as noted in Chapter 3, an incoming CSA went further and wound up DSAC and started from scratch with a new council.

5.4 Industry

5.4.1 What do we need to know?

In industry, there is great variety in terms of research needs and finding ways of meeting them. Some sectors, pharmaceuticals, for example, will have large in-house research structures, though even in that specific case, front-line research is to an extent 'delegated' to start-ups and the successful ones can be bought or invested in. Perhaps the only way to handle the variety is to note the scale of research on industrial organisations in business schools, typically on a case-study basis. Perhaps there is a case for research on this vast set of case studies to seek generalisations and good practice.

In all cases, whether developing structures for the core business of an organisation, or in research, an initial 'big picture' and 'systems' focus will be essential.[17] The 'What are we for?' questions progress to 'What do we need to know?' and this will connect core business to research, whether in-house or bought in. We pursue this in more detail in Chapter 7. In all cases, the structure will be represented in a (relatively flat?) hierarchy which makes clear where responsibilities and accountability lie. There will be a 'CEO' at each level. Devolution, as ever, is critical in establishing an effective structure and in association with financing and budget rules, can be a key driver.

5.4.2 GMAP Ltd

Finally, a small but perhaps helpful personal example. As one of the founders of GMAP Ltd, I did much of the early marketing (along with my colleague Martin Clarke).[18] At a slightly later stage, as the company grew, we thought a particular structural change was important: it would reduce the load on Martin and myself. We appointed a Director of Marketing. What emerged was that potential new clients really did need to see the company's principals, largely because of our knowledge base and our ability to shape a potential project more precisely to target what the client needed – rather than promoting a 'product'. The change didn't work and we had to expand by a different route! There was a need for some of the more senior technical staff to take on promotional roles.

5.5 Research

In the preceding sections of this chapter, we have focused on particular examples. It is more difficult to attempt to generalise when we consider 'research' and 'industry' more broadly. Research institutes, in Mintzberg's terms, are adhocracies and are likely to be project-oriented. There are particular challenges such as the need for new blood, often, but not always, meaning 'younger staff'. There is a particular transition to be made from PhD: post docs often wanting to continue with their PhD research (perhaps for good reason), to becoming more mature researchers, transferring skills to new projects. There is a problem at the other end of the age spectrum: finding roles for 'permanent' staff as their research momentum diminishes. This can be particularly acute for research institutes – less of a problem for universities or wider industry, as productive new roles can be found more easily. This, of course, illustrates another challenge for organisations that are not purely research-oriented. In universities, to take an obvious example, there is a well-known challenge to find and guarantee research time in relation to teaching and administration. These are all structural challenges that will have to be solved in different ways in different kinds of organisations – adhocracies – and for larger organisations with wider briefs than research, adhocracies within more traditional structures!

At the heart of research is invention, and the conditions for encouraging this are many and varied and not well understood: supporting a lone researcher through to ensuring that there are groups that are large enough to tackle the biggest challenges. Collaboration may create 'size'. Experience is likely to be a guide, including learning from others.

5.6 Lessons learned

A variety of structures will always be possible. Here we have built on understanding the big picture (Chapter 2), strategy (Chapter 3), and finance (Chapter 4). These should all be understood and driven from the top, but also communicated to (and listened to), at all levels in the hierarchy. Hierarchies should be as flat as possible, agile, silos should be avoided, responsibilities devolved where possible – avoiding accountability sinks. Be aware of the Mintzberg and Christensen principles and challenges. Be aware, and learn from, successes and failures in other organisations – both 'like' and 'different'.

Notes

1 Devolution from central to local government is argued at length by Sam Freedman (2024).
2 Mintzberg (1989).
3 Mintzberg (1989) argues this for 'professional bureaucracies' but I think it is more widely applicable.
4 Christensen (1997).
5 Barber (2015).
6 The professionalisation of HR can lead to bureaucracy and unhelpful 'rules' imposed from the centre! There is a delicate balance to be struck in maintaining standards and being effective and agile.
7 King's College was an even earlier adopter, and Stewart Sutherland, then the Principal, gave us some excellent advice.
8 This process involved me in many visits to departmental staff meetings. In the case of Philosophy, there were many objections to the proposals but I discovered late in the meeting that what they were really worried about was losing the title of 'School' of Philosophy. I agreed there and then that the title could be retained and the other objections fell away!
9 JANET is the UK's national research and education network, connecting 20M users, run by JISC (Joint Information Systems Committee).
10 However, I would argue against heavy professionalising of 'project management', driven by software.
11 In fact, Howard Newby, then CEO of HEFCE, said to me that he predicted that I would have more staff working on HE than he had in HEFCE, and I believe he was right!
12 Off-the-record meetings with a students union!
13 See Department of Health (1994; 1995).
14 NDGBs are non-departmental government bodies.
15 ISTA: independent science and technology advisers.
16 See Defence Science Advisory Council (2014), Ministry of Defence.
17 A more formal way of looking at this can build on Beer's argument that a good information/intelligence system is what most organisations lack.
18 Clarke (2020).

Bibliography

Barber M. (2015) *How to run a government*, Penguin, Harmondsworth.

Beer, S. (1972) *Brain of the firm*, John Wiley & Sons, Chichester.

Beer, S. (1994) *Designing freedom*, John Wiley & Sons, Chichester.

Christensen, C. M. (1997) *The innovator's dilemma*, Harper Business, New York.

Clarke, M. (2020) *How geography changed the world, and my small part in it*, Sweet Design Ltd, Bristol.

Davies, D. (2024) *The unaccountability machine: Why big systems make terrible decisions – and how the world lost its mind*, Profile Books Ltd, London.

Defence Scientific Advisory Council (2014) Triennial review report, 24 March. Ministry of Defence, London.

Department of Health (1994) *Being heard: The report of a review committee on NHS complaints procedures*, Department of Health, London.

Department of Health (1995) *Acting on complaints*, Department of Health, London.

Freedman. S. (2024) *Failed state: Why nothing works and how we fix it*, Macmillan, London.

Mintzberg, H. (1989) *Structure in fives: Designing effective organisations*, Prentice-Hall, Englewood Cliffs, NJ.

6 Integration: what works?

6.1 Making things work

We can now attempt some drawing together, taking the four pillars of Chapters 2–5 seeking to integrate – what has to be added to 'make things work'. Practice beyond the theory! At this point, as we investigate, we will see that the four pillars all connect. To recap: SSFS:

- S: the *system of interest*: understanding the big picture – along with the PDA/STM framework (policy, design, analysis/systems, theory, method)
- S: a clear long-term *strategy*
- F: *finance*: follow the money
- S: *structures* that deliver; devolution

and we might add, being *ambitious*.

We introduced Michael Barber's check list[1] in Chapter 5, but it bears repetition here. As noted, he has 57 points and, here, we extract a subset which complements the four pillars, adding practicalities:

- decide priorities
- consult without conceding on ambition
- set up a delivery unit
- understand the potential drivers of change
- have a plan that is good enough to get started
- anticipate the implementation dip
- diagnose problems precisely, and act
- take all excuses off the table
- invest deeply and continually in skill and capability
- periodically adopt a bold clean-slate approach to budgeting to liberate resources
- big data and transparency are coming!

None of this works without good *people* and good *teams* – the right 'culture'. And perhaps above all, appropriate means of working with, and handling, the

DOI: 10.4324/9781003673149-6

politics and the Politics. We need people who can lead at all levels of the structure, and these leaders need to have all elements of the four pillars in their minds. Indeed, at the top levels of management, we will need refinements in our structure that recognise this. Changing the order slightly, the leader needs a good structure that facilitates devolution, access to an information system that provides the basis of the big picture, and indicators of organisational and individual performance,[2] a strategic plan, and a financial plan. The leader needs a top team that is able to support this integration, one that is not too large. He or she needs to ensure that all this works flexibly and in an agile way, and needs to be able to allocate new tasks to time-limited project teams rather than adding to the management structure. The leader needs to be sufficiently close to Finance and HR directors to ensure that they don't become, under the pressures of professionalisation, management silos that take on bureaucratic roles that restrict agility.

There are some specifics to bear in mind: the Mintzberg (1989) and the Christensen (1997) arguments to ensure that front-line professionals are well connected to the management and can, if necessary, launch potentially disruptive new initiatives as 'experiments' that can be merged into, indeed, take over, existing elements of structure if they succeed. The latter is also a good example of the need for a leader to run such an experiment. We need to be aware of the need for effective communication from the top down and have mechanisms for 'listening' for comments and ideas from the bottom up. Mechanisms for bidding for development funding can help this.[3]

There is an important principle that can be usefully made explicit here. I have often been frustrated with meetings that range over important possible projects or initiatives, and then no action follows. I sometimes argued that I was more interested in 'projects' rather than 'meetings'. The way forward is to ensure that someone is deputed to lead the potential project and to take responsibility for it. I can offer two related examples of this. The three Vice-Chancellors of Leeds, Sheffield, and York wanted to set up an applied research collaboration. We had a name: 'White Rose Ltd'. Nothing happened until we agreed to contribute jointly to a fund which enabled us to appoint a Chief Executive for White Rose. It then expanded very rapidly, exploiting the opportunities from the government at the time being enthusiastic about collaboration and supplying seed funding. We later added the World-wide Universities Network (WUN) and the experience was repeated: it took off when we appointed a CEO.

6.2 Education

I will look at the university case in some detail as this is where most of my experience in managing change was located. 'Making things work' is best illustrated by the fact that I had a very long 'running agenda'[4] with a wide variety of tasks, big and small. This only works of course with effective delegation, not only to the Senior Management Team (SMT), but across the university. We have seen in earlier chapters that key changes had to be made to refocus strategy, to change the culture in relation to finance from 'cuts' to 'growth', and to redevelop the 96 departments, via a reduction to 55, into a devolved 33-unit resource centre system. The 'how to' was challenging. It is fair to say that I had a 'honeymoon' first year and then as the changes kicked in in the second year, there were many objections as colleagues realised they were going to happen and that it was sometimes painful. Managing this was a serious challenge and at one point, one of my Pro-Vice Chancellors told me that 'people were finding me difficult to work with'. My wife and I even had discussions about how much time we had to serve ahead of an honourable departure – and we judged 'three years'! However, this did not materialise and I survived for 13 years. As we moved into the third year, and the changes were largely in place, many of the 'objectors' took early retirement, and others stepped back from management roles to return to a more normal academic life of teaching and research.

The main changes in the administration (and by implication, in the strategy) – reorganised on the basis of key foci – were brought about by strengthening the central management team through the appointments of additional Pro-Vice-Chancellors (PVCs) (for Teaching and Learning, Research, IT, and Staff) and the appointment of a new Registrar[5] with the role redefined from something like a Chief Operating Officer to something more purely administrative.[6] The PVCs had more central management responsibilities and staff reporting to them rather than the Registrar. The committee structure was duly reorganised. There were over 100 committees listed in the University Calendar and this was reduced by half, but with only three main committees: Academic Development, Planning and Finance, and Estates. The Council (chaired by the Pro-Vice-Chancellor, a lay member of Council) was responsible for the overall strategy and key financial decisions, but delegated the academic business of the University to the Senate. The Academic Development Committee reported to the Senate; and Planning and Finance and Estates reported jointly to Senate, first, and then to Council. The Council was too large and we did manage to reduce it in size – from around 80 to 30. The Senate was very large – around 200 members, and I retained this, and it had to approve all academic business. This had the great advantage that it was possible to 'govern by consent'. It was quite representative and provided a forum for dissenting opinions to be voiced. It was managed by introducing anything controversial through a 'green' paper, and then in the next meeting, with a 'white' paper, taking account of the debate. The proposals were usually accepted, most of the time without a vote. There were occasions when there was a vote and the outcome was close – the proposal to modularise teaching was an example.[7] Very occasionally, a vote was lost. The only defeat I recall is a proposal to close the Department of Archaeology. I took the view that it was good for the management to lose a vote occasionally as it showed that the Senate did retain its influence.

At the top level, I did have an SMT, meeting weekly, though it was called then 'VC's strategy group', made up of the PVCs, the Registrar, the Director of Finance and the Director of HR. Everyone knew it existed but it had no formal decision-making role. Of course, the VC and the senior officers could make day-to-day decisions but anything significant was the responsibility of one of the main committees. It was essential that committee business was supplemented by informal meetings, communicating intentions, gathering supporting and noting opposition (or alternative ideas), many of which could be dealt with ahead of a formal presentation to a committee. To make this work, and to keep the system agile, I was an enthusiastic user of 'Chair's action' which enabled me to take decisions ahead of Senate or committee meetings on more routine matters on the condition that they were always reported at subsequent meetings. In practice, these decisions were never questioned, indicating that they had been properly judged as either routine or consistent within an already-agreed strategy. I also managed to introduce the word 'normally' in most university regulations and this provided both committees and 'Chair's action' a helpful degree of flexibility.

The Vice-Chancellor's 'running agenda' is focused on the core academic strategy, with lots of informal meetings with colleagues, and in departments – and this was one source of integration. I had at least termly meetings with the staff unions, and the Students' Union Executive. I had regular '5 p.m.' drinks meetings of all Heads of Department – invaluable for exchanges of views. One example sticks in my mind. I said at the beginning of one meeting that I wanted the day's focus to be on outreach. One colleague said something like, 'We can't do everything, Alan, last month it was research and the RAE, this time something new.' This led me into propounding 'excellence with multiple objectives' as a mantra. This didn't solve the focus issue as seen by some, but it did get all the challenges on to the table.

There was a lot of formal business – degree ceremonies, for example, which sometimes needed quick thinking.[8] More broadly, 'responding to events',[9] for example, the David Blunkett visit,[10] student sit-ins,[11] gas fires without certificates,[12] caravans at Boddington.[13] There were opportunities for innovative problem solving: from the minor but important,[14] to widening participation through adding Bradford hospitals to the Leeds Medical School.[15] And being opportunist: setting up White Rose Ltd, and the Worldwide Universities Network (WUN), both initiated by availability of 'regional/collaborative' funding; and the introduction of work-based learning.[16]

It was not easy to assemble a team to produce a strategic plan. Even senior colleagues tended to be focused on their own areas and there was no expertise. In this case, I recruited a colleague from Geography, Sally Macgill, and we worked together on the plan that is described in Chapter 3. Later, I made another appointment that was internal in the university but external to the administration, Jonathan Adams, as Director of Strategy. Interestingly, neither were popular appointments, possibly because they were seen as 'interfering' in colleagues' areas of work. But it did help integrated thinking. It also provides an example of where top-level leadership fills a vacuum. I thought that much future development, in terms of student recruitment, for example, should be interdisciplinary. Leeds had a good record of Combined Studies degrees which was a significant contributor but while it might be argued that biochemistry and biophysics, for example, were interdisciplinary single degrees, it seemed there should be other opportunities. I proposed and implemented such degrees – a good example of 'experiments': Environmental Studies, Communications Studies, European Studies, Medieval Studies. Two succeeded very well, the others chugged along.

In terms of 'making things work', a lot of effort was needed to implement the changes that had been introduced and described in earlier chapters. These include the impacts of the introduction of resource centres, particularly in relation to the 'losers' in the early stages. (Needless to say, Medicine was very challenging: as is true of many universities, on any kind of allocation rules, Medical Schools are usually overfunded.)[17] We had to handle the notion of 'our money', for example, in relation to the Funding Council unit of resource. This was resolved by setting up a task group which met annually to determine what we called the Leeds unit of resource as opposed to the HEFCE one. We had to resolve maintenance vs development challenges – in this case, by making one big cut which provided an investment fund for development. Devolution of budgets drove student number growth, and along the way we had to solve problems of teaching space, in this case, by 'charging' departments for what they considered to be their own theatres, which quickly led to departmental theatres becoming university ones, available on the wider timetable. We had to build research capacity to ensure that research grew more rapidly than student numbers. Much of this demanded additional financing, and we took on loans – based on HEFCE guidance of a limit of 4% of turnover in interest payments – and this provided substantial capital funding.[18]

A major element of implementing the strategy, and the Vice-Chancellor's role, was the development of the University's estate.[19] There was a large backlog maintenance challenge and expansion plans demanded new buildings, not least teaching and library space and student accommodation. (We built new student accommodation at Clarence Dock in central Leeds.) We needed a substantial amount of capital. This was achieved through a mixture: some budgeted university funds, some one-off UGC/HEFCE funding (SRIF), some loans (as noted above), and, with some luck, some substantial philanthropic donations. We bought a large church for £1 from the Church of England and converted most of it to teaching space using some fortuitous £2M of government funding for teaching space, and at the same time, we expanded the University Library. We negotiated with a large retail company to take over the playing fields part of our Boddington site. A condition for applying for planning permission was that we had a site available to replace the playing fields, and for this purpose we bought two farms in North Leeds. The negotiations on Boddington then fell through! It was at this point that Leeds Grammar School decided to move and we were offered their site – 10 acres adjacent to our campus. They were happy to accept our farms[20] as their new site as part of the purchase price, and Mrs Keyworth's donation – see Chapter 4 on philanthropy – helped us to develop the buildings on the old school site which became our new Business School. We won a competition to launch a nursing degree, and we used the capital grant that came with this to refurbish the old Biological Sciences Building for a new Department of Health, thus, in passing, solving a large backlog maintenance problem. In the same part of the campus, a large grant from the Clothworkers Company allowed us to renew the Great Hall and the nearby courtyard. We solved another maintenance problem for a student hall of residence at Weetwood Hall by converting it into a hotel. This was self-funding and indeed profitable – run as a commercial hotel.

My other education examples can be dealt with more briefly. The Leeds Schools Commission was set up by the City Council and I was appointed Chair. The local paper ran a story with the headline: 'Man appointed to prevent Leeds schools from being removed from local authority control'! This of course was seen as the objective of Leeds Council and its Leader, Jon Trickett. However, it was presented as 'A new partnership for schools'. It had already been agreed that most of the Schools' budget would be delegated and it turned out that most of the Commission's work was on whether the remaining elements could be delegated. However, we took a lot of evidence and I learned a tremendous amount about schools systems, including policies on admissions. The main objective, however, was not achieved: the Conservative government of the day proceeded to establish more or less autonomous academies.[21]

6.3 Government: ministers, civil servants, practitioners, and users

In the DfES case, there was a reasonably established starting point: the 50% target for student access to HE and the Research Assessment Exercise (RAE) were in place; there were outreach objectives, particularly linking research with industry applications. However, there were some particular challenges, all noted earlier: a big one was the introduction of tuition fees in 2004; sharpening the schools science offer, and starting to build a national STEM programme;[22] and PQA.[23] I did have to quickly adapt to working in a new culture: overcoming some of the rigidities in the civil service with project groups.

For light relief, I can record one initiative that ultimately failed, involving the Open University (OU) and the funding of part-time students. Ruth Kelly was the Secretary of State and Baroness Betty Boothroyd, former Speaker, and the Chancellor of the OU, arranged a meeting with Ruth, along with Joel Barnett and another peer – essentially arguing that the OU was underfunded because of the Department's policy on part-time students. I attended. Lady Boothroyd launched into a major attack on the Department and threatened motions in the House of Lords. Ruth looked increasingly flustered. I intervened and said: 'Why don't I go up to Milton Keynes and explore the situation in more detail?' A very relieved Ruth said: 'Yes, Alan can go to Milton Keynes' and the meeting drew to a close.

The aftermath, the visit to Milton Keynes, was interesting. I travelled with a young civil servant, Helen Brooks, and as our taxi entered the campus – which looked like a 'normal' university campus – I said to Helen, tongue in cheek: 'Where are the students?' At lunch with the senior management, I suggested to them that they might recruit 10,000 full-time students, at the capital cost only of student accommodation (which others would pay for), and their financial problems would be solved and they could develop a new kind of very exciting university – teach their students with their OU distance-learning materials and focus staff time on a very superior tutorial and seminar system. One of the PVCs present said, 'But that isn't our mission' and another said, 'And you should be aware that there is a proposal to build a University of Milton Keynes'! I made no progress. I should probably have pressed the idea harder in the Department. Years later, the financial troubles of the OU have continued. There is now an active development of MK:U – the Milton Keynes University – and the OU have declined to be a partner. The lead partner university is Cranfield. The OU can be seen as being a dramatic early success, and a later failure – not seizing opportunities and not recognising that its 'unique' delivery model was going to be taken over by a host of new competitors.

The DSAC case was interesting. As we have noted in Chapters 2, 3, and 5, the review highlighted the main functions of the DSAC as being available to advise, quality assurance, and horizon scanning and it was important to organise the work that distinguished the short term from the long term. The need to find efficient ways of working was particularly acute because of the diverse and complex nature of the MoD's agenda.

6.4 Industry and research

Creating structures and making them work form an iterative process. We can simply repeat what we learned and summarised at the end of Chapter 5. We built on understanding the big picture (Chapter 2), strategy (Chapter 3), and finance (Chapter 4). These should all be understood and driven from the top, but also communicated to (and listened to), at all levels in the hierarchy. Hierarchies should be as flat as possible, agile, silos should be avoided, responsibilities devolved where possible – avoiding accountability sinks (!). Be aware of the Mintzberg (1989) and Christensen (1997) principles and challenges. Be aware, and learn from, successes and failures in other organisations – both 'like' and 'different'.

Again, repeated: at the heart of research is invention, and the conditions for encouraging invention are many and varied and not well understood: supporting a lone researcher through to ensuring that there are groups that are large enough to tackle the biggest challenges. Collaboration many create 'size'. Experience is likely to be a guide, including learning from others.

6.5 Lessons learned

In terms of lessons learned in relation to industry and research, I will make one comment from personal experience and then some general observations. In the case of the Alan Turing Institute, the main point about making things work – for example, in expanding the universities' network – is that it does take a lot of, mainly informal, meetings. A colleague needed some information from me as part of writing a report to the Engineering and Physical Sciences Research Council (EPSRC) – for some reason I didn't understand – about how many meetings I had had over the previous two years. I handed over my diaries and she counted a total of around 400 meetings in that period. As agendas for these meetings, there was the essential need – see Michael Barber[24] – to maintain focus on achieving objectives.

In terms of lessons learned more broadly, I would note:

- the need for 'leaders' – 'CEOs' – in different parts of the organisation, especially when seeking to achieve new objectives;
- the Christensen challenge: handling (technological) change, for example, in AI and data science – obviously disruptive technologies;
- changing the dynamics: the 'DNA';
- the value of project groups to create and sustain agility.

Notes

1 See Barber (2015).
2 See Onora O'Neil (2002). Oversimplifying, and, in my words, she argues that over-zealous performance management can result in the diminishing of trust.
3 In the research council case, this is the 'responsive mode' (bidding) vs the strategic.
4 I was mocked by my management team when I produced a 22-page 'running agenda' for myself!
5 When I took over, both the Registrar and the Bursar (who was responsible for both finance and estates) took early retirement 'to give me the opportunity to make a new start'. However, neither of the appointments of a new Registrar and Finance Director were wholly successful and this demonstrates the challenges of high-level recruitment and that it can take time – in this case, three or four years.
6 Indeed, later, the title of this post was changed from 'Registrar' to 'University Secretary'.
7 In subsequent years, one member of Senate, Adrian Hastings, Professor of Theology, at its first meeting of the year, no doubt with tongue in cheek, always proposed a vote of no confidence in the Vice-Chancellor because of modularisation. I always then asked for a seconder to the motion, and no one responded.
8 An honorary degree ceremony began and I noticed to my horror that the two honorary graduates were missing. The Chancellor, the Duchess of Kent, had started her speech. I beckoned to a very nervous porter, asked him to go to the back of the Hall and bring the two in down a side aisle. The Duchess didn't notice and I hoped the audience thought it was part of the ceremony! There was another ceremony when, at the end, the organist forgot to play the national anthem, even though we had all stood up and started to sing. We quickly shifted to processing out.
9 Echoing Harold Macmillan's response to the question about what determined his diary: 'Events, dear boy'!
10 David Blunkett, then Secretary of State, had been invited to give a talk by a small student society. He accepted. Half an hour before he was due, I was telephoned in my office and given the message that the lecture theatre was packed but there was uproar with demonstrations. I rushed over and managed to get to a point where, with some difficulty, the lecture could actually take place.
11 There was a student demo and a large crowd assembled outside my (locked) office, planning to 'occupy' it. I sent a message that if they all retreated to a nearby large

committee room, I would join them for a discussion. This is what happened and I persuaded them to disperse!

12 Some very quick action was needed. I instructed the Estates Department to contact gas engineers from anywhere in the country and have the problem fixed within 24 hours. It was fixed.

13 This followed a crisis at the start of the academic year in 1989 when we had over-recruited. We solved it by locating 100 caravans on the Boddington site, attracting national publicity at the time!

14 See Hicks (2021).

15 Young women in some communities were not 'allowed' to leave the city and adding Bradford to our University hospitals group solved this. We had a minor and, in the end, comic version of this. We had a group of Ogden Scholarship school students visiting for the day. At the end of the morning, two were reported as 'missing'. This was a big scare for us, but it turned out that they had never seen the centre of Leeds and so decided to take an hour out!

16 It proved necessary to create a new faculty to avoid a Christensen problem.

17 There is an old joke: a Vice-Chancellor dies and goes to Hell. He is waiting to see the Devil to be told where he will be sent to. He is told he will be a university vice-chancellor – 'Not so bad', he thinks; but then: 'And this time you will have two medical schools'!

18 If the turnover was £400M p.a., the maximum 'sensible' level of interest payments, would be £16M which would allow a loan 'book' of, say, £60M easily.

19 This was a big challenge. Another university vice-chancellor once said to me, with feeling: 'Have you ever managed to sort out your Estates Department?'

20 The school celebrated its 25th anniversary on the new site in 2023.

21 See Leeds Schools Commission (1993).

22 See National Science Learning Centre (2008).

23 Post-qualification (mainly A-levels) admissions.

24 Barber (2015).

Bibliography

Barber, M. (2015) *How to run a government*, Penguin, Harmondsworth.

Christensen, C. M. (1997) *The innovator's dilemma*, Harper Business, New York.

Hicks, C. (2021) Experience: I was orphaned at Christmas – and saved by kind strangers, *The Guardian*, 17 December.

Leeds Schools Commission (1993) *The new partnership: Quality, governance, choice and resources*, Leeds City Council, Leeds.

Mintzberg, H. (1989) *Structure in fives: Designing effective organisations*, Prentice-Hall, Englewood Cliffs, NJ.

National Science Learning Centre (2008) *The STEM framework*, University of York, York.

O'Neil, O. (2002) A question of trust, The Reith Lectures, BBC, London.

7 Future challenges: radical change

7.1 Introduction

The argument so far has been presented in terms of past experience and 'lessons learned' with a focus on the 'four pillars' of the SSFS (system of interest, strategy, finance, and structures) and the policy, analysis, and design/system of interest, theory, and methods (PAD/STM) frameworks, along with some 'tricks of the trade'. In this chapter, we move on to apply the framework to future challenges. Our main sections work through the usual example areas – education, government, industry and research, and hence shift the focus to applications of the 'four pillars' in substantive areas.

In Section 7.2, we begin with education and review the challenges facing universities which will provide the 'knowledge base' for the future. Many of the challenges for leaders and managers demand responses from government. In particular, given the ever-present challenge of interdependence, we focus in Section 7.3 on 'joined-up' government. We proceed in this section in two stages, focusing first on planning systems in the context of 'levelling up' between cities, and then on the wider question of the government integration – the 'joining-up' challenge more broadly. Industry (Section 7.4) faces the challenge of developing new business models through technological and other dimensions of change – notably the impacts of data science and AI. We explore future research priorities in Section 7.5. As with education, this is cross-cutting and relevant to all sectors.

The grand challenges identified in earlier chapters provide an ongoing context as cross-cutting threads: climate change, security, pandemics, social inclusion, along with the continuing evolution of technology, and they figure in each section. In Section 7.6, we draw together the threads and implications for the development of leaders and managers in the future, with particular reference to out-of-the-box thinking and the necessity of radical change in relation to major challenges.

The focus is on the UK experience, and in many cases, on England, as equivalent problems in the devolved administrations are sometimes different. However, while the challenges in different countries around the world will obviously have different emphases, not least in relation to levels of development, the ideas presented here can be translated to a variety of circumstances.

DOI: 10.4324/9781003673149-7

7.2 Education: building the knowledge base – universities as a key system

7.2.1 Universities

We will only be able to 'manage' the future if we have an adequate, indeed fantastic, knowledge base. This means having a comprehensively well-educated population, supported by an effective system of schools through to universities. We focus first on universities as key (though not the only) curators and creators of knowledge. Their principal functions, delivered by academic and supporting staff, are teaching students, research, and reaching out – communicating to wider communities – all supported by an adequate infrastructure, managers, and administrators. Typically, the 'managers' are academics, or some might say, ex-academics, and the management can in principle embrace the wider academic community, thus overcoming the Mintzberg (1989) challenge. The Christensen (1997) challenge is still to be overcome, for example, in relation to promoting interdisciplinarity, pedagogy, and IT.

In supporting the future, universities currently are not in a good place! The staff are overstretched and underpaid; the students have had a difficult time through COVID-19, and the fees and financial support system are sending them out into the world with large debts; university finances are in poor shape as a result of inflation, increasing interest rates, and inadequate government funding. This has placed a heavy reliance on the recruitment of overseas students, setting up a new problem for the future. Since a large part of future income derives from fees, universities compete with each other to recruit students and this produces the element of a 'race to the bottom', for example, with degree grade inflation. At a broader level, this has led to a loss of confidence in university management: the purpose of a university becomes less clear: a 'good' education versus the instrumentalism of training for future work, and good wages and salaries.

We can explore ways of moving forward – the challenges for university leadership and management – by working through the headings of our four pillars – though, as we'll see, it is convenient for the fourth, structures, to precede the third, finance!

A useful starting point is to examine the system and build the big picture using the Cisco formula:

$$C[(T, C, A, L), S, P, Tech]$$

Recall that this provides first, in relation to students, good teachers (T), an effective curriculum (C), with accountability (A), and Leadership (L), all in the context of skills (S), the best pedagogy (P), and making the best use of technology (Tech). We can apply the formula to research (as in Chapter 2), bearing in mind the complication that in many universities, the same staff are responsible for both teaching and research.[1] In general terms, the staff remain of high quality, notwithstanding poor (relative) pay and increasing workloads and hence time pressures: academic life is, fortunately, still potentially attractive to some. The time pressures make it difficult to ensure that research potential is being realised. The curriculum is almost certainly too conservative, particularly in undergraduate teaching. The opportunities for interdisciplinary and critical thinking are being missed. Accountability can be good but in some cases is being overtaken by a form of managerialism which is not helpful as a basis for academic life. Leaders, as noted, have often lost confidence, perhaps overwhelmed by the challenges facing them, possibly with an unhappy staff who might be reluctant to take on necessary change.

Student recruitment is a starting point for building a strategy. Recall the Baghai, Coley, and White (1999) (BCW) framework introduced in Chapter 3, aimed at supporting growth and income generation. It has seven elements:

- existing products to existing customers
- new customers
- the possibility of new products and services
- new geographies
- development of new technologies
- a new industry structure – that is in the 'environment'
- new competitive arenas.

Most universities have development possibilities framed by the BCW agenda. A notable one is ensuring that they are making effective contributions to life-long learning – a point we pursue below.

Growth in student numbers ensures maximum opportunities for education in broad terms – future proofing – and provides a skilled employment base. However, it is in the S, P, Tech part of the Cisco formula that it may be possible to achieve some efficiency gains without losing essential quality. We proceed to explore these possibilities in this case, bringing the strategy pillar together with some preliminary remarks on structures. We focus on the (T, S, P, Tech) elements of the formula. How can we be more efficient and effective in teaching by using the best IT-driven Tech, developing our pedagogy and associated skills? One spin-off from COVID-19 is the wider availability of on-line lectures and teaching resources. This offers the possibility of flipped lectures[2] and offering students more contact time through seminars and tutorials: the restructuring of teaching. There is much 'best practice' but this is not effectively diffused across the system.

A bigger and more challenging step is to review the curriculum. Is it too narrowly discipline-based? Do we try to pack so much into a course that it shifts into exam-driven remote learning for the student rather than providing the basis for exploration? Can we be more explicitly interdisciplinary? An example – anticipating the need for structural change – merge departments to form a unitary School of Humanities and Social Sciences. This would enable the development of a stronger link between, say, Sociology and Economics with History. It is also in this territory, more broadly, that leaders can explore new courses, building on the continued growth of the life sciences, and the emergence of new major areas such as AI and data science. The latter areas are likely to imply serious restructuring of mathematics, statistics, and computer science, for example, take a large chunk of the three departments to be a School of AI and Data Science. More broadly, many traditional departments are likely to be 'tired' and investment and restructuring can be invaluable.

The research agenda has to be explored separately, tackling a number of questions: allowing room for individual blue-skies thinking; and putting structures together to facilitate the building of large-scale research groups for major challenges, possibly through inter-university collaboration or university-industry collaboration. This may need the creation of research structures than are separate from teaching. This is often partially achieved at present through interdisciplinary research centres, though these are often not at a sufficiently large scale to be effective, and also have to take on the teaching of Masters' courses (as well as PhD students) to be financially viable. Of course, this can be positive: supporting a new cohort of potential researchers (and 'briefing' them) to support other careers.

The third arm of universities – effective outreach – will also demand its own structures as part of the strategy. Many universities already have umbrella companies as a basis for incubating start-ups and spin-outs and/or consultancy companies to offer academics' services to industry and public authorities. These organisations, and Vice-Chancellors and senior managers, need to identify academic entrepreneurs who can play major roles. Outreach can embrace both teaching and research, in the first case, especially given the availability of online resources. Effective policies in this area can also generate income, notably in work-based learning as a contribution to life-long learning and skills development. Conversion courses fit in here. It may also be possible to be more ambitious and develop in such a way that staff can be more mobile and better paid and the links between the university and industry and public services, running what is in effect a careers and recruitment agency to make the connections. These initiatives can be combined as appropriate in different situations. It should be possible to have significant and close relationships with major employers, the NHS and local government, for example. This leads to the idea that the 'teaching hospitals' model – a close collaboration between hospitals and a university medical school – can perhaps be applied more widely.

New and extended initiatives are likely to demand some *structural innovation.* For example, as noted in Chapter 3, there is a case for universities having a College of Corporate Learning, a College of Life-Long Learning and a company – University Consultants PLC – as argued 15 years ago in the Cisco HE 3.0 White Paper! These would contribute new opportunities on the three key fronts: teaching, research, and outreach – feeding from each other in these new units.

A major management challenge is implicit in this analysis: that the time of academic staff has to be divided between teaching, research, and outreach, and to these we should add administration. To what extent should there be divisions of labour and specialisation? What are the dangers that distinguished researchers can buy themselves out of teaching, and thus deprive students? This can be illustrated anecdotally. I once did the welcome speech for a large research conference in Leeds, and I was followed by Robert May as the keynote speaker. (At the time, he was President of the Royal Society.) He said that when he was doing this kind of talk, he liked to review the conference programme and see what might be missing. In this case, it was any reference to 'teaching'. He went on to say: 'What have we come to that to be bought out of teaching is seen as a mark of esteem?' Wise words.

For our third pillar, finance, we start from the position of underfunding, and in many cases, crises with institutions with substantial recurrent deficits and no reserves for investment. I noted in Chapter 4, a senior industry executive saying that in these circumstances, you had only two options: 'cut your costs and/or increase your income'. In so far as costs have to be cut, the possibilities of new technologies in teaching kick in. We have already highlighted the BCW framework to enhance student recruitment. In recent years, particularly encouraged by low interest rates and therefore low borrowing costs, universities have invested in new buildings. In the present circumstances, capital spend may have to be switched to human resource development and meeting the kinds of restructuring challenges discussed here. More broadly, we have to recognise that cuts are likely in many circumstances. It is then vital that these are sufficiently large to free up funds for development and investment, including those needed to handle redundancy and early retirement. While it may be convenient to draw from reserves, a review of 'reserves policy' will be important so they are not run down to be too low.

All of this implies substantial challenges for leaders. In the formula, 'accountability' implies 'government by consensus' and extensive consultation in circumstances where it might be difficult to achieve agreement, along with avoiding accountability sinks. A priority for making this work will be to ensure effective *devolution* and that the main agents of management at all levels are incentivised. Given the demands for change in departments and centres, and the creation of some new units, it will be important to ensure that senior management at that level set up project groups to devise and implement the necessary changes.

7.2.2 *Education and the knowledge base*

We have emphasised the importance of education and life-long learning in the development of both a knowledge base and a skills base. The context is complex. The economy will develop, as always, through technological change, particularly through data science and AI which are fundamentally changing production processes and notably – by hollowing out employment needs – automating the 'middle'. In our horizon scanning, we need to add to this background the economic and labour market transformations needed to meet the grand challenges: sustainability and climate change; security (local to global, data, cyber); pandemics; and social inclusion. It is not clear whether these challenges are being helped by the current nature of the capital market, notably the influence and short-termism of much private equity.[3] These issues raise serious challenge for universities and for government at all scales.

7.3 Joined-up government

7.3.1 Introduction

Systems thinking, as we have seen, demands 'joined-up government'.[4] We explore this in relation to future challenges, first, by examining the planning of cities and regions in the context of 'levelling up' – tackling the social exclusion challenge (Section 7.3.2); and, second, more broadly, to explore the means of meeting the challenges of joining-up in government (Section 7.3.3). In UK terms, we use an example of the goals of the former government, up to the election of July 2024. These easily translate into the five 'missions' of the current government. In particular, the focus on 'growth', as the basis for meeting a set of key challenges, demands 'levelling up'. This is a multidisciplinary challenge, and growth will not be achieved until the performance of 'poor', mainly northern, cities is raised, particularly in relation to productivity and a variety of social goals. It is not difficult to translate this agenda from the UK to a variety of international contexts.

7.3.2 An example: 'levelling-up'

We use an example that illustrates the magnitude and difficulty of a particular future challenge: 'levelling up' 'poor cities' to become 'good cities'. This not only provides a valuable illustration of a major challenge, it also represents an invaluable element of context for leaders and managers in virtually any sector: social exclusion impacts in all sectors. It is introduced first through the development of an appropriate 'big picture'. We emphasise the importance of interdependence by using the housing subsystem as an example. We then move on to the next three pillars for this example – strategy, finance, and structures. 'Levelling-up' is a politician's mantra of the kind that no one can be against: if your town or city is 'poor', levelling-up will make it better. The 'north vs south' problem in the UK – the 'poor' vs the 'prosperous' – will be solved. However, this is oversimplifying and in broad terms, impossible – a myth. But the challenge is real and, in all its complexity, can be unpicked: we can articulate what is needed and move on to what can be done about it. We will show that levelling-up is impossible without a dramatic improvement in skills, and that is inconceivable without a major rethink in education, targeted at areas of greatest poverty and deprivation. We will show that there are many interdependent challenges and that levelling-up demands policy and planning integration, both nationally and locally.

To establish the foundations and build the big picture, we deploy our usual categories of system elements: people; the organisations that represent the economy; infrastructure – buildings, transport and communications networks;

the environment – air quality, energy and utilities. People are housed, derive incomes from work or pensions; use a wide range of services; the economy delivers employment, goods and services – some public, some private. Both social and economic activities are anchored in the infrastructure. The quality of the environment can be measured in various ways. All of this, of course, underpins another grand challenge: climate change and sustainability.

This works through different geographies: at scales from the local to the international: neighbourhoods, suburban towns and villages, city regions, through to countries and the global system. We can explore communities, economies, and infrastructure at any of these scales. Levelling-up is about shifting any of the key elements from being 'poor' to being 'good'. These are subjective terms, of course, but we can give them meaning in ways that make them useable. To make progress, we can work at two scales: the system of towns and cities; and at the finer scales of neighbourhoods within a particular place. This means that there are two kinds of 'levelling-up': between cities and within cities. We focus first on the 'system of cities' which is the most common scale of application of the idea of 'levelling-up' – in the UK, for example, encompassing 'North vs South'; 'London and the South-East' vs 'the rest'.

We can characterise people, and how they live, by age and gender, their work (and hence, for most, their income), their use of services – from retail, health, and education through to leisure. We can build measures such as accessibility: how someone who lives in a place has access to work and services; which in turn depends on where these facilities are located and the nature of the transport and communications connections. We can immediately see that all parts of this picture, how people live, are connected, are interdependent. This means that policies and plans to improve one element will be dependent on connections working.

We can begin to articulate what we might usefully mean by 'poor' and 'good'. A starting point for the 'people' dimension is the *Index of multiple deprivation* (IMD). This is built for larger units such as local authorities with elements including: income, employment, education, health, crime, barriers to housing and services, and environment. The indices can be used individually but are usually combined into a single index – the IMD. The measures are inevitably rough, but they are useable, and between them give a reasonable picture of the 'poor' and the 'good' for places and areas, small and large: a starting point for thinking through 'levelling-up'. Although this is focused on people, it connects to the other elements of the picture we are building and can be connected to other data: where are good places for service providers and the whole range of economic units? These places have all to be linked in effective ways – and hence the importance of connecting infrastructure and accessibility measures. Do the environment indicators correlate with good and poor IMD measures? A second broad measure which is focused on incomes through employment, is gross domestic product (GDP) per capita, which also serves as a measure of productivity. This indicator can be calculated by city and then summed to provide a national figure for urban GDP. The change in the national figure over time gives an indication of economic growth and we can explore future scenarios in these terms which provides an envelope on what is possible in terms of levelling-up. There are alternative approaches that can be brought to bear. For example, Sen's capability framework[5] and the UN SDGs.[6]

If we plan to intervene in a problem area, there will be both preconditions to be satisfied and consequences for other areas – so we need to look for key points in what we can call interdependency chains. We also need to take into account the time-scales on which objectives can be achieved in the short, middle and long runs. A UK Government levelling-up White Paper[7] was based on 10 missions: (1) close gaps on pay, employment, and productivity; (2) increase domestic public investment in R&D outside the South-East; (3) raise standards of local public transport to those of London; (4) provide gigabit-capable broadband; (5) raise primary school standards, 30% improvement in worst-performing areas; (6) high quality skills training – adding 200K in higher skills, 80K in lower; (7) reduce the gap in healthy life expectancy; (8) improve well-being and close gaps; (9) increase pride of place, e.g. satisfaction in town centres, local culture, community; (10) housing: renters have path to ownership, reduce numbers of non-decent rented homes. However, this is very much an unstructured shopping list; it is partial and offers little detail on how these missions can be achieved, or the full costs or benefits. It is not joined up, much is missing; it is too full of generalities. It can be rewritten and structured if we use our 'big picture' effectively: we need to aim to develop a more systematic framework, embracing interdependencies and time-scales of impacts, with short-, middle-, and long-run perspectives. Unfortunately, the same comments can be made about the current UK Government's (2025) five missions: (1) growth; (2) clean energy; (3) health and the NHS; (4) safe streets; and (5) maximising opportunity through child care and education – an unconnected and limited shopping list.

We can illustrate interdependence more specifically by picking up the housing challenge. There are not enough (decent) houses, though this is not explicit in the mission. To make progress, a reasonable conjecture is that a key aspect of the housing problem is less about building more houses in general, but more about incomes. In areas where there are good household incomes, there is less likely to be a housing problem; in areas where there is a housing problem, people do not have sufficiently adequate incomes to purchase and maintain their housing needs. In this case (and it is similar for other challenges) solving the housing problem means solving the income problem. Good incomes come from good employment; good employment is based on good skills; good skills are developed through an education system founded on life-long learning. The levelling-up challenge, therefore, has its roots in education and there is a chain: from education to skills, to employment, to incomes, which in turn will support housing and, indeed, many other objectives. This is a necessary condition but not, of course, sufficient. There are many other aspects to solving the housing problem: supply-side and planning failures (particularly in respect of social housing), taxation policy, the property rights of landowners – and, of course, these are linked, including, for example, the possibilities of instituting a land tax.

Policies and plans have time dimensions which complicates the analysis: investment in primary education will have impacts on incomes 20 years into the future – dependent, of course, on other elements being in place – secondary and higher education, for example, and teacher recruitment and training. Given that it is necessary to make progress in the short term, this implies different kinds of investment in education – training and re-training as part of a life-long learning strategy. The same chain will support better food, diets, and health. Other chains will determine the delivery of effective services, another crucial dimension of levelling-up, not only in relation to local delivery and quality of life, but as key influencers of inward migration and investment, and the building of the skills base.

We can work towards a strategy, and more explicit integrated policies and plans, to support levelling-up. We can work with our PAD framework – policy, design and analysis. The previous section has provided the beginnings of analysis. We should work through iterative loops – towards plan evaluation and the exploration of alternatives in the short run; and for monitoring and adjusting plans in the light of experience.

A first step is to examine 'poor' and 'good' through the Index of multiple deprivation. We take poorer cities to be those where the population is concentrated at the lower end of the UK-wide income distribution, which means, in turn, at the lower end of wages and salaries in employment. The differences are further sharpened by poorer cities needing relatively greater shares of welfare benefits from the national pot – in effect, people in the better-off cities subsidise those in poorer ones. The two scales are linked, of course: poorer cities will have more neighbourhoods with high indicators of multiple deprivation, and this makes them less attractive in terms of migration and investment. When we focus on city GDP per capita, we can explore improving the mix of sectors in each local economy, particularly those that export either in the UK or internationally, on the assumption of an improving skills base. Typically, skilled people, notably graduates, will migrate away from poorer cities; such cities will be unattractive to investors, for not offering a suitably skilled labour force, and, more broadly, with a poor environment. Economies thrive on exports and a positive balance of payments, something that is well known for countries but is also true of cities. To level up, therefore, cities need a strategy to be attractive enough to encourage net in-migration of skilled people, to attract investment, and to be effective exporters, establishing a positive balance of payments.[8]

This analysis indicates a preliminary conclusion on finance: that a priority for government investment to level up should be in education at all levels, including local access where necessary to higher education, and including a commitment to life-long learning. Investment in housing, and public and private services, providing new employment through the greening of the economy, are all important factors in reducing out-migration and encouraging in-migration and inward investment. Improved transport infrastructure and communications networks, particularly at the regional scale, can offer suburbs and smaller towns the benefits of agglomeration economies. This can all be set out in detail for different kinds of towns and cities. This is the easy part. The more difficult part is dealing with the challenges of budget constraints and the availability of skilled labour; and, indeed, having available the capabilities to devise strategies and implement plans – bearing in mind the old management mantra, already noted in earlier chapters, that strategy is 5% of the problem, implementation, 95%! We follow this up in Section 7.3.3 in the context of joined-up government.

The two tiers of levelling-up intertwine when it comes to planning and implementation. The latter has to be local: plans need to be in place for education, housing, access to employment and availability of skilled labour, services, infrastructure and the quality of the environment. These need to be integrated within a spatial planning framework. It is reasonably straightforward to articulate policy in broad terms. It is possible to generate alternative ways of achieving objectives and solving problems on each dimension, and to understand the interdependencies between them. There are two key difficulties: the first and most obvious is reviewing alternatives relative to budget constraints (while also preparing the material to bid for increased financial allocations); the second is to investigate the possibilities of attracting private capital investment, particularly in the short run. We proceed, therefore, to explore possible government policies for levelling-up, with a focus on some radical directions of change before facing up to the budget and investment challenges involved in radical change.

7.3.3 How to join up

The levelling-up agenda is quite precisely focused on the futures of particular people and communities in particular places. This fits closely with one of the broad grand challenges of the time: social inclusion. However, there are other broader grand challenges with a wide range of impacts: climate change and sustainability, future pandemics, security and geo-politics. Policies in these areas should be coordinated with the levelling-up agenda. Urban development to support levelling-up should also be consistent with sustainability. Indeed, the need to 'green' the economy provides levelling-up opportunities. The argument that follows is in terms of current UK Government structures but can easily be transferred to other environments.

The Treasury and the Cabinet Office have key roles to fund and to coordinate – getting the macro-economics right, essentially generating and coordinating the fiscal, regulatory, and spending framework for government policy. If taxes cannot be substantially increased, or growth is slower than anticipated, then it will also be important to cut or stop some funding in order to release enough resources to invest and make levelling-up work. This can be complemented by incentivising private investment, for example, from pension funds (as exemplified in Legal & General's investment in social housing). As ever, we need short-, middle- and long-run perspectives, and, in particular, to identify the most serious and urgent problems for the short run. In order to be radical, it will be necessary to set up task forces within and across civil service departments, starting with zero-base budgets. This will involve exploring a wide range of policies, plans, and investment and establishing an agreed framework for the evaluation of alternatives: measuring impacts of, and returns on, investments: in particular, the impacts on people and their 'utility functions' would help integration of policies and plans. The Treasury and the Cabinet Office must work together, bearing in mind the three kinds of thinking that are needed – policy, design, and analysis: as noted earlier, it has been argued that these are rarely found in the same room at the same time!

We work in turn through the elements of the key chain introduced in Section 7.3.2, using education as an example: education to skills, employment, incomes, housing and services. There is a serious tail of underachievers leaving secondary school, and this tail is significantly longer in poorer cities. It is also known that success in education is highly dependent on the quality of the teachers. Levelling-up therefore, turns on the supply of, and investment in, good teachers. Premiums may have to be paid to attract teachers to poorer cities. Schemes such as Teach First, which has been very successful, particularly in London, could be expanded. Particularly for primary schools, parents and families should be supported where necessary. Pupils should be tracked effectively and those falling behind offered additional support. Needless to say, all of this is expensive – note Sir Kevan Collins' recommendation to the government on the additional support needed to overcome the problems created by the COVID-19 pandemic (which was rejected by the government on cost grounds).[9] These initiatives have to be worked through at all levels: poorer cities have to have local access to the high-quality Further Education and Higher Education. While some high-level courses will be directly related to the professions, nonetheless, the best form of future proofing is high quality education which lays the foundations for different kinds of training for future employment.

Serious investment in education in poorer cities will begin to transform the local labour market and, potentially, attract inward investment that creates new jobs. There are very complex processes at work here for levelling-up policies to succeed. There needs to be sufficient growth in attractive jobs, along with the offer of a good quality of life though housing availability, effective services, and a good environment, to reduce outward migration and to encourage inward migration. Direct government investment to provide employment is obviously one of the levers, whether through moving civil service employment out of London, and encouraging other employers – potentially attracted by not only a good environment with high-skilled workers available, but which is also cheaper in investment terms. Innovative experiments are needed to tackle unemployment, particularly focused on vulnerable groups: adults who have been in care, those who have been failed by the education system, ex-prisoners, the disabled. Government-funded schemes, such as the now-privatised Remploy scheme offering employment to the disabled, could be introduced in such a way that the savings from unemployment benefits would pay for the investment. Policies on employment need to be supplemented by effective welfare benefits and pensions. The labour market, and hence access to a wider range of job opportunities, can be expanded through efficient transport services. These kinds of accessibilities can be measured quite effectively and provide a basis for transport infrastructure planning. Plans have to be delivered locally but the Department of Transport and the Department for Culture, Media and Sport provide the policy framework and investment allocations for transport and communications respectively.

Accessibilities can be calculated to measure the effectiveness of delivery of services: education as above; health and social care (the Department of Health and Social Care, and the Department for Business, Energy and Industrial Strategy through research); and retail, for example – and, of course, there is a much longer list. Availability of, and access to, housing need to be linked to the whole set of accessibilities sketched here. The major services beyond education need serious reorganisation and investment, notably health and social care and a range of local services. These are all important in generating the attractiveness of an area, but also directly as a source of employment: education, health, and other government services are between them usually by far the largest employer in a city.

Levelling-up involves improvement in all these areas. We can combine our conclusions here with those of Section 7.2.2. There are measures of the quality of schools, FE colleges, and universities and these become part of the accessibility calculations – access to good schools and good hospitals. There are trade-offs to be explored locally: is a system of a smaller number of high-quality facilities 'better' than a finer-scale spatial distribution of smaller units which may not be able to provide the range of specialisms that might be needed? There are hybrid systems, of course: smaller units complemented by much larger 'central' ones. In the health case, for example, general practices are the smaller units, in place to refer patients if necessary to hospitals. Would it be better to locate GPs in hospitals to facilitate rapid diagnosis and treatment? No more six-week waits to see a consultant?

This brief analysis shows that levelling-up has be approached through integrated policies. An important feature of this is planning at the local level, in part, through planning in the narrower sense: land use and the spatial organisation of areas. This links closely to sustainability challenges. This is reflected in housing policy: densities of new housing developments are too low and are often located in areas that are inaccessible to employment except through car travel. There are sources of land available which would improve things in this respect: railways' land, some NHS and other government-owned land, other brownfield sites. These are all potentially available for new kinds of investment such as business parks and science parks as well as housing. The development costs in these areas are relatively high and central government support and investment are important.

To achieve this kind of integration effectively, some hard thinking needs to be done on the balance of responsibilities between central and local government. Increased devolution is necessary on the basis of some clear principles of subsidiarity. Judgements need to be made about what can be achieved on different time-scales. The immediate problems of vulnerable groups should not be neglected through longer-term investment projects. Inventive solutions are needed, for example, in responding to staffing issues which currently bedevil health, social care, education, and other public services. One of the advantages of increased devolution is the possibility of more local experiments that would build intelligence on 'what works'.

Investment in education is crucial to levelling-up but we have shown that integration of policies across all areas of government, national and local, is crucial too. This broad analysis is underpinned by detailed and applicable analytics. We can systematically explore what can be achieved in various timescales. Any government could and should absorb this knowledge and use 'levelling-up' as the basis to become truly joined-up in its policy development.

We can develop the argument further by examining the wider challenge of handling interdependence. From a central government perspective, a dozen or more departments are involved in a variety of chains. The Treasury and the Cabinet Office, as noted, have key roles to fund and to coordinate – essentially generating and coordinating the fiscal, regulatory, and spending framework for government policy. Education sits in the Department of Education (DoE) but with inputs from the Department of Energy and Industrial Strategy (BEIS) in relation to skills, training, apprenticeships, Higher Education, and the labour market. Policies on employment, and therefore most incomes, along with welfare benefits and pensions, rest with BEIS and the Department of Work and Pensions (DWP). Related areas include health and social care, the Department of Health and Social Care (DHSC), and, again, BEIS, through research; environment – from sustainability to food security – with BEIS and the Department for Environment, Food and Rural Affairs (DEFRA). The delivery of services, including retail, are partly planning matters, and, along with housing, lie with the Ministry of Levelling-up, Housing and Community (MLUHC), which is also the core of the levelling-up agenda, as its name implies. Accessibilities provide the connectivity and transport and communications systems that are critical to this: Department of Transport (DoT) and the Department for Culture, Media and Sport (DCMS), which has IT and communications responsibilities. What is needed is integrated government policy, and an associated White Paper, rather than an unconnected series of departmental, usually short-term, initiatives. This will be replicated in different forms at local levels – though there is often more 'joined-upness' locally than in Whitehall. There are also a significant number of non-departmental government bodies, and of course charities, contributing to elements of this agenda, and a review of these in relation to levelling-up would be appropriate.

In central government, it is very difficult to move effectively beyond the siloed functioning of individual departments. There has been more success in restructuring to meet this challenge at local and regional level but there is still a long way to go: for example, integrating health service delivery with social care. To achieve significant change in central government involves radical restructuring: a reduced number of departments, each much smaller – say, for the sake of illustration involving 20% of the civil service; the 80% could then be distributed in project and task-and-finish groups, some central. Some devolved to local and regional authorities. This illustrates the scale of the task which is not likely to be achieved by the addition of overarching 'mission boards' while not radically changing the rest of the structure.

7.4 Industry

'Industry' is a complex system of organisations producing goods and services, interacting with each other and with their markets. There are many kinds of ownership, and hence a variety of objectives. In looking ahead, leaders and managers have at least four time horizons: now, the short term, the medium term, and the long term. This provides one element of the futures' agenda. The next step is to review, and maintain a review, of the challenges over these time horizons. The context is provided by the grand challenges, which will have some impacts on most organisations. The examples we have used here are climate change and sustainability, pandemics, defence and security, and social exclusion – all interacting with changing technology, particularly AI and data science. A specific example relating to sustainability in the financial sector is the set of ESG objectives. This is a contested area within investment, for example. I once asked the CEO of a bank why she would seek to invest in ESG-compliant stocks even it was evident that they offered lower returns. 'Because my clients want me to,' she said. Growing concerns of customers and clients are themselves impacting organisations' behaviour.

We can build on this initial thinking through the four pillars (SSFS) framework. We have begun to sketch the big picture, but this needs to be done more formally by articulating the position of an organisation in its wider ecosystem. This agenda includes competitors; central and local government (regulation, fiscal policies, capital spend, city and regional planning); markets; investors; technologies; production technologies, and supply chains. The board should have 'futures' as a regular agenda item, enabling it to lead on strategy and financial planning while the executive can both support this and put structures in place to recognise the futures' thinking needs: data, systems, research, perhaps in a horizon-scanning unit which, like the rest of the organisation, can draw on, and add to, an effective management information system. It is now clear that new technologies, in particular, AI and data science, are being transformative. First-mover advantage is creating big and dominant players. For many organisations, Christensen's (1997) argument will be important as they are 'invaded' by disruptive technologies. There will be huge scope for new kinds of investment in 'experiments', even new business models. This all connects to research more broadly.

7.5 Research

Over the years, I have had a range of research council grants and one Innovate UK grant; I have been a member of one research council and have chaired another; and have had responsibility for the Quality-related Research (QR) part of government research funding. This range of experience provided an opportunity to think about – not quite 'think through' – the overall structure of government funding of research. Many challenges can be identified. The 'basic' and 'applied' labels are not always helpful, particularly because the research community typically associates prestige with the former. Perhaps the biggest challenge is the immense complexity of the funding system: dual funding – HEFCE QR and research council grants; Innovate UK; government departments with their own budgets and systems; and industry – all in all, a complex ecosystem.[10] As with many ecosystems, this can be very strong – much better than one central system. However, constant vigilance is needed in this case to ensure that the system is working, and ongoing reviews of the big (ecosystem) picture are vital. To some extent, this requirement has been met in relation to government research funding in the UK, notably with reviews commissioned by Paul Nurse, the President of the Royal Society, and significant changes have been made, including the setting up of UKRI (UK Research and Innovation) as an overseeing body with a strategic capability – embracing research councils, Innovate UK, and Research England (which now administers QR). UKRI is a key node in a complex UK, indeed, international research ecosystem. It can offer strategic direction and, for many, it will be a key funder.

How are the strategic priorities of an ecosystem categorised? The big picture remains the obvious starting point. We can seek the potential game changers in research. Some will be rooted in pure science, while others will be related to wider societal challenges. We can note Brian Arthur's 'combinatorial evolution' argument: that most innovation comes from the lower reaches of a system's hierarchy; and discoveries at lower levels can often be transferred to other domains.[11]

Computers offer a dramatic example: invented as calculating machines, they are now ubiquitous in a wide range of systems. Contributions to strategy can come top-down from institutions (reading the landscape and scanning the horizons) or bottom-up from individual researchers.

These challenges, questions, and approaches have to be addressed at each node in the ecosystem. Then the nodes must be effectively connected. For example, money has to flow in the direction of the potential game-changers and the high impact innovations. Each node, from the individual piece of research up to UKRI, has to have a strategy, grounded in experience, but employing horizon scanning and imagination. In the UK, the ecosystem has not been functioning effectively for some time – notably in the transfer of research findings into industry and the public sector. To build an effective strategy, UKRI (or any central government equivalent) will have to do the following:

- identify and build on strengths and opportunities – both the people with track records and the early career researchers with skills, imagination, and ambition – there is a top-down vs bottom-up aspect here;
- find ways of avoiding the conservatism of peer review (which has been enforced by the Research Excellence Framework). I believe that universities

do not always provide the right incentives by insisting on both the volume of publications and on 'top journals' as the basis of their promotions' criteria. This has skewed the motivation of researchers, particularly by neglecting applied research whose outputs do not qualify for the 'prestigious' journals.

Industry also has a role to play. Where are the modern equivalents of Bell Labs? Perhaps Deep Mind? How much important R&D is now being done in start-ups with the big players relying on purchasing success? While there are many excellent examples of industry-university joint working, there could be many more.

Another strategic question which demands sensitive judgement relates to the size of research groups. What should be located at the 'big science' end of the spectrum? There are established successes, from CERN to Sanger; there are new Institutes like Turing and Diamond, with others in development. However, a big question: is the average size of a research group in a university too small? Are there potential 'big science' areas that are not funded in universities? My own area of 'cities', for example, falls into this category. Indeed, how do we value different fields of research for public funding? Health, education, justice – all are obviously important. Basic research is needed to support future industrial development. Should there be more applied research as well, both in industry and the public sector?

We can recall the Warren Weaver argument: In the 1950s, he was the Science Vice-President of the Rockefeller Foundation.[12] He argued that systems of interest fell into three categories: (1) those that were simple; (2) those of disorganised complexity; and (3) those of organised complexity. Roughly speaking, the first two represented (among other things) the physical sciences of the time, while the third comprised biology. He switched much of his funding from physics to biology. That was a prescient decision. Is there an equivalent diagnosis to be made now? UKRI's strategy needs to be connected to the social questions of our time – the grand challenges: climate change and sustainability; pandemics; security; and the future of work and incomes, along with growing social inequalities. Does this agenda demand a Weaver-like shift? While the focus has been on questions specifically relating to UKRI strategy, in reality, every element of the research ecosystem needs strategic thinking: from universities and institutes, through industry and government departments, to individual researchers. All of it needs to be strongly connected to translational and development ecosystems.[13] All of it needs a big picture framework.

7.6 Making it work: meeting the grand challenges

The four pillars, SSFS, along with the PAD and STM frameworks, provide a core. The big picture now needs to draw on the impacts that the grand challenges, along with technology, are having on all sectors. This means investment in the knowledge base on a spectrum from government to individual organisations. It means recognising that meeting the challenges needs both different kinds of investment – in green energy, for example – and the capacity to engineer social changes, many of which seem to be politically impossible! It will be very difficult to redirect investment to find the money, and the people, to implement all this.

Notes

1 This is different in some other countries, Germany and France, for example.
2 Flipped lectures: the students view the lecture off-line ahead of the 'lecture': the lecture time is used for discussion and Q&A.
3 Notwithstanding the contested environmental, social, and governance (ESG) agenda.
4 A mantra of the Blair government in 1997.
5 See Sen (1999).
6 The United Nations Sustainable Development Goals.
7 See Department of Levelling Up, Housing and Communities (2022).
8 We should bear in mind Jane Jacobs' (1970) argument that import substitution may be a more important driver of growth than exports!
9 See Education Policy Institute (2021).
10 The British Academy/Royal Society report (Royal Society, 2019) adopted an ecosystem view for the education sector and this illustrates the complexity which applies to a wide variety of situations.
11 See Arthur (1988; 2009).
12 See Weaver (1948; 1958).
13 See Wilson (2018).

Bibliography

Arthur, W. B. (1988) Urban systems and historical path dependence, in Ausubel, J. H. and Herman, R. (eds) *Cities and their vital systems: Infrastructure, past, present and future*, National Academy Press, Washington, DC.

Arthur, W. B. (2009) *The nature of technology*, The Free Press, New York.

Baghai, M., Coley, S., and White, D. (1999) *The alchemy of growth*, Perseus Publications, Cambridge, MA.

Christensen, C. M. (1997) *The innovator's dilemma*, Harper Business, New York.

Department of Levelling Up, Housing and Communities (2022) *Levelling up*, HMSO, London.

Education Policy Institute (2021) Analysis paper: Preliminary research findings on education recovery, Education Policy Institute, London. Available at: https://epi.org.uk/publications-and-research/analysis-paper-preliminary-research-findings-on-education-recovery/.

Jacobs, J. (1970) *The economy of cities*, Jonathan Cape, London.

Mintzberg, H. (1989) *Structure in fives: Designing effective organisations*, Prentice-Hall, Englewood Cliffs, NJ.

Royal Society (2019) *Harnessing education research*, British Academy and the Royal Society, London.

Sen, A. (1999) *Commodities and capabilities*, Oxford University Press, Oxford.

Weaver, W. (1948) Science and complexity, *American Scientist*, 36, 536–544.

Weaver, W. (1958) A quarter century in the natural sciences, in *Annual Report*, The Rockefeller Foundation, New York, pp. 7–122.

Wilson, A. (2018) Research and innovation in an ecosystem, *FST Journal*, 22, 9–10.

Annex 1

Analytics

A1.1 Ways of thinking: systems and models

A1.1.1 Systems

I have had versions of the idea of a 'system' in my toolkit since I was a student. My subject was mathematics but under the rubric of 'applied maths', there was a lot of physics. Virtually every lecture by a physicist, started with something like: 'let us define our *system of interest*'. A key point in doing this was to identify the simplest system – usually a very artificial one – that could be used to illustrate some law of physics. It was always necessary to define the elements of the system, and how they related, but it also introduced an important principle, one that is important for teaching but also for 'thinking things through' more broadly: what is the simplest 'system of interest' I can construct to make my point, to illustrate the problem? Since systems in physics can also be thought of as (usually) mathematical models, it also introduced me to the idea of a toy model – a demonstration model – to get started with a problem. The detail and the depth could be added later.

Since we have the 'elements' – say, people or organisations, in my case – a starting point is often to place them in categories, and to count them – population by age and sex, for instance. These counts can be systematically arranged. In relation to a working population, for example, we will have residential and work locations for each person and thus have locational information but also interaction between two locations. This information can be arranged in a matrix and form the journey to work *accounts*.

In seeking to define characteristics and categories, we quickly become aware of the need to define *scales*. We usually have to handle three dimensions of scale: (1) the granularity of groupings of elements – how many age groups, for example; (2) the spatial scale; and (3) the treatment of time. Spatial systems, for example, are made up of area units – from an individual address, a neighbourhood, a city, or a country. Temporal units might be minutes or hours at the micro scale, through to light years in cosmology! In each case, there will be a *hierarchy* of scales from the macro via the meso to the micro.

As we specify relationships between system elements, it becomes clear very quickly that there are high levels of *interdependence*, and this in turn means that we will usually be working with *complex* systems. We have noted Weaver's classification of complex systems and we can expand on it here. Obviously, the number of elements in the systems gives a measure of complexity and this gives us the first of Weaver's three categories of complex systems: if this number is relatively small, this can be designated as a *simple* system; if the number is large, the system is complex and he identifies two types of complexity: systems of *disorganised complexity* and systems of *organised complexity*. The first of these has large numbers of elements but they are weakly interacting; the second consists of systems where the elements are strongly interacting. These distinctions turn out to be very important in developing mathematical and computer models of systems of interest. Weaver, at the time he was developing these ideas, noted that, possibly oversimplifying with hindsight, the first two kinds of system were represented in physics, the third, organised complexity, in biology. He used his analysis as the science Vice-President of the Rockefeller Foundation to shift funding from physics to biology on the basis that this is where the most challenging research problems lay.

This focus, of course, is the basis for what I have described as the *STM framework* introduced in Chapter 1. To recap:

S: system definition
T: theory, what do we know about the system?, how can we build on this knowledge?
M: what methods can we apply?

A1.1.2 Simulation and modelling: a perspective from cosmology

Being interdisciplinary involves elements of serendipity: reading in areas apparently unconnected to one's own research or problem-solving interests, but which trigger ideas that can be incorporated into an interdisciplinary toolkit. A recent personal experience was reading Andrew Pontzen's (2023) brilliant book, *The Universe in a Box*, an account of contemporary cosmology and how new methods, particularly new uses of some that were controversially neglected some time ago, are enlarging our knowledge of the universe. A number of his ideas resonated with me – either extending and reinforcing concepts that I use – new and extended insights into those concepts; and in some cases, new ideas for me to explore. In the following account, I will oversimplify Andrew's work, but in apology for this, I would strongly recommend reading the book!

Andrew's system of interest is the whole universe and at this scale, while in some sense, there is rich data and theory, in terms of the big picture – in relation to distant parts of the universe, for example – data is poor. His method to progress depends on computer modelling and simulation. He needs a spatial structure as a base for his models and he uses grids and subgrids. To handle billions of galaxies in the far reaches of the universe, he uses the idea of grouping them into idealised entities called 'smarticles' and models these through the mathematics of fluid dynamics. His model outputs can then be seen as simulations of the universe through a sequence of points in time. These can then be input to machine learning algorithms in a search for patterns, and these patterns compared with earlier histories and in relation to parts of the universe for which there is some data.

I was particularly taken by his emphasis on the importance of setting the initial conditions for dynamic simulations. This resonates strongly with me. I have sometimes argued that this is an under-researched area in my field, and indeed, it may be possible to construct an interesting typology of cities through specifying different structures of initial conditions for dynamic models and this would have implications for 'levelling up' analytics. I haven't had the time, or probably the ability, to progress this idea and have so far failed to find any takers for a collaboration! His modelling also seeks to handle competing forces – gravity and pressure in his case – and this connects to my use of adapted Lotka-Volterra equations from ecology to model, say, retailers and developers competing for consumers. I liked his idea of handling uncertainty through Bayes' theorem which led me to speculate on whether his was an area where entropy-maximising might help. I mentioned this to him, and he sent me a paper showing his exploration of this – but he didn't think it was ultimately useful to him. Nonetheless, it showed another way in which apparently disparate areas can connect. His use of the concept of scenario development also resonates. In my case, it provides a way forward when the levels of uncertainty mean that forecasting is not sensible, while explorations of possible scenarios are potentially productive – raising planning questions such as 'how to plan in the short run to steer away from bad long-term scenarios and towards good ones?'

Because I often have to work with imperfect or missing data, as a general take on Andrew's work, I like his idea that simulation is a new way of doing science. He explicitly recognises that simulation will not solve everything, but he does say 'simulations offer a way to structure scientific knowledge, insight and collaboration'. He adds: 'No individual could construct a simulation and compare it to data from a modern survey telescope. The range of expertise is too vast – covering hydrodynamics, star formation, black-hole formation and growth, quantum mechanics, optics and artificial intelligence' (Pontzen, 2023, pp. 211–212). This emphasises interdisciplinarity of a kind within a discipline. If I try to develop a similar list for my own field of urban research, it strongly makes the interdisciplinarity case, but also the vastness of the enterprise! But I do like the idea that mathematical and computer modelling of cities helps to structure the broader knowledge base of urban science. Simulation as science gives me a new argument to help explain a lot of what I do, and I would now advocate simulation as an important element of an interdisciplinary toolkit! In conclusion, I reiterate my earlier comment: I strongly recommend Andrew's book!

A1.1.3 Looking ahead: AI and data science

AI and 'big data', in their ubiquitous use, certainly function as superconcepts. Daily reports in newspapers and media draw our attention to the revolutionary transformations being brought about by AI in our digital, data-driven world. Here, we seek to disentangle what is driven by 'big data' and data science, and what is, in some way, 'real' AI – seeking to understand their uses in our interdisciplinary toolkit. Much of what is claimed as 'AI' is basically elementary statistics but implemented with more and better data. Indeed, 'data science' is sometimes described as 'statistics re-invented'! Data science and AI do overlap of course which makes naming the methods used in particular projects difficult, making the use of the AI label more likely. It sounds more exciting! Data science certainly makes statistics more powerful. It often needs hi-level maths.[1]

AI has a long history, dating back at least to the 1950s. Its original drive was to replicate human intelligence. It has had 'summers' and 'winters', the latter probably driven by the failure of the human intelligence metaphor. In its new mode, driven by the productive algorithms of machine learning, we can perhaps now envisage a long summer? Its algorithms can 'see', 'read', 'write', 'speak', 'hear', and 'recognise' images. It can deliver analysis, especially through clustering, and identifying patterns which a human might miss – examples ranging from medical imaging to money laundering. It can read text and 'learn' grammar, as, for example, with ChatGPT. These 'skills' can then be combined with hearing and speaking in chatbots. It can implement rules-based systems, 'taking decisions' much faster than a human. Most of these functions are delivered through machine learning and, the training database is crucial: usually the 'learning' is achieved through the labelling of the data – the so-called supervised learning using a pre-labelled data set; clusters can also be identified through unsupervised learning. Most of the machine learning algorithms are based on the construction of neural networks, mimicking brain structures. These can be huge, with many layers, accounting for hidden variables not seen in conventional statistics – the so-called 'deep learning'.

To seek to understand both what has been achieved, what is on offer, and the challenges, we proceed first on a sector basis. In consumer-serving business, many processes, certainly those that are rules-based, can be automated; chatbots can deal with a large percentage of inquiries, and the customer base can be analysed, generating routes to targeted marketing. In finance, invoicing and accounting can be automated as in the 'big data' information systems of banks, for example. These systems provide the basis for detecting anomalies, and hence fraud and money laundering, and facilitate compliance with less human intervention. Stock-market trading can be algorithms-driven in real time and much of this is in place now – taking advantage of arbitrage opportunities. Through this transformative period, data science and AI skills are in short supply and this has created a large market for consultants offering expertise.

In public services, in government or public bodies, as in business, many routine processes can be automated. In education, health, and work and pensions, students, patients and clients can be tracked in 'big data' information systems and these can be the basis of personalised services. We find major challenges in these sectors where we can explore whether AI and data science can be revolutionary. We can identify grand challenges: climate change and sustainability, security – from defence to police – developing preventive strategies, pandemics, social inclusion – and, above all, the economy.

How much are data science and AI contributing to 'new science'? We address this in three stages: first, the impact of data directly, and generative AI; second, what can be added to prior knowledge – taking on what I will describe as the Mike Lynch challenge; and third, what is 'real' new science?

In many areas, more and better data, and associated information systems, are key drivers. Through a mixture of scanning and simulation, generative AI produces new 'data' – ChatGPT again. Superior image processing can be complemented by AI analysis to root out what is interesting. Solving large systems of nonlinear differential equations generates 'results' which can then be analysed with AI algorithms, producing 'patterns' which would otherwise be undetected. This all illustrates another kind of value to scientists: new tools to speed up analysis.

The second heading: Mike Lynch, an early AI pioneer, once argued, at the end of a brilliant lecture which was a history of AI and its winters and summers, that the integration of prior knowledge is the biggest challenge for machine learning. In my field, that would include the mathematical modelling of cities where the AI/data science contribution is the possibility of real-time model calibration together with a reformulation of the core model by analogy with health. A second personal example comes from elementary particle physics. I once applied statistical methods to analyse bubble chamber events from synchrotron experiments at CERN. This can now be done by AI image processing – though this stops a long way short of 're-inventing quantum mechanics'! There are also additions from AI and data science to areas such as engineering – now represented as data-centric engineering; and operational research, particularly with complex optimising problems.

It is not easy to define, relative to the examples above, what constitutes new science. We have already mentioned the basic applications of automating rules-based systems, for example, or the way in which pattern recognition can offer new insights from simulation model outputs. However, in each of these cases we should probably recognise deep-learning applications of AI that are so dramatic as to constitute new science. In the 'rules' case, chess and AlphaGo offer good examples of significant achievement. In the simulation case, Andrew Pontzen and his colleagues in cosmology have shown how simulation offers more than pattern recognition. Deep Mind's demonstration of the mechanisms of protein folding is an outstanding achievement. We might include drug discovery in the pharmaceutical industry. In medical science, the idea of 'learning machines', demonstrated in proof-of-concept research, can offer augmented intelligence on diagnosis and prognosis to clinicians; perhaps later, almost achieving automation. The same ideas could be applied in social science – learning machines for urban planning – but this research is still on the drawing board.

The argument has largely focused on the opportunities. There are major challenges, of course, which should be confronted at the outset. In social terms, new efficiencies and automation are already producing job losses – the 'hollowing out' issue. This always happens in times of technological change but the losses are relatively quickly replaced by new jobs. It is not clear that this will happen in this case. In decision processes, if there is bias in the data, there will be bias in the learning, and in the outcomes. Generative AI is brilliant but can be unreliable at what may be critical points. It is very difficult, at present impossible in many instances, to interpret the results of deep learning algorithms. The technical challenges – bias, reliability, and interpretation are all subjects of major research projects. Will the results of these be available fast enough to meet the challenges?

A1.2 The knowledge base

Different types of organisation have different needs, though there is of course a big overlap. We can begin to explore with the usual 'industry' classifications, and then add 'government' and the public sector. We can seek to distinguish 'business to people' from 'business to business'. It is very difficult to classify conglomerates, and it may be better to work with their component parts. We can look at a wider range than we have used as illustrations to date so that the uses of the analytics toolkit can be fully illustrated.

We will work through the categories of the standard industrial classification, starting with business-to-people organisations, supplying goods and services. These include a wide range of sectors: auto; banking, insurance, investment companies and finance; construction and property; consumer goods; leisure; media; retail; telecoms; transport; and utilities. Business-to-business organisations include (with some repetition) auto; banking, insurance, investment companies, and finance; construction and property; engineering; industrials; natural resources; professional and support services; real estate; technology; telecoms; transport; utilities. Then we can add, under the heading of 'government', public services to people: health; education; defence; security and, police; and many others.

We can then ask the question: what does management need to know? As ever, we need to recall, and start from, the four pillars:

- systems – understanding the *big picture* – providing focus. What are we for? What are our challenges? The PDA/STM systems (policy, design, analysis/systems, theory, method) framework.
- a clear long-term *strategy*
- finance: follow the *money*
- *structures* that deliver; *devolution*

and add, *making things work*.

The first of these is about system definition – the foundation stone of analytics. We can then start to build a knowledge base. For all sectors, this will include:

- demographics
- economics – costs, prices, critical paths, markets and competitors (consumers, clients, users of services)
- engineering (in a broad sense): the production technology (including supply chains)
- geography (linking markets and production – networks, nodes, flows)
- sociology
- politics
- along with indicators of 'performance' and 'change'.

This provides a starting point and as these perspectives are all linked, we will need an interdisciplinary synthesis for the variety of applications.

It is commonly recognised that there is a 'data' revolution and organisations are urged to maximise the knowledge that can be derived from 'their' data. This knowledge, in our terminology, is what we derive from our analytics tools, using the data. In other words, the analytics comes first, and then we can ask the question, what data to we need for our analytics? We begin with an overview of what is on offer, based on the 'disciplines' list above, and then follow through with a number of examples. The city has two major systems which then divide into interacting subsystems: demographics and the activities of the population; and the economy as the supplier of goods and services (and in this case including government-provided public services). Transport and communications subsystems provide the interactions' infrastructure and connect the two major systems. The geography and the politics are ubiquitous.

We can use this framework to begin to respond to the question: what does the management need to know? In outline:

- *demographics* – the make-up of the population and how it is changing, including migration;
- *economics*, including trade – imports and exports – regionally, nationally and internationally; how these connect and translate into markets (consumers, clients, users of services, including the markets in labour and housing, for example, exhibited by the journey-to-work);
- *engineering* and the underpinning technologies;
- *geography* is ubiquitous: the location of activities – both supply and demand – is a crucial part of the knowledge base along with spatial interaction.

Add to all this a knowledge of the competition. And, of course, the sociological and the political contexts.

When all this is in place, along with an appropriate synthesis for different applications, management will need to refine this into an information system and sets of indicators of performance and change. The former includes measures of costs, profits, and efficiency and effectiveness of delivery. The latter embraces economic trends, and changes in production technology, including intelligence on the behaviour of competitors. More broadly, we can designate what is needed beyond the core quantitative information system: adding a wider range to build an intelligence system. We can now review what is available to build a comprehensive analytics-based intelligence system.

A1.3 The analytics toolkit: building an intelligent information system

A1.3.1 The system of interest

As we start to assemble the toolkit, we begin by returning to the task of defining the system of interest, the big picture. We can do this in relatively abstract terms to provide the basis for exploring examples. A critical starting point is that our system articulation will depend crucially on the level of granularity we choose to work with. For example, how do we categorise people and organisations, space and time?

There are many potentially relevant descriptors of people: age, sex, social class, and education for example. We have already noted the sectors used for the classification of organisations in industry in Section 7.1 in Chapter 7, along with the major public services. We could in principle classify individual people or organisations, and sometimes it may be appropriate to do this; more often we will use clusters – person types or industry or public service sectors. These clusters can be in more or less detail – and sometimes the level of detail we can use is determined by data availability; or sometimes the reverse – how to handle very large quantities of data that can arise from using very finely specified descriptors.

To handle space, we usually divide areas into zones: (1) at an international scale, these will be countries; (2) at a national scale – the whole nation as a unit, and perhaps subdivided into (3) city regions; at a finer scale, (4) neighbourhoods within a city. In terms of the intelligent information system, there are many instances where we need all four scales represented: the international context for migration and trade, national gross domestic product (GDP), indices of development in different cities and regions of the country; neighbourhoods for detailed market analysis or to understand the demand for public services. Within neighbourhoods, zones can be so small as to represent individual addresses, but more likely they will be local authority wards or Census units.

Time units can range from the very short run, for example, in managing emergency services, or can range from hours, days, months, or years for different purposes. We may depend on decennial Census data, for example.

All of this needs serious forethought! However, we can assume that these decisions have been made and now turn to what is on offer for an analytics toolkit. The description here will be narrative rather than technical, the point being that managers need to understand all this at least in broad terms, and need to be able to assemble able analytics teams to build and run the intelligent information system, and to apply the tools which will offer crucial insights. We work through our core headings in turn.

A1.3.2 Demographics: communities

The core of the demographics knowledge base is the modelling of birth, death, and migration processes. There are long-standing elaborate models that function at all spatial scales for these purposes.[2] It is probably most common for managements to rely on published data, for example, the latest Census data or Office for National Statistics (ONS) population projections (from national down to local authority levels). The ONS typically publish 'median' estimates with ranges from lowest to highest. In areas such as insurance, management relies on actuarial data, calculated in terms of life expectancy for different groups of people.[3] The most difficult element of course is to estimate migration, nonetheless, particularly important given its political salience. There are definitional problems here as well. International migration is well defined as it involves crossing borders with flows ideally, but not always accurately, measured. Intra-national migration is more difficult. Between cities, perhaps beyond a certain distance apart, this may be defined as migration. For a move within a city region, this may be regarded as residential relocation.

For many management purposes, we would like to know much more about our populations than the demographic cores of age, sex, and maybe location. This is the case for many purposes, but notably targeted marketing and this is very much where 'big data' kicks in. There are now many more records of individual data, mostly in private sources such as supermarket purchases or in public, but unavailable sources, such as NHS data. The characteristics might include education and skills attainment, employment (including location) and occupation, income, housing (location and type), leisure and retail (locations again), health data and something about family structures. The greatest value is achieved when it is possible to link data from different sources through some kind of personal identifier. We also need to connect to qualitative research on, for example, people and behaviour, and cultural change – looking to sociology and perhaps a wider range of commentators.[4]

Data science has to meet substantial challenges in handling this kind of data. If this kind of list of characteristics is indexed against individuals in a database, it is very high dimensional. It is customary to combine individuals into clusters, for example, of 'market types', or those particularly vulnerable in social or health terms. This was originally the task of geodemographics[5] but this has more recently been enhanced by the deployment of AI and machine learning-based clustering algorithms.[6] The high dimensionality challenge has been tackled through a method known as microsimulation,[7] converting population characteristics into probabilities and then generating an artificial but realistic population that can be stored much more efficiently than the raw data. This also has the advantage that it can be used as an anonymisation procedure. It has a relationship to agent-based modelling.

A1.3.3 Economics and technology

The second core perspective comes from economics. Classical economics provides the behavioural fundamentals for individuals and organisations, the former maximising utilities, the latter, profits. It is now more widely recognised that these are huge oversimplifications: individuals are more varied than is recognised and in particular do not have the perfect information demanded by the theory; organisations may well have objectives that supplement profit maximisation. Public services organisations do not have profit as a prime objective, but efficient and effective delivery, and we need indicators to measure these. Economics is being rewritten! However, as will see, the classical basis gives us a starting point that can be modified and developed.

For organisations, it is helpful to focus on what we might call the 'production technology' – 'engineering' in a broad sense; and of course, individuals and families are 'organisations' and the same concept can be applied here. We need information on how goods and services are produced, including supply chains, costs, prices, and the patterns of supply and demand. At broader spatial scales, mainly national, occasionally regional, even more occasionally, urban, input-output models can be brought into play.[8] In relation to investment for maintenance, development and innovation purposes, the methods of cost-benefit analysis (CBA) should be at hand.[9]

Cost-benefit analysis provides a good route into economics. However, there are more core concepts from economics that have wider applications beyond the discipline, and therefore function as superconcepts, and I review some of them here. Economics is a big and important discipline but has largely been a self-contained community and, at least implicitly, hostile to interdisciplinarity. The core tools included demand, supply, markets, utility, profits, accounts (and input-output modelling). The subject is divided mainly into micro- and macro-economics with little focus on the 'meso', which was what was most useful to me in urban analytics. Indeed, when economists did venture into spatial analysis, they tended to treat space as continuous rather than as a set of discrete zones. This made the mathematics more difficult and forced assumptions such as the requirement that a city was monocentric – hopelessly unrealistic. Consumer behaviour was modelled in terms of utility maximisation along with '*rational man*' assumptions, and firms were 'profit-maximising' – in both cases, again hopelessly unrealistic. However, the ideas of utility and profits can be developed and function as superconcepts. As noted, 'accounts' were important and the basis of important indicators such as GDP. However, there was a weakness here which connects to 'profit maximising' and what was largely the absence of equivalent measures in relation to public services – something dealt with in important ways by Diane Coyle,[10] for example, calling for new measures of GDP.

Economics has moved on, of course, with stronger connections to sociology and psychology, refining the over-simplistic models of 'behaviour'. There have been noble attempts to refine the core models – introducing time in a more effective way through activity-based models. However, much of the core is still in place, with its inadequate assumptions, and there is a continuing role for all of use both to work with economics and to locate it in a better interdisciplinary framework. My own experience shows the nature of the battles still to be fought. The development of entropy-maximising models of spatial interaction (Chapter 4), has largely been unaccepted by economists. What has happened is that an 'economic' version of the models has been produced – using a 'random utility concept' with an assumption that the 'error' term – the economists' way of handling uncertainty – is a Gumbel distribution. The mathematics then produces a usually unacknowledged entropy-maximising model which offers, in practice, a better interpretation of 'behaviour' than the economic account.

When we define any system of interest, we are building on the STM framework (Chapter 2), and we are assembling a toolkit for analysis, we should always scour the economics basket. We will usually find valuable contributions. A final comment: there is a huge opportunity for research to integrate economics with all contiguous and potentially valuable disciplines, to locate it in a full interdisciplinary framework.

A1.3.4 Geography

These sources of intelligence begin to be drawn together through the perspective of geography. Virtually every piece of data has a location associated with it (or multiple locations through spatial interaction), linking markets and producers through networks of nodes and flows; migration, trade (input-output relationships); work, linking residence and employment; retail; business-to-business; handling competition; modelling money flows, migration and trade. The core of the analytical capability is provided by the spatial interaction model and we will see many examples in Section A1.4. In broad terms, its key components include measures of (1) trip origins, (2) the attractiveness of destinations, and (3) the impedance of interaction (such as travel costs and time), all in the context of handling competition and rents and prices in the light of this. This model is sometimes misleadingly known as a 'gravity model' from its early history, but in its present form, it is based on Boltzmann mathematics and statistical averaging rather than Newton.[11] It has been widely applied and tested and proved to be accurate at least for short-run forecasting in many situations.

A number of indicators can be calculated from the core model outputs: catchment areas, or measures of accessibility, for example. For many services, it is possible to calculate estimates of both efficiency and effectiveness, and it is particularly interesting to identify circumstances where a facility can be efficient but not effective in delivery. There may be a very efficient dental surgery for example, but it may not be available to much of its catchment population and is therefore ineffective in its delivery to its potential user base. (See the note on 'dentist deserts' in Section A1.4.)

The spatial interaction model also contributes one of the foundations for dynamic modelling and analytics. This deploys the mathematics that Lotka and

Volterra[12] used to model prey-predator and competition-for-resources models in ecology, and as we will see through examples below, this gives us a basis for identifying phase transitions – sudden changes in structure such as the introduction of supermarkets, or gentrification. A useful footnote – an example of early dynamic modelling, is Hotelling's response to the question: where is my best location? The answer is: next to your strongest competitor![13]

A1.3.5 Politics

All individuals, families, and organisations function in a political environment, and indeed, some organisations, at different levels, represent the government or are government agencies. Intelligence on this context is vital. Broadly speaking, the agencies themselves have four levers available to provide an environment in which all can flourish: fiscal, regulation, revenue spend, and capital spend.

This broad account of the requirements of an intelligence system draws attention to what will by now be an obvious point: the elements of the system are all interdependent and though we have introduced concepts through disciplinary perspectives, the overall management perspective has to be interdisciplinary. We have to take stock and put the question: is everything in place?[14] The answer to this question is complicated: while the principles are clear, different kinds of organisation will have different needs. Perhaps what management needs is the equivalent from medicine of the doctor who is a good, even specialist, diagnostician, to identify the elements of the toolkit that are most needed. This is not easily found in medicine, given its siloed specialisms and is probably largely non-existent in management![15]

A1.3.6 Overview: requisite knowledge

We can now return briefly to our core framework:

- the big picture – providing focus. What are we for? What are our challenges? The PDA/STM systems (policy, design, analysis/systems, theory, method) framework
- a clear long-term strategy
- finance: follow the money
- structures that deliver; devolution
- making things work.

What we achieve by assembling data and analytics in an overarching interdisciplinary intelligence system is a statement of the big picture. We can jump two steps within the 'four': this will certainly incorporate full and detailed links to the financial accounts – and will provide the basis of understanding flows of income, costs, and investment; and the flows can be linked to the structures of the organisation. This all provides, therefore, the basis for thinking through strategy and developing the structures that will make things work. And it is worth adding that, from a management perspective, even without detailed technical knowledge, model-based analytics does provide a good conceptual framework – a good overview.

The interdisciplinary drive is captured through an important superconcept: *requisite knowledge*, developed from Ross Ashby's notion of 'requisite variety'. This has its origins in control engineering. If an engineering system is to be controlled, its control system has to be at least as complex as the system it controls. 'Variety' is a measure of complexity and 'requisite variety' is a measure of the minimum level of complexity required in the controller. This is intuitively obvious in the engineering case: complexity, aka variety for present purposes, can be measured in terms of the number of states that can be reached by the system of interest. We can get another intuitive perspective in a different way. Consider a country which is being run by a dictator. It is impossible for his or her government to have requisite variety that would be required for full control. The response is to diminish the variety of the country by making it much more rules-bound. The same argument might be applied to the Chief Executive Officer (CEO) of a large organisation: either the management structure has to be strongly rules-based, perhaps as in the military case; or responsibilities have to be devolved to smaller autonomous units with requisite variety in place both at the top in each of the units. Devolution again!

The argument can also be applied to research – and indeed to tackling any complex problem. This is the sense in which requisite variety becomes requisite knowledge: what do we need to know to tackle the problem? This immediately drives us to an interdisciplinary perspective for most problems. We can search disciplines to assemble an intellectual toolkit for the problem. If I am working on a city-planning problem, in principle, I need to draw knowledge from economics, geography, sociology, psychology, physics, engineering, biology, mathematics, and computer science! It may be argued that this is impossible – certainly in terms of depth of knowledge – but it can be argued that the researcher has to have a broad understanding of at least the insights that can be drawn from the range. It may then be a matter of building a team with a range of 'in-depth' skills but whose members are flexible enough to understand and work across the broad front as well as contributing these skills. It is also worth introducing the notion of 'interactional expertise'.[16] If we spend long enough working with those who are expert in fields other than our own, we can acquire serious knowledge to complement our own areas – a means of developing interdisciplinary thinking and working.

Requisite variety drives us to an interdisciplinary approach and, not surprisingly, the framework sketched here draws together many of the superconcepts introduced in earlier chapters. More detail is available in *Knowledge Power* (Wilson, 2010a) and *Being Interdisciplinary* (Wilson, 2023).

A1.4 Applications

We now assume that, for any organisation, an intelligence system along the lines sketched in the previous section, is in place. This is a big assumption, of course! We will initially focus on organisations that are serving people – as consumers, or more broadly, as clients. Goods or services will be delivered through facilities and networks and geography will be of critical importance. The 'production technology' and associated economics – costs, prices, and means of delivery – will be well understood. We will work through examples to show how such intelligence systems can work, beginning with retail (and supermarkets) as a relatively simple example to fix ideas.

Consider a city region and its supermarkets as a system of interest. Each facility will be located along with its characteristics, such as size and range of products – and the costs of running it. The region will be divided into small zones, and for each of these, the population of potential consumers, and their characteristics, will be articulated. A computer model will be available that predicts the revenues attracted to each supermarket in terms of the flows from each population zone – this is the spatial interaction core. The model will be calibrated on the company's own data, which allows reasonable assumptions to be made in such a way that flows and revenues can also be calculated for competitors. Suppose now that the company wants to explore the possibilities of investing in a new supermarket somewhere in the region, and it will have identified a number of possible sites. For each such site in turn, it can locate the prospective facility on the computer system and the model will calculate not only the revenue that would be attracted to the site but also the revenues that would be lost at the company's existing sites. Given the knowledge of the costs of running the new site, an estimate of the profit or loss of locating in a particular place can be calculated. If profitable at the 'revenue minus cost' level, the company can then determine the price it would pay for the land to make a good business case. This process could be repeated if there was more than one possible site. When a positive decision is made, the company could then use the flow information from the model to optimise its stocking and local marketing. There would be available, of course, an analysis of the 'click and collect' potential of the site to support the company's internet shopping. The system could also be used by local authorities to map access to supermarkets, for example, to identify supermarket 'deserts' (or indeed to map access to dental services to identify 'dentist deserts'!).

This range of analytics range can be expanded in that it applies to a wide variety of retail organisations – 'retail' in the broad sense – including banks and car dealers, for example. It can also be applied widely by planners, starting with the contribution of urban structures to the quality of life of the citizens. It can be applied in education, for example, in relation to school catchment areas, parental choice, and competing schools; universities can use it to understand their student 'markets' in relation to their competitors, and they can usefully estimate their local and national economic impacts. Indeed, it can be applied in a wide variety of public services: health; defence, security and police.[17] It could even be applied by research councils exploring the distribution of funding across the country. A good recent example of the development of a comprehensive model is Batty and Milton (2021).

It can be applied widely across industry – it is left as an exercise for the reader – and potential user! – to do this across, say, professional and support services; construction and property; telecoms; utilities; transport; and business-to-business organisations including insurance, investment banking and asset managers; and in engineering, industrials, and natural resources.

A1.5 Lessons learned

Many authors have argued the need for organisations to have units that supply their intelligence system under a variety of names – from Beer's 'war room' to Barber's 'delivery unit'. It is, or course, a moot point about whether this should be centralised or distributed to operational units, or something of both. Note the education example earlier: in the Department for Education and Skills (DfES), the central analytics capability was broken up and distributed to directorates; in the Ministry of Defence, there is more than one central intelligence unit, and the 'commands' certainly have their own. There is a challenge of how to optimise these structures to avoid expensive duplication. In all cases, there is a balance to be struck between 'analytics for the here and now' and the short term, and 'future-proofing' activities such as horizon scanning and the exploration of future scenarios.

Notes

1 For a cautious and interesting overview, see Jordan (2019).
2 A classic reference is Rees and Wilson (1976).
3 There are enormous variations in this at local levels.
4 The best journalists are as good as the best academics, see John Harris in *The Guardian*, for example.
5 Singleton et al. (2018), Harris et al. (2005), Webber and Burrows (2018).
6 There are many references on AI and machine learning, see Alpaydin (2016) for a brief overview.
7 Tanton and Edwards (2013).
8 Miller and Blair (2022).
9 There are lots of references on cost-benefit analysis, as an example, see Layard and Glaister (1994).
10 See Diana Coyle (2025).
11 See Wilson (2012) for an overview.
12 Lotka (1925) and Volterra (1938).
13 Hotelling (1929).
14 Beer (1972; 1994).
15 There is. of course, a wider toolkit – optimisation methods through operational research (OR) and statistics – particularly in relation to the analysis of uncertainty and risk.
16 'Interactional expertise' was propounded by the Cardiff sociologist, Harry Collins, who was introduced to me by Carl Gombrich.
17 See Baudains and Wilson (2016) and Guo et al. (2019).

Annex 2

Employment and key publications

A2.1 Employment

A2.1.1 The first ten years: Harwell, Oxford, and London

Rutherford Lab (Scientific Officer, 1961–1964)
Oxford University Institute of Statistics (Research Associate, 1964–1966)
Ministry of Transport (Mathematical Adviser, 1966–1968)
Centre for Environmental Studies (Assistant Director, 1968–1970)

A2.1.2 The next 30+ years: Leeds

University of Leeds (Professor, Geography, 1970–2004; Faculty Board Chair, 1982–1984; Pro-Vice Chancellor, 1989–1991; Vice-Chancellor, 1991–2004)
GMAP Ltd (Director, executive, then non-executive, 1990–2000)

A2.1.3 10+ years: mainly London

Department for Education and Skills (DfES, Director-General for Higher Education, 2004–2006)
Corpus Christi College Cambridge (Master, 2006–2007)
Centre for Advanced Spatial Analysis, UCL (Professor, CASA, 2007–2018; Visiting Professor, 2004–2006, 2018–present)

A2.1.4 7+ years: London and Norfolk

The Alan Turing Institute (Fellow, 2016; CEO, 2016–2018; then Director, Special Projects, 2018–2023; Honorary Fellow, 2018–present)
The Ada Lovelace Institute (Executive Chair, 2016–2019)
The Institute of Finance and Technology, UCL (Director of Research, 2022–2023)
The London Interdisciplinary School (Director of Research, 2023–2024)

A2.2 Non-Executive

Labour Party (Oxford constituency, General Management Committee, Executive Committee, 1962–1967)
Oxford City Council (Councillor, 1964–1967)
Assistant Editor, *Transportation Research* (1967–1970)
Editor, *Environment and Planning* (1969–1983)
SSRC (Environment Committee, member, 1972–1975)
Dewsbury District Health Authority (member, 1977–1981)
Kirklees Area Health Authority (Vice-Chair, 1981–1985)
Yorkshire Regional Health Authority (member, 1994–1996)
British Academy (Fellow, reviews, 1994–present)
White Rose Ltd (Chair, 1999–2002)
e-University (NED, 2000–2002)
World-Wide Universities Network (WUN) (Co-Chair, 2000–2004)
Economic and Social Research Council: ESRC (Council Member, 2000–2004)
Royal Society (Fellow, sometime Council member, reviews, 2006–present)
SCORE: Science Community Representing Education, Royal Society (Chair, 2007–2010)
AHRC: Arts and Humanities Research Council (Chair, 2007–2013)
Home Office Science Advisory Council (HOSAC, Chair, 2012–2018)
Ministry of Defence Science Advisory Council (DSAC, member, 2012–2018)
Centre for Cities (NED, Trustee, 2015–2018)
Prospective Labs Ltd (Chair, 2015–2021)

A2.3 Consultancies, visiting appointments

International Institute for Applied Systems Analysis (IIASA), Laxenberg, Vienna (1970s)
University of Pennsylvania (Adjunct Professor, 1977)
Polytechnico di Torino (1970s)
Oakleigh Ltd: SOAS; University of Wales, Newport; Dubai (2008–2010)
Cisco (Higher Education, post-Katrina New Orleans redevelopment, 2006–2008)
Milton Keynes Council: Commission for MK 2050 (Honorary Adviser, 2014–2015)

A2.4 Reviews and inquiries

Channel Tunnel (Committee Member,[1] 1980s)
NHS Complaints Procedures (Chair,[2] 1993–1994)
Leeds Schools Commission (Chair, 1992–1993)
Biotechnology Clusters (Group member,[3] 1998–1999)
Department for Education and Skills: Science Education, PQA (2005)
AHRC: leading the world: the economic impact of UK arts and humanities research (Chair, 2008–2009)

British Academy: Punching our weight: the humanities and social sciences in public policy making (Chair, 2008)
JISC: Joint Information Systems Committee (Independent reviewer,[4] 2010)
Defence Science Advisory Council, Ministry of Defence (Independent inquiry, 2011–2012)
Government Office for Science: Foresight Future of Cities (Chair, 2013–2015)
IIASA: International Institute for Applied Systems Analysis, Laxenburg, Vienna (UK membership review, 2017)
British Academy and Royal Society, Harnessing Education Research (Group Chair. 2017–2019)

A2.5 Some key publications

Wilson, A. G. (1967) A statistical theory of spatial distribution models, Transportation Research, 1, 253–269.
Wilson, A. G. (1970) Entropy in urban and regional modelling, Pion, London. (Translated into Russian and Chinese).
Wilson, A. G. (1974) Urban and regional models in geography and planning, John Wiley, Chichester. (Translated into Spanish).
Wilson, A. G. (1978) Equilibrium values and dynamics of attractiveness terms in production-constrained spatial-interaction models, Environment and Planning, A, 10(4), 371–388 with Britton Harris.
Wilson, A. G. (1981) Catastrophe theory and bifurcation: Applications to urban and regional systems, Croom Helm, London. (Reissued by Routledge in 2011).
Wilson, A. G. (2000) Complex spatial systems, Prentice Hall, Englewood Cliffs, NJ.
Wilson, A. G. (2010) Knowledge power: Interdisciplinary education for a complex world. Routledge, Abingdon.
Wilson, A. G. (2012) The science of cities and regions: Lectures on mathematical model design. Springer, London:
Wilson, A. G. (2015) Explorations in urban and regional dynamics, Routledge, Abingdon.
Wilson, A. G. (ed.) (2016a) Global dynamics: Approaches from complexity science, John Wiley, Chichester.
Wilson, A. G. (ed.) (2016b) Approaches to geo-mathematical modelling: New tools for complexity science, John Wiley, Chichester.
Wilson, A. G. (2022) Being interdisciplinary: Adventures in urban science and beyond, UCL Press, London.

Notes

1 Chair: Sir Alec Cairncross.
2 For Secretary of State, Virginia Bottomley.
3 Chair, Lord Sainsbury, then Science Minister.
4 For Sir Alan Langlands, Chief Executive, HEFCE.

Annex 3

Working life: A personal memoir

A3.1 Oxford

A3.1.1 Harwell

I started at the Rutherford Lab at Harwell as a 'Scientific Officer' (a Civil Service professional grade) on the 3rd of July 1961. I buried myself in work. I was assigned to the Bubble Chamber Group in Theoretical Physics and found that the work I'd done the previous summer as an intern hadn't been touched. I picked that up again and started programming properly, this time in Fortran with the programming running on an IBM 7090 at Aldermaston – debugging having to be undertaken on the basis of single overnight runs. No wonder it took so long to get things right: a single typo in the program meant a day lost. Bill Walkinshaw, the Head of Theoretical Physics, was very kind: he knew I really wanted to do theoretical physics and encouraged me to find time to do some serious reading. I guess this is how the time was filled during the 'waiting' for results from the computer. The task was in three stages. First, from the topology of the tracks, identify the range of hypotheses that the event could be – bearing in mind the possible production of neutral particles which didn't leave tracks, though which sometimes revealed themselves in secondary collisions. Second, for each hypothesis, the kinematical analysis: estimate the momentum of each charged particle. Third, run a chi squared test on each hypothesis. By some magical process that I never quite understood, an event could usually be identified by a chi squared that was much smaller than the alternatives. In some cases, it was possible to identify the mass of a potentially 'new' previously undiscovered particle, and if this could be done for many events, that constituted a discovery. We were looking for neutral and negatively charged Ξ^- particles and ultimately, the Ω^-, both predicted by theory but not 'seen'.

I made the judgement – and interestingly, I was 'allowed' to make the judgement – that I would write a general program that could analyse an event of any topology. It was more common at the time in other labs to write programs for specific experiments. This may have been more sensible, but with some difficulty, I succeeded. Within a year, I had a working program and data from three experiments from the European Organization for Nuclear Research (CERN), one from each of three groups we worked with: Oxford, University

College London (UCL), and Padua. I established good working relationships with each group, particularly with the Oxford one. Christianne Wilkinson, the wife of the Head of Nuclear Physics in Oxford, was assigned to work with me. Mike Eastern was my UCL contact and I had my first visits to UCL (Malet Place, I recall) at that time. In March 1962, I spent three weeks abroad, mainly at CERN in Geneva but with a few days in Padua working with Marcello Cresti and his Italian group. (It was my first trip abroad, and the first time I had flown.) The depression I felt when I first started working lifted with the interest in, and success of, the project. I made a second trip to Italy in May to produce some results for the Padua Group. The computing was done on the IBM 7090 at the Euratom Lab at Ispra on Lake Maggiore. All very pleasant. We were 'given' the computer for the night or at weekends. In the former case, we could set up runs and leave the machine running while we slept. In the latter case, we set up the runs in the morning and then repaired to a restaurant on Lake Maggiore for lunch. In July, the Oxford Group led by John Mulvey needed some results for a conference and Aldermaston was proving too slow. So John decided – 'over a pint in the Lamb and Flag' my diary reports – to move camp to Ispra, which we did. I had two trips to Paris in November 1962 and February 1963 supporting conference presentations and by this time, I was being offered jobs in Oxford and the Argonne National Lab in Illinois. I assume that people wanted my program with me to develop and run it. A taste of success. It was good for me to develop an understanding of big main frame computing and this, of course, was a precursor of the handling of 'big data' – data science. John Burren, whom I worked for, was also prescient: he envisaged experiments being done in a week rather than a year and that our methods could be applied by the NEDC – the then National Economic Development Council. Nothing came of this at the time! There was one other work dimension: I had two weekly tutorial groups, one second year, one third year, of four students each from St Hughes – teaching nuclear physics – my first experience of university teaching.

A3.1.2 The Labour Party, and Oxford City Council

I must have started looking for something 'new' around the turn of 1961–1962. I had started applying for jobs in which I could still be a mathematician but would be socially useful. I must have applied for 20 or 30, always turned down. It was not fashionable in those days, as it is now, to move from physics to the social sciences. Given this problem, I thought I would move into politics – not sure whether this was explicit, or is it post hoc rationalisation? The big move was to join the Labour Party (LP) in February 1962. A 'catch-up' bit of my journal diary records that I did this out of 'frustration with the Tories rather than a sudden drive to socialism'. It was, probably still is, Labour Party practice, this meant joining the local ward Labour Party, in my case, Summertown Ward in North Oxford. This was very Tory of course, and the Ward membership was small – only just double figures. However, there were two significant consequences. First, within a year, I slowly became heavily involved in local politics. A massively important new friend was

Tom Richardson – part of Summertown LP – married to Alice Hooson, niece of Emlyn Hooson.

By the beginning of 1963, I was Secretary of Summertown Ward LP and (possibly ex officio) a member of the constituency General Management Committee (the GMC). By the end of January, I found myself the Labour candidate for Summertown for the May elections. Each ward in those days elected two councillors each year for three-year terms. We had selected our candidates but at the end of 1962, they left Oxford. The Party 'rules' then said that with time so short, the Chair, Kath Wignall, and the Secretary, me, would be the candidates. (This had the later advantage that I never had to be interviewed as a possible candidate for future elections as I had already stood.) A 'catch-up' entry in my journal after a long gap captures the rest of 1963 pretty well.

> Summertown was fought with reasonable efficiency with Andrew (Stibbs) making an excellent Election Secretary. The election took me to the stage where Labour politics was so ingrained as to be beyond the possibility of change. A month or so after the election, I left for Geneva on the 4th of July. I was there for two and a half months until the 14th of September. I stayed in a large rented flat in the old city with Mitch and his wife, and Jean, a young assistant. I started taking driving lessons, and by the end of the year I had a car. I rose in the City Labour Party – a member of the Election Committee, and elected to the Executive Committee.
>
> (Right and left put out 'slates' of their preferred candidates for the Executive. I was on both lists and came top of the poll!)

In January 1964, I was selected (with Tom Richardson) as a Labour candidate for East Ward in the May 1964 Council election and by March, serious electioneering was underway. This was not only important for East Ward, which seemed winnable, but for the city, because Oxford was a marginal Parliamentary seat, held by the Tories, and was considered winnable in the upcoming June General Election. Getting the Labour vote in for the Council election provided the intelligence to do the same for the Parliamentary election. I worked very hard, canvassing more or less every evening.

Diary again (slightly edited):

> East Ward elected me as a Councillor. Unfortunately, any celebration was very muted … because Tom wasn't elected. The Tory was first, I was second and Tom third with three votes between each. We were almost famous by having five counts, but some ward in Stratford had six. There were three counts on the night. I was in on the first two and out on the third. The Town Clerk then ordered all the ballot papers to be returned to their boxes for a new count in the Town Hall the following morning. I was in by 2 or 3 votes each time and the Clerk then called an end to it. Fortunately, Tom was immediately selected for a by-election in Headington in June, and was duly elected with a large majority.

I was 25 when I was elected to the Council, probably at least 30 years younger than any other members bar one – John Briscoe. It was an exciting time. In those days, Councils still had Aldermen, senior figures, almost always ex-Councillors, who were elected by the Council itself. I remember that at the first Labour Group meeting before the first Council meeting, we worked out that if we replaced two Conservative Aldermen, we would have an overall majority of one on the Council. We did that – an occasion of some embarrassment as those 'unseated' had to leave the Chamber. For me, I recall the whole experience as important staff development: I was treated as an equal by the other members. I was assigned to the Education, Water, Childrens, and Library Committees. I was a Governor of three schools. I had a couple of successes on the Council – both supported by the *Oxford Mail* – real success. The first was to argue that the Council should move to five-year budgeting; the second that the new Town Clerk would not necessarily be a lawyer. Council meetings and committee meetings were all held in daytime and I'm not sure how I managed this with my Harwell work commitment but I must have done. It was an interesting time to be in local politics. The big issue in Oxford at the time was, using our majority of one, to shift to comprehensive schools.

Even more time went into Labour Party activities. This occupied most evenings. As noted, I was on the GMC and the Executive Committee; and I was responsible for postal votes as a member of the Election Committee for the upcoming General Election. In the early days, I spent many evenings canvassing first for Tom in Headington, and then for the Parliamentary election. Tom was elected, but we lost the Oxford Parliamentary election.

After the June elections, things must have settled down somewhat, though there was a second General Election in October. Work was going well and I was running my program for real experiments – travelling round Europe to seek out free time on IBM computers.

A3.1.3 The Institute of Economics and Statistics

Further changes came in the summer of 1964. It must have been around the spring that I decided to try again to find a job where I could still be a mathematician but do something more socially connected. I applied for lots of jobs, unsuccessfully. In July I applied for a research post in the Institute of Economics and Statistics in Oxford. It was drawn to my attention by Tony Harrison – an old school friend – and I was successful. It was a small group of economists led by Christopher Foster, working on the cost-benefit analysis of major transport projects. They were not at all quantitative and the deal was that I would do all their maths and computing and they would teach me economics – and so I converted to the social sciences through a kind of apprenticeship. I started formally on 1 October, a few days before the General Election.

The Institute of Economics and Statistics, with hindsight, was an unusual organisation. It must have been part of the Department of Economics in Oxford, but I had no interest in those days in constitutional arrangements and didn't pursue this. It seemed to house, for research purposes, lecturers who had (all small) research groups, and perhaps those who were fellows of colleges but who did not have University appointments. Its Director was 'Teddy' Jackson, I think a development economist and economic statistician – a mildly eccentric, rather affected classic bow-tied Oxford don. I saw very little of him. I was one of a group of three working for Christopher[1] – Tony Harrison and Jane Black were the others. I had a very diverse set of material thrown at me on transport and traffic and it must have taken me quite a while to sort out what I needed to be working on. All the relevant research seemed to me in the United States and in September 1965, I embarked on a whirlwind tour of Canada and the United States with Christopher and Michael Beesley. The main object of the exercise was to meet the modellers and, to a lesser extent, planners and policy developers. (This must have been very perceptive of Christopher because neither he nor Michael were modellers but obviously recognised the need.) For me, it was extraordinarily successful and I met many who became iconic figures in the early days of transport and urban modelling.

We flew initially to Toronto to visit TRC (the Traffic Research Corporation), then to Chicago, Los Angeles (Santa Monica), San Francisco (Berkeley), and Boston. I don't have a detailed record of who we met on that first trip and I think other trans-Atlantic trips followed pretty soon after. Key figures were Britton Harris at Penn, I. S. (Jack) Lowry at RAND in Santa Monica, Walter Hansen, T. G. (Laksh) Lakshmanan, and Alan Voorhees in Washington.[2] Interestingly, only Brit was an academic, the others were consultants. This was a measure of the urgent need for modelling to underpin the planning of the US highways programme – and the market response. TRC and Voorhees (Alan's company) had full-blown transport models. Walter and Laksh introduced me to the retail model. And Brit and Jack Lowry introduced me to the idea of building a comprehensive model that linked transport and land use and that such a model was the basis of urban planning. In a very short time, between 1965 and 1967, the framework for the research programme that has occupied me for the next 60 years was established.

It was in this period that I did a piece of work that established my academic career and opened up 'academic life' – game-changing for me! Modelling the spatial distribution of trips was a crucial part of the transport model and this was done by analogy with Newton's theory of gravity: the number of trips between any pair of areas (zones) was proportional to the 'mass' at each end – for the journey to work, residents at one end and jobs at the other – and inversely proportional to some function of the distance between them. The model didn't fit the data very well and the American pioneers, mainly engineers, added some factors to improve the model. In my student days, I had taken statistical mechanics very seriously and I recognised these factors as something like partition functions in Boltzmann's theory of gases. I was able to rewrite the derivation of the model in Boltzmann terms rather than Newton's and produced what became known as the entropy-maximising model. This turned out to be a powerful general method with a wide range of applications. I must have been doing this work around the middle of 1966 by which time I was already working almost full-time in London. The story in more detail.

I discovered 'entropy', and its beginnings as a superconcept, through a combination of an accident of circumstances and through some apparently disconnected piece of knowledge from my student days. The existing transport models had been mainly developed in the United States and were based on an analogy with Newton's law of gravity. That was my starting point. Unfortunately, the basic model was inconsistent in that when the flows from an origin were summed, they did not add up to the known total number of flows from an origin; and similarly for flows into destinations. The engineers solved this problem by adding 'fudge factors' to the flow equations. This was the basis of a lucky break for me. As a student, I had spent serious time on statistical mechanics and in particular on Boltzmann's theory of gases and I recognised these factors as something like – not exactly like – the partition functions used by Boltzmann. I recognised that there was a possibility of shifting the underpinnings of the flow model from its Newtonian basis to Boltzmann. I reworked the mathematics of classical statistical mechanics to produce a consistent flows' model and this was achieved by maximising an entropy function, generating the fudge factors from a formal procedure. This became a standard method for producing – renamed from the 'gravity' model – a spatial interaction model.

It is worth trying to describe the key idea without the maths. Boltzmann was dealing with systems of gases made up of very large numbers of atoms or molecules, far too large a number to model the individual states of these elements. What Boltzmann was able to do, was to characterise more aggregate properties of the *system* such as temperature and pressure and show how they could be calculated from a whole set of individual states. He then considered an ensemble of *system* states and showed that of an astronomical number of these, in terms of the aggregate properties, one state was overwhelmingly the most probable. In the transport case, each individual can be assigned an origin and a destination, and the ensemble is the collection of these for all individuals making trips. An extreme example, would be the case where all individuals were assigned to the same origin-destination pair, clearly highly improbable. However, by finding the most probable system state, and recognising that this is overwhelmingly the most probable, the array of origin-destination flows can be calculated. This is done through an optimisation process, and it turns out that, in physics, the quantity to be optimised is the entropy; and hence this is the name that is still used in building a transport model. If W is the number of system states that can be generated from a particular assignment of origin destination pairs, then $S = k\log W$ is the equation which is the formal representation of the quantity to be maximised. S is a measure of entropy in thermodynamics. This equation is engraved on Boltzmann's grave and is precisely the basis of transport modelling, with different definitions of the 'elements' – people instead of particles.

The idea, in the first instance, was developed as an analogy, and might seem that transport modelling is based on physics. However, it turns out that the entropy-maximising process is general in the sense that it can be applied to any system with a large number of elements that are only weakly connected – particles in a gas, people in a city, and many more. It is a superconcept that sits above disciplines. Relatively quickly, I realised that the method could be applied more widely in urban analytics, and later, in areas as diverse as ecology, archaeology, and history. There is another lesson in developing research ideas here: if you happen to stumble on a good idea, work out how it can be applied much more widely than you might have originally thought.

The original idea was published in Wilson (1967) 'A statistical theory of spatial distribution models', *Transportation Research*, 1, pp. 253–269; and in Wilson (1970) *Entropy in Urban and Regional Modelling*, Pion, London (republished by Routledge in 2011). Peter Gould wrote a 'pedagogic review' of the book in the *Annals of the Association of American Geographers*, 62, pp. 689–700, which sets out to explain the idea to a wider, less mathematical, geography community. The history of its application in urban analytics is recorded in detail in D. Boyce and H. Williams (2015) *Forecasting Urban Travel*, Edward Elgar, London, note Chapter 3, pp. 90–99. There was a special issue of *Geographical Analysis* (2010) recognising the 40th anniversary of the publication of *Entropy in Urban and Regional Modelling*, which included Wilson (2010) 'Entropy in urban and regional modelling: retrospect and prospect', *Geographical Analysis*, 42, pp. 364–394; a more recent personal review in a book recognising the 50th anniversary, is Wilson (2021) 'Entropy in urban and regional modelling', in *Handbook on Entropy, Complexity and Spatial Dynamics: A Rebirth of Theory* (Eds Aura Reggiani, Laurie A. Schintler, and Sammy Czamanski), Edward Elgar, Cheltenham, 2021, pp. 20–31. A more recent review and exposition is by Laurie Schintler (2023).

I also had a second experience of university teaching. As researchers, we were encouraged to do up to six hours a week of teaching and I had three tutorial groups, each of two young women students, teaching quantum mechanics and statistical mechanics.

A3.2 London

A3.2.1 The Ministry of Transport

Around the end of 1965, Christopher announced to the three of us who constituted the researchers in his group that he had been appointed as Director-General for Economic Planning in the then Ministry of Transport (MoT). The project clearly had to be wound up and we were given the choice of moving to London with him, or not! Tony and I opted to move to London, Jane to stay in Oxford. It must have been part of Christopher's 'deal' that he could take people with him, Tony and I on the basis that we would be Economic Advisers – a professional Civil Service grade equivalent to that of Principal. It also produced a welcome salary increase. However, there was a difficulty in my case. Tony's case was fine because he was an economist; the economists in the Ministry refused to accept me because I wasn't. I clearly had to be appointed and I was summoned to see John Moores, Assistant Secretary and head of what would now be called HR. He had clearly been instructed to solve the problem. 'If you're not an economist, what actually are you?,' he asked. 'I'm a mathematician,' I replied. 'That's easy then,' he said, 'you can be the Mathematical Adviser!' and so I became, probably uniquely, just that. This gave me my first taste of team building and management.

I began, four-fifths time, in February 1966 and commuted three or four days a week from Oxford. It was a bit of a trek: how did I get from Headington to Oxford station – a journey in itself? Then train to Paddington, Bakerloo Line Tube to Waterloo, and a long walk down Southwark Street to the aptly-named St Christopher House. Barbara Castle was the Minister and Stephen Swingler the Minister of State. Sir Thomas Padmore was the Permanent Secretary – a sign of the times being that he was always seen in a morning suit: black jacket and striped trousers, no doubt accompanied by a bowler hat, though I never saw him outside the Ministry. The Deputy Secretary was J. D. Jones – genial and easy to work with, always known by his initials, though later he became 'Sir James' as Permanent Secretary at the Ministry of Housing and Local Government. The Assistant Secretary with whom I had most dealings was Peter Lazarus – always helpful – later 'Sir Peter' as Permanent Secretary at the Department of Transport in 1982. In fact, all the senior people I worked with rose, John Garlick became 'Sir John' as Permanent Secretary at the Environment Department. We were easily absorbed into the Civil Service rather than, as might have been expected, treated with suspicion as outsiders.

The Ministry had an objective at the time to ensure that transport modelling was available to underpin road and public transport planning in British cities. Roy Spence was the civil servant charged with bringing this about and it was decided that we should build some in-house capacity for doing this. This became my responsibility and led to the creation of the Mathematical Advisory Unit – the MAU, as it became known. I set about building a team and we took on the job of building a model for the Manchester region as a demonstration – the SELNEC (South East Lancashire and North East Cheshire) model. The team included David Quarmby (who later became Managing Director of Sainsbury's) and Derek Waggon (whom I poached from the Rutherford Lab and who later led modelling for London Underground). London County Council, as ever, were ahead of the game and brought Brian Martin from Alan Voorhees in Washington to lead the building of a London model – followed a year or so later by Tony Ridley. Brian and Tony were British engineers, now returning, and part of my job was to keep in close touch with them. The London model was implemented by Freeman Fox Wilbur Smith Ltd which must have been a joint venture set up between the British engineering consultants who had no modelling experience and the American company which had. Jim Tressider, British, was the leader of that company in building the London model.

There was one piece of work carried out by the MAU in 1966 which differed from conventional transport planning: the analysis of freight flows through a proposed new port at Portbury near Bristol. We carried out a model-based analysis which was accepted by Ministers – to the extent that the reasoning was published in a White Paper in July that year, setting out the reasons for turning down the investment proposal. This included the algebraic equations of the model and all the data that we had used – in effect, offering a challenge to those who disagreed with the scheme to rework our analysis. In the event, it wasn't challenged, though a few years later, with a new Government, the scheme went ahead (cf. the Clarke et al. 1986 paper).

Although I was spending four days a week in London (and travelling round the country a lot) – at least in theory, I managed to keep my head above water as an Oxford Councillor and to be heavily involved with the Labour Party in Oxford. It amounted to doing three or four jobs depending on how to count them. In academic terms, the 'entropy' paper and ideas were at least sketched in this year. The paper was published in September 1967 – a subject to return to below and this was followed by a stream of publications in 1968 and 1969. It was also a year in which I did my third stint of teaching and lecturing – starting a ten-lecture course at the then Northern Polytechnic.

At the beginning of 1967, I became full-time at the Ministry. Somehow I survived as a not-very-active Councillor in Oxford until the May elections and of course did not stand again. (If I had done, I would have lost, having been elected with a majority of two in a year of peak Labour victories.) This was a year when we built a transport model and used it for the SELNEC Study: there was much travelling up and down to Manchester – and indeed more widely around the country. The MAU grew and at some point we ran out of space and we were moved, rather oddly, to a top floor suite of offices in Church House in Great Smith Street.

In this year, it is research and academic memories that stand out. I gave a course of lectures on cost-benefit analysis for the Greater London Council. I did a ten-lecture course, I guess on models in planning, in the Planning Department at University College London (invited by Peter Cowan). My diary records one-offs scattered around the country. By this time, I must have grasped the state of the art in urban modelling and was invited to lecture on this basis. The formal publication of my entropy paper didn't come until September, and then by a rather odd route. Somehow – I don't recall any detail but it must have been a recommendation from one of a small number of people who became mentors – Peter Haggett? – I became Assistant Editor of a new (Pergamon) journal called *Transportation Research*. The Editor was a Californian, Frank Haight. There were to be four issues in 1967 and as the deadline for the third issue approached, Frank contacted me – post, phone? – and said that he didn't have enough material, could I help? I must have been drafting my entropy paper – 'A statistical theory of spatial distribution models' – and I offered him this, which he gratefully accepted. So what became my most-cited paper and the one that established my academic reputation, appeared in a new journal, un-refereed, to fill a gap. By the following year, I was publishing a lot. I began to be invited to give papers at conferences, an important milestone being the 1967 conference in London of the Regional Science Association. I was naïve, and I wrote a ridiculously long paper for it. The chair of the session was a fiery Welsh Professor – John Parry-Lewis – and I vividly remember him telling me, as I came to the end of my introduction, that I had five minutes left. I survived somehow but it was a lesson learned.

A3.2.2 Centre for Environmental Studies (CES)

A turning point came around the middle of the year. I gave a talk in the Civil Engineering Department at University College London. In the audience, unknown to me – I didn't know him at all – was Henry Chilver, then Professor of Civil Engineering at UCL. I left after the seminar and turned into Gower Street. Henry caught me up and offered me a job! 'I have just been appointed as the part-time Director of a new research centre,' he said, 'the Centre for Environmental Studies. Would you like to be the Assistant Director?' Not exactly how universities would proceed now under the watchful eyes of HR. This led to several further conversations over the next few months, and I accepted. There must have been some negotiation with Christopher and the Ministry and I started at CES part-time the following January. My 1968 diary clearly demarcates CES and MoT days.

So for most of 1968, I did two jobs. The MAU had involved building a team from scratch, and the process now started again. The CES had very elegant accommodation in Regent's Park – 5, Cambridge Terrace. It was part-funded by the Ford Foundation, part by the Ministry of Housing and Local Government. Its Governing Body was chaired by Richard Llewellyn-Davies – by then a Labour peer. (An oddity in my diary was an entry for January for lunch with Richard at Brooks in St James's – preceding the first meeting with Henry by several months! On reflection, perhaps this was the root of my meeting with Henry later.) Christopher was a member. Martin Meyerson was the 'international' member, presumably representing Ford. (In our 1965 tour, Martin had given us a rather splendid lunch in the Chancellor's Dining Room at Berkeley – he was Chancellor for the whole of the University of California. It was beginning to be a small world.)

A diary entry for July shows a meeting with John Ashby which added another dimension. He was Managing Director of a small academic publishing company – Pion Ltd. – which led to me becoming the Editor of the journal *Environment and Planning*. This had its first publication – two issues in 1969 and it pretty rapidly grew to 12 issues per year. I think in this case, they had approached Peter Haggett, who had declined, but suggested me. I had no experience, but learned on the job. Editing other people's papers taught me a lot about writing – particularly achieving clarity – and improved my own enormously.

The Centre's brief was to be a focus of social and economic research in relation to urban and regional planning. I must have persuaded Henry that we needed an in-house team and this built up rapidly. It was very much focused on model building and the use of models in planning but in the early days, surveyed a wide range of possible, mainly quantitative, methods. One of my recruits was Doreen Massey whom I now see as having 'rescued' from an advertising agency. She wrote papers on linear programming and game theory – not something she flagged in her later and very distinguished career! The external funding was much more widely spread in its scope and included some (later) famous names – Peter Hall (who recruited Eric Cripps, who later worked with me in Leeds), Peter Willmott, Melvyn Webber, Ray Pahl, Lionel March, Barry Cullingworth, and Peter Cowan. They represented the cream of planning researchers, so we selected well.

So we had a good team and we did some good work. I enjoyed working with Henry. He had considerable ability but no real knowledge of planning. As a Professor of Civil Engineering, he refused to fly – it was 'too dangerous'! – and I recall him being very nervous when we were being driven over the Clifton Suspension Bridge in Bristol – in both cases his professional opinion was that flying, and some bridges, were unsafe! With hindsight, my lack of experience showed and there were rumblings in the Governing Body (which I didn't attend – with hindsight, a mistake on both Henry's part and my part) about how effective we were being. Christopher Foster called into my office one day on his way to a Governing Body meeting and told me that he was pretty sure that at the meeting, Henry would be asked to stand down from the Directorship – and he said by way of warning, that he wasn't sure about my position! Henry did depart and I survived. David Donnison became the Director. We got on well but priorities changed and I started thinking about moving on. Henry must have returned to UCL full-time, but then rose and rose. He became the founding Vice-Chancellor of Cranfield University, which post he held for 19 years; he was a Fellow of the Royal Society, was knighted, and became a peer in 1987; and became Chairman of English China Clays (and maybe other companies). Was it a characteristic that he always took on new jobs for which he had little experience?

A3.3 Leeds

A3.3.1 To the University of Leeds

For all the concerns about focus in CES, quantitative social science was the height of fashion. This had been mainly led by the introduction of statistics but it began to be recognised that mathematical modelling might be very significant in the future. My name was obviously in currency as people were asked for recommendations for Chair appointments – I suspect again led in my case by Peter Haggett, Professor of Geography at Bristol. This led to serious approaches from Alan Walters at the London School of Economics for a possible Chair in Urban Economics, John Parry Lewis at Newcastle for a Chair in Planning, and Bill Birch at Leeds for a Chair in the Department of Geography – actually advertised as a Chair in Spatial Analysis. I opted for Leeds by a process of elimination – and possibly influenced by Peter Haggett – feeling that the economists would never accept me – recall the MoT experience – and that

Geography was wider than Planning, and indeed, a broad church. It was a pivotal decision. I was interviewed in Leeds in what must have been the Spring (I think, possibly the summer). The Chair Committee was chaired by Sir Roger Stevens, then in his last year as Vice-Chancellor. There had been a previous attempt to fill the Chair which had clearly failed, and I was the only candidate. The interview must have been OK and I was offered the job. I don't remember it in any detail but I do recall two things. A member asked me how long I would stay – clearly noting that I had to date failed to stay in a job for as long as three years. I said with the arrogance of youth, that I would stay at least five years. (I stayed in Leeds for 34 years.) The Vice-Chancellor, at the end of the interview, asked me whether, if appointed, I would be happy with the title of Professor of Spatial Analysis? I said that I thought there would be a problem of people understanding what it meant, and if the geographers would accept it, I would prefer a title which included 'Geography'. He asked me what I suggested. I noted that Peter Haggett at Bristol was Professor of Urban and Regional Geography, which sounded very good. It was agreed there and then – I later learned to the consternation of Bill Birch.

So, in September 1970, I moved back to live in the North for the first time since I had left for Cambridge 13 years earlier.

A3.3.2 Geography

I can think of the 1970s as 'the best of times and the worst of times' – a phrase that was to occur later in a different context. In academic terms, I was proud to be a young professor. It was my first 'permanent' job and I threw myself into it with enthusiasm. Although I had arrived from entirely outside academic geography, I was welcomed by my Leeds colleagues and with the wider community. There was quite a lot of curiosity and I was invited to give talks in a number of other universities. In 1972, I was invited to give a talk to the Royal Geographical Society on 'Theoretical geography'. I was accepted. The idea that geography was a broad church, which had motivated my decision to go to Leeds, was justified. A few years down the line, most people 'forgot' that I was anything other than a geographer. The atmosphere in the Department was (largely) congenial. I enjoyed the undergraduates – enjoying teaching. There was no shortage of research students. I had a pleasant office in a small building that was the original university refectory – and there were still cockroaches in the kitchen in the basement. I had a secretary and a funded research assistant. The only problem was the Head of Department, Bill Birch. He was rather domineering and many of the staff were frightened of him. Monthly staff meetings were held in the name of 'democracy' but the outcome was always what Bill wanted. This reached a point where, two or three years' in, I was thinking about moving on. However, early in 1975 – this is jumping on – Bill was appointed Director of Bristol Polytechnic. I became Head of Department, and the atmosphere changed. One of the things I learned then about being head of anything was the extent to which one's own behaviour determined the atmosphere of the place – the unwritten part of the job contract.

In those days, all professors were members of Senate and the appropriate Faculty Boards – in relation to the latter, because of the nature of Geography, we were jointly in two Faculties – Social Science and Science, and hence involved with two Boards. Social Science was part of a Joint Board of three Faculties – of Arts, Social Science, and Law. A bit of luck was that I started at the same time as the new Vice-Chancellor, Edward Boyle, and I got to know him, not well, but well enough, and I think this led to me being nominated to various University and external roles. Meetings of the Senate – attended by maybe 100 people – were long and smoke-filled. I learned later that Boyle, as Chair of the Senate, would estimate the length of time for a meeting and set out in front of him the appropriate number of cigarettes. There were a number of rather grand figures, still part of the age when Heads of Department were appointed until retirement rather than, as became the more appropriate fashion, for a fixed term. It must have changed by 1975 when I was appointed as Head of Geography – for a three-year term. One or two of the 'barons' cultivated me a bit – someone to get into their camp? – Adam Neville in Civil Engineering, for example; some were simply friendly – Sydney Dugdale in Physics. There was curiosity about me – from older professors about a very young one.

I took on various University roles beyond the ex-officio ones. There was a problem with student accommodation for the future. As was the University's wont, a special group was established to tackle this, chaired by Fred Holliman – a benign and very nice 'baron'. This must have reported to the sub-committee on Student Accommodation – a sub-committee of Estates Committee – already establishing at least three layers of administration to look at the problem. However, this was recognised as a geography problem and I was commissioned as a member of the group to produce a report which I did, with part-time research assistance from Geography of John Pay, a research student. I'm sure Bill thought this was a good thing – he was always one, rightly – for wanting Geography to be seen to have influence within the University as this would help to produce support when it was needed. The accommodation connection must have led to me being appointed to a couple of Hall Councils – Ellerslie and Lyddon. By 1972, I was a member of the Research Degrees Committee and by the late 1970s, I was the Chairman, succeeding Sydney Dugdale. This was very much administrative business, but sensitive and complicated with a serious 'human' dimension – postgraduate students who had not been well treated, members of staff who had supervised inadequately, and so on. I once had to interview – in his office – a very senior Professor about some misdemeanour. I was very nervous, but, accepting the charge, he took it all very well. It was in the middle of the 1970s that I learned how to chair meetings – not in any way consciously, but when I reflect, the monthly Geography staff meeting settled down very quickly; the Research Degrees Committee was a bigger challenge, but again was OK pretty quickly.

After Lord Boyle died, I was appointed as a member of the Committee to appoint the new Vice-Chancellor, so I was clearly part of the University establishment by then. In the event, I was the only person on the Committee in the final vote, to be against the person who was appointed (and with whom, later, I had to have a decent working relationship). I'm not sure whether my vote was ever publicised – I have no evidence that it was.

I spent a lot of time in London (and elsewhere) being drawn into various national groups. I was involved with the SRC[3] – possibly as the holder of a large SRC grant and I was a member of the SSRC[4] Computing Committee and the RGS Research Committee. I also spent a lot of time at CES – unfinished business, I guess. There was a Group on 'Developing Patterns of Urbanisation' run by Peter Cowan which I went to many meetings of, and I clearly had appointments with David Donnison from time to time. My diary shows at least two weekends in Norwich and I haven't the slightest idea in my memory what they were about. I became a member of a Group chaired by Sir Alec Cairncross which was considering the case for the Channel Tunnel. I was appointed as the techie modeller who would be qualified to review any forecasts that were produced. We deliberated, we called for evidence, we interviewed various groups. At the beginning of what became our final meeting, we were told, in confidence, that the Government had decided that they would not go ahead with the Tunnel. We were scheduled to hear evidence that day from a group called the Defenders of Kent. We had to go ahead with the meeting without disclosing what we knew. When the announcement was made a few days later, they must have thought that they had had a tremendous influence on the decision!

I enjoyed teaching. It was very much research-led. Most of the students only had O-level maths but this did not stop me taking modelling seriously. I recorded having 'mathematics' tutorials as well as conventional ones. And, with Mike Kirkby who had modelling interests in physical geography, we jointly wrote *Mathematics for Geographers and Planners* which was published by Oxford University Press and even ran to a second edition. Indeed, I had plenty of scope for writing and I combined what amounted to a research monograph with a textbook, *Urban and Regional Models in Geography and Planning*, published by Wiley in 1974. Some of the early undergraduates became research students (or research assistants) – notably Mark Birkin and Martin Clarke. Through the 1970s, I must have had of the order of a dozen research students together with researchers working on a large SRC grant on transport modelling. I tried to establish a research programme that systematically covered the field. Phil Rees, who joined at the same time as me with a PhD from Chicago, happily switched into spatial demography and we published *Spatial Population Analysis* in 1976. I wanted to get seriously into regional input-output modelling and tried to do this with a research student who dropped out. I picked it up again later with Sally Macgill. The core of spatial interaction modelling was developed by a number of people – Mark, Martin already mentioned, Graham Clarke, especially in retailing. I did some good work on mathematical programming with Martyn Senior that has stood the test of time. Huw Williams, a convert to the field from physics as part of the SRC Programme, did outstanding work in transport modelling – partly on uses in cost-benefit analysis, partly in linking entropy-maximising models to the 'choice' models that began to appear as an alternative, driven by economists' perspectives. I was very taken with using microsimulation to tackle problems of high dimensionality of the matrices we worked with and made some progress with Carol Pownall and we published a good paper. I was anxious to demonstrate that the models could be applied in the Leeds region and Chris Leigh, Phil Rees, and I organised the work into a book, *Models of Cities and Regions*, published in 1977. I was strongly connected internationally, much of this facilitated through Regional Science Association conferences in Europe and North America. The RSA was run from the University of Pennsylvania and I worked closely with Britton Harris and for a period, I spent three weeks each year in the Spring in Penn as an Adjunct Professor. Indeed, it was working with Brit that led to a joint paper with him, published in 1978, on urban dynamics, which is an area I still work on and which I consider my second significant contribution to modelling. Martin Clarke and I started to work closely with a group of Italians centred on the Polytechnico di Torino and made good friends there – in my case, notably with Giorgio Leonardi. Throughout this period, I was the Editor of *Environment and Planning*.

This is a sketch of a very intensive period of research. The Leeds modelling group has remained a landmark in a field – through the period when it became less fashionable – though it is now the height of fashion again. Martin, Mark, Graham, and Phil all became professors in Leeds; Huw and Martyn became Professor and Reader respectively in Cardiff. By the end of the 1970s, we became less fashionable. There was the oil crisis and a recession and the Callaghan Government was not enthusiastic about planning. City planners didn't take up modelling on the scale we hoped and there was a significant shift in academic geography – following on, slightly late, to a corresponding shift in the social sciences more broadly, to a more radical Marxist position. Andrew Sayer wrote what became an influential paper arguing for the end of large-scale urban modelling. Modelling was attacked as being 'positivist', a term of abuse which at the time embraced anything that contained equations. This was absurd, of course, and I cited distinguished Marxist economists like Sraffa who worked with mathematical models. In order to be able to respond adequately, I read a lot of Marxist and, more broadly, structuralist literature. This was certainly good for me. I learned a lot about power structures and what models didn't do – allowing me to articulate better what models *could* do. The structuralist movement invaded many disciplines, notably English literature to the bemusement of the Leeds English Department. Probably following a conversation with John Barnard, then Head of English, I even found myself leading a seminar on structuralism in the English Department. In spite of all this, our research programme was strong and survived into the 1980s and beyond – and now remains a beacon decades later, as fashions have swung back.

If I extend the decade slightly at both ends, the 1980s was a time of extraordinary transition for me. I had a sabbatical for the 1979–1980 year and didn't manage it well. For 1980–1981, I had a 'normal' academic year. For 1981–1982, I was Head of Department again for three years and in 1982, I became

Chairman of the Joint Board of the Faculties of Arts, Social Science and Law for a two-year spell (1982–1984) – the equivalent of a Dean in modern terminology. (This was a mouthful, and it was always known for short as 'The Board of Arts'.) From October 1989, I was (the sole) Pro-Vice-Chancellor (PVC). In each of these cases, the posts were by election by Senate, but there was only one candidate as was the tradition at the time. Presumably 'soundings' had been taken. By the summer of 1990, in July, I was Vice-Chancellor-Elect. Research was maintained. I published five books – two single author, two joint author, one edited – and almost a hundred papers. I continued to edit *Environment and Planning A*. Martin Clarke and I established, from about 1985, what became GMAP Ltd. I spent quite a lot of time in London: I was Vice-Chairman of the SSRC Environment and Planning Committee. I was Vice-Chairman of a Health Authority. When I look at my diaries, I was simply phenomenally busy. I kept a detailed diary for the 1983–1984 year, the second year as Board Chairman, and at the end of almost every day I recorded myself as 'very tired and irritable'. There was a kind of driving on without any planned ambition.

In my 1983 diary, I recorded the Department as 'more or less running itself once all the (admin) jobs had been allocated'. There was a variety of work – and a lot of it: teaching (more or less four full lecture courses), research (including administration – grants, studentships, etc), writing, supervision, joint research in Italy, editing *Environment and Planning*, GMAP (later), Department and University admin, SSRC, Dewsbury Health Authority. My diary was packed – London sometimes for half a day, research consulting trips to Italy – Rome in May, Turin a few days later were examples. There was a period when I was making three or four of these trips in a year. At the time, when I wrote down the list of areas of work, I also, for the record at the time, wrote down my worry/to-do list for the following day: it had 17 items on it, all to be combined with a Board briefing at 9 30, a Department lunch, a lecture at 4 and the Board at 5.

Research[5] in the 1980s was very much a run-on from the 1970s. Many of the same people continued in various posts, Phil Rees already a Lecturer from 1970, Martin Clarke was appointed to a 'new blood' Lectureship in 1983. Roger Mackett, Martyn Senior, Eric Cripps, Huw Williams, and Jose Coelho all overlapped the decades. Carol Pownall was one who moved on – to a Health Authority. We had a modelling toolkit available to us – continually extending the entropy-maximising framework – this particularly through Huw teaching us a lot about mathematical programming formulations, and Martyn Senior and I produced a couple of related papers. We attempted to get into new sectors for which these modelling methods could work. We put a lot of effort into retail which became our 'test' model for experimenting (Graham Clarke, Martin Clarke) and extended into energy (John Beaumont, Sally Magill), education (Sarah Irwin, Bob Croutchley), health (Paul Forte, Sarah Harvey, Martin Clarke), and water (Adrian McDonald, Graham Clarke). Graham and I produced a couple of good papers on performance indicators – showing that it was possible to be 'efficient' without 'delivering' effectively, for example, dental services.

Work continued on structural dynamics building on the method I had developed with Britton Harris. An undergraduate, Mark Oulton, did his thesis work on the 'sudden' evolution of supermarkets – the first piece of empirical evidence that the theory of more or less discrete change worked – taken up by a range of people in the UK, the USA, and Italy during the 1980s. We made an attempt to link this to the then-fashionable 'catastrophe theory' (Graham Clarke, Martin Clarke, Tim Poston – the last as a visitor from the Chris Zeeman School). I was introduced to a new formulation – using master equations – by Gunther Haag. This dynamics work opened up some new areas of application – notably in ancient history through Tracey Rihll, then a postgraduate student in the History Department. This enabled us to 'predict' the likely populations of settlements in ninth-century BC Greece and is a thread of research which is still expanding. We continued with microsimulation work – integrating with accounting approaches – and this is another thread which is still maintained in Leeds. Mark Birkin and I used the dynamics framework to rewrite much of classical geographical theory – a piece of work which has not really been recognised in the teaching of geography! Martin and I continued to do a lot of work in Italy with Sergio Bertuglia's group – Giorgio Leonardi (then mainly at the International Institute for Applied Systems Analysis; IIASA), Roberto Tadei, Giovanni Rabino, Sylvia Ocelli, and Sylvana Lombardo[6] and this involved frequent trips to Turin and, more occasionally, Rome.

My involvement in University business reached its peak in the 1982–1984 period. I was already Head of Department and Chair of the Research Degrees Committee and in October 1982, as noted, I took on the Chairmanship of the Board of Arts. This mean that I was an ex-officio member of the main University committees: Planning, Development and, General Purposes along with Academic Staff Committee and I chaired numerous Board committees – Examiners, Transfers, Masterships, Courses. I also chaired many special groups including those on AV Services, the Centre for Applied English, Archaeology, and the Workshop Theatre. There was a Board Advisory Group and of course there were briefing meetings for RDC and the Board. I was a member of the Board of the Colleges. That added up to at least three meetings per week plus briefing meetings and all the 'special add-ons', plus Department meetings.

A3.3.3 GMAP Ltd

At the ends of the 1983–1984 academic year, I ceased to be Head of Department and Chair of the Board of Arts. Around the same time, some major research grants ended. I must have felt like a free agent. Was it to fill a gap that produced the idea that became GMAP Ltd? I think I know the exact time that this happened. Martin (Clarke) and I were in the habit of going racing at Wetherby on Boxing Day and in December 1984, we were in a racecourse bar watching Borough Hill Lad (ridden by John Francombe) win the King George Chase at Kempton. It was in a conversation then that we decided to try to 'go commercial'. We had good retail models that in principle would predict the revenue attracted to a store and we thought the industry might jump at it. We had a very slow start. We assumed that if we took the idea to the big management consultants, they would employ us as consultants to set the model up and then deliver it to their retail clients. We made trips to London for this purpose, but to no avail: we were well treated and apparently listened to, but there was no follow-up. We realised that we had to go it alone. We agreed with Bernard Stone, the Managing Director of ULIS,[7] that we would channel any contracts though the University company. Our first contract was with the Post Office. We visited their Head Office in London and explained how we could optimise their retail network. What they actually wanted was to know the average length of garden paths – presumably in different kinds of areas – to plan postmen's walks! We were good enough embryonic businessmen to accept the £5000 contract we were offered to do this and returned to Leeds celebrating with gins and tonic on the train – smiling as we acknowledged that neither of us knew how to do it. However, with a group of students and string and maps, we wrote an appropriate report. We did another small job with the model to estimate the population that would be attracted to a proposed dry ski slope near Birmingham and, notwithstanding a near disaster that involved rerunning the model because of some faulty data input hours before we were due to present, we had a second success. My diary records some work on flows to health facilities, a subcontract with MVA Ltd.[8] Otherwise, nothing serious until well into 1986.

We attempted to find jobs by searching the job advertisements in the *Sunday Times*. When anyone was needing a market analyst, we wrote and said that we were not applying for the job, but we had a novel and powerful method for doing the analysis. We struck lucky with Toyota and W H Smith. Toyota had just established their new manufacturing plant at Derby and needed to build a dealership network, and Smiths were trying to do the analysis we were offering internally but couldn't make it work. In this latter case, we were offered a £12,000 contract to analyse West Yorkshire – serious money for us at the time. They had 12 stores in the County; they gave us data for six and said that if we could predict the revenues of the other six to within 10%, we would get a national contract. We managed to get them to ask their own team to do the same exercise. Three months later, we exchanged results: the in-house team couldn't do better than 50% and we had five out of six under 10%. We were given the national contract for £120,000 and we worked for them for a number of years. The Toyota contract was of the same order and so we were really in business, with retail and auto, and we started to employ staff. We added breweries and pub estates, and banks. A large Building Society used the system to model the impacts of mergers and acquisitions. The big breakthrough came with a contract with Ford in late 1989. Over the years, they effectively contracted out to us the optimisation of their dealership networks in 13 European countries. By 1990, we were turning over £1m p.a. – and at this threshold, we were allowed to spin out from the University and set up GMAP Ltd. Martin drove the business – seconded out from the University as Managing Director. By 1997, the annual turnover was nearly £6M and we were employing over 100 staff. At this point, the auto part of the business was taken over by an

American company; the rest of the business struggled until it was taken over by a Building Society in 2001. This is all jumping ahead into the 1990s, of course, but it is better to have the core of the GMAP story in one place.

A3.3.4 Pro-Vice-Chancellor

In the late 1980s, I had various lives outside the university. I was the University's nominee on the Board of Kirklees Area Health Authority (covering Huddersfield and Dewsbury). When this was split in what was an early NHS reorganisation, I became Vice-Chairman of Dewsbury Health Authority. These posts were quite time-consuming with many hospital visits and meetings, not least because this was the point at which the NHS converted hospital administrators into managers and hence a new structure had to be implemented and bedded in. I was also a Governor of Ilkley Grammar School. More widely, I was a member of the SSRC Environment and Planning Committee and combined with GMAP business, this meant that I spent quite a lot of time in London.

In 1987, I became Head of Department again – nominally for a three-year term, though this became two years as I became Pro-Vice-Chancellor in October 1989 (for a two-year term). I was actually PVC-elect from December 1988 and I think from that point, I attended all the major committees again in preparation for the 1989–1990 year. In the Spring or early summer of 1989, it was announced that the then VC, Sir Edward Parkes, had been appointed as Chair of the Committee of Vice-Chancellors and Principals (CVCP) and this caused some consternation in the senior management as this would involve him spending much of his time in London. The Registrar, Jim Walsh, said: 'Edward has never delegated anything: how can this work?!' A dinner was convened in a suburban hotel: the Pro-Chancellor and Chair of Council (Alan Roberts), Registrar, Bursar (Ray Head), the PVC (Donald Lee), and myself as PVC-elect. At that time, there was only one PVC whose job was mainly to chair various staff committees. The VC chaired all the important ones. No one at the dinner could see any obvious solution. I said: 'Let me go and talk to him', and this I did a few days later. Notwithstanding the Registrar's fears, he happily delegated about half of his job to me! I agreed that in order to do this, we should appoint a Dean of Staff (Douglas Watson) who would take over all the staff committee duties. I took over the Chair of Academic Development Committee.

The new academic year started in a hectic way. It was the convention that the university of the chair of the CVCP would be represented at CVCP meetings by a PVC, and so this duty fell to me. The September CVCP Conference was held in Leeds, at Boddington Hall. The University had overshot on student recruitment and we met an acute shortage of accommodation for new students by putting a large number of caravans on the Boddington Hall playing fields and this, of course, attracted the attention of broadcasters who were there for the conference. I was deputed to do the TV interviews, and I duly appeared – for the first and last time in my career – on the BBC News at 1 p.m., 6 p.m., and 10 p.m. This was before I had my media training. The VC was not keen on degree ceremonies, and so the next piece of early delegation was for me to preside in York Minster for the College of York St John degree ceremony on the 10th of October. I was extremely nervous, not helped when Brian Hogan, a previous PVC and a distinguished lawyer, always confident, said to me as we left Leeds: 'Always a knee trembler this one!' The Registrar told me afterwards that I had not shown any sign of nerves, and this had been good for everyone else! I must have been a good actor. There were 400 graduands and about 1600 people in the Minster. The Archbishop, John Habgood, was there, and processed in front of me and sat behind me on the stage. I did get through it without incident, and did think then that 'if I can do that, I can do anything'! I do have a fragment of diary for that time which records in some detail what I thought I needed to do as PVC in terms of developing the University. I set out a reasonably structured plan and then drew up an initial action list (university, external, departments) along with an immediate list, for example, Chair Committees, something else which had been delegated to me. I was always a 'planner'.

In the first Term of that year, a committee was established, chaired by the Pro-Chancellor, to make a recommendation for the appointment of the next Vice-Chancellor – from 1 October, 1991, so well ahead of time. As PVC, I had an ex-officio seat on the committee. However, a number of colleagues began suggesting that I should be a candidate. It was in late October that I had spent a day at Brunel University at their invitation as one of two possible candidates to be VC there, so I guess the idea was in my mind. (After the Brunel day, I declined to pursue it and withdrew. They then more or less immediately appointed the other candidate, perhaps fearful that he would withdraw as well.) The upshot was that I withdrew from the Leeds VC Committee. This was like making a public statement that I was a candidate. The final formal interviews were not to be held until July and so, in effect, I had a year of being inspected as a possible VC. As I remember it, notwithstanding this, I enjoyed the year. It was a high-level version of my Board of Arts experience a few years earlier – all the main committees, but sometimes now with me chairing them.

The VC Appointing Committee met for the last time over two days in July – Saturday and Sunday – at the Station Hotel in York. (Brian Hogan, a member of the Committee said that he had been kept awake for most of the night with platform announcements at York Station!) Two candidates were interviewed on the Saturday, and I was the third, interviewed on the Sunday morning. I had to do a substantial presentation on how I saw the future of the University and the whole session lasted the best part of a couple of hours. I was back home in Burnsall by lunchtime, waiting for a phone call on the outcome. There was no call all afternoon and finally, about 6 p.m., Alan Roberts, the Chair of Council, did ring and told me that I was offered the job, which I accepted. I still have no idea what that Committee must have talked about over several hours, but it must have been a close-run thing. So for my second year as PVC, I was also VC-elect. This gave me excellent preparation time with the possibility of hitting the ground running the following year.

This was probably my heaviest workload decade, not least because of the variety of roles. There was a kind of structure in all this: teaching, research, writing, editing as more or less constant in different proportions at different times; and with a progression through Head of Department, Chairman of the Board, the beginnings of GMAP, and Pro-Vice-Chancellor; and finally, Vice-Chancellor-elect. This wasn't a planned progression. It was a continuing expansion of experience. None of it was planned in the sense of 'It's my ambition to do this or that'. It was all a rush, but I probably moved into a more thoughtful, if still hectic, phase in the next decade.

A3.3.5 Vice-Chancellor

On 1 October 1991, I arrived early and greeted my staff and walked into the Vice-Chancellor's office. (Edward Parkes occupied it until the 30th of September!) In the previous two years, as PVC, I had done most of the jobs that a VC would do – but it still felt different. Jim Walsh, the Registrar, left a note on my desk to welcome me by wishing me 'Good luck' and leaving a Churchill quotation on my desk:

> At the top there are great simplifications. An accepted leader only has to be sure of what it is best to do, or at least to have made his mind up about it. The loyalties which centre on the number one are enormous. If he trips, he must be sustained. If he makes mistakes, they must be covered. If he sleeps, he must not be wantonly disturbed. If he is no good, he must be pole-axed!

I learned (again) on day 1 something that is not in the job description: the Vice-Chancellor's behaviour can go a long way to setting the ethos of the place. I had to sort something out with the Deputy Registrar. I walked down the corridor to his office, we did the sorting out and as I left, he said: 'Well, that's a first, the Vice-Chancellor has never been in my office before.' I always tried then, at least for informal meetings, or to see Heads of Department, that if at all possible, I would go to their office. My predecessor always summoned people to his office and, combined with his depression and pessimism about university funding, created an atmosphere of uncertainty and, at times, gloom.

Because I was an internal appointment, had been PVC for two years and VC-elect for a year, I had a well-prepared start. What became the major driving force for the growth of the University was already in place: the devolution of responsibilities from the centre to departments – the resource centre system. The beginnings were in 1989. I was PVC-elect and the then PVC, Donald Lee, and myself were deputed to explore the idea of introducing cost centres. This was accepted as a good idea but, via the idea of budget centres, it evolved into 'resource centres' – the crucial idea being that departments were given income-generating incentives as well as the responsibility to manage budgets. In the following year, as PVC, I had the responsibility of driving its implementation. There were many difficulties, not least the argument from the administration that it would take 3 or 4 years to implement because of the challenges of design and lack of appropriate accounting software. The first of these was overcome through persuading a colleague from Geography, Sally Macgill,[9] to design the system; and the second through the purchase of an American accounting system to supply the software back-up. And then, of course, when the budget allocations were calculated, there were winners and losers with Medicine being by far the biggest loser. In retrospect, it was a triumph to bring everything into balance.[10] Decades later, there are still universities that have failed to bring their Medicine budget under control. We also had to tweak the Funding Council's unit of resource by subject: the units seemed to be too high for some departments and too low for others. We introduced the 'Leeds Teaching Unit of Resource – the LTUoR', and then appointed a group of three 'wise' people to review it year by year – a process that was accepted within the University. The system was implemented in my second year as PVC (1990–1991), no doubt with some transitional arrangements in the most challenging areas. This also provided the opportunity to merge smaller departments into units of viable size: 96 departments became 55 resource centres with the major mergers creating Schools of Medicine, Biological Sciences, and Modern Languages. We also merged the University's Department of Dentistry with the NHS Dental Hospital in a creative development. In 1996, there was a further major restructuring and the 55 were reduced to 32. None of this was without difficulty. The School of Philosophy was very reluctant to be subsumed into a Sub-Faculty of Arts. In the end, I attended one of their staff meetings and heard many arguments about their need for independence – but in the end, it dawned on me, on the basis of one comment, that their real worry was that they would cease to be a School and would become a Department, which they saw as less prestigious. I agreed that they could remain a 'School' and all opposition disappeared!

We had to have growth – both of student numbers and of research income – to overcome the University's recurrent financial crises. The resource centre system drove this. An increase in a student numbers meant an increase in departmental income of 60% of the LTUoR per student recruited – 40% being retained as a University overhead. Heads of Department soon realised that this was a very effective way of building resources to increase academic staff, and to build a new research base. There were also minor tweaks. For example, a department had been given an 'incentive' of being allowed to keep 6% of overseas student fees. With the advent of the resource centre system, this was increased to 60% and produced a significant increase in international recruitment. In the 1988–1989 year, it had been agreed that a student number target of 12,500 should be set for 1994–1995. In fact, the student population rose to 13,000 by the 1991–1992 year. In the five years from 1989–1990 to 1993–1994, student numbers grew from 11,000 to 18,000, a 65% increase. Given our staff numbers, I once cited the university, with its relatively small inner-city campus, as being like a small town of 25,000! Research income grew by 125% in the same period – the latter part facilitated by the expansion of interdisciplinary centres and the creation of research schools. This was all supported by substantial capital investment, notably in the Library, student accommodation, and IT.

But back to October 1991.The resource centre system wasn't the only reform that had to be put in place. There were other changes both in culture and in organisation. In my introduction in my first Senate as VC on 16 October, I outlined a number of principles. Our main activities were teaching and research, and expanding both was not only in the University's interest but were also in the students' and the national interest. However, while we were not a 'business', we had to be 'business-like' to achieve our objectives. This demanded a better-organised management and the restructuring of the central administration and a sharp cutting down of the committee system. However, I was very happy for this management to be fully accountable to the wider University and therefore proposed to retain a large Senate, more or less in its present form – with a membership approaching 200 and about 100 regular attendees. This would provide the opportunity for colleagues to review critically any proposals for change that were brought forward. This was in some ways seen as a bold move but it did provide the basis for moving forward relatively rapidly and by consensus. I developed the practice of taking anything likely to be controversial to Senate in 'green paper' form with a white paper to follow based on a judgement of what was likely to be acceptable following the first debate. This mostly worked out, and there were very few votes. One exception was 'modularisation' of teaching which led to a heated debate and was only just carried. Indeed, one or two members, for a while, sought to bring it back year after year. Occasionally, the 'management' lost a vote in Senate – for example, on the proposed closure of Archaeology – but I argued to the team that this was good for us: it demonstrated to the Senate that it was more than a cipher.

A second bundle of principles was based on the notion that the University could only succeed if its departments succeeded. A corollary was that the central administration's role was in large part to support departments. It was indeed odd that the administration had no units to support either teaching or research and that was put right. By Year 2, I was supported by four PVCs – for Research, Teaching, Staff and Students, and IT. They took some responsibility for the reformed units within the administration, jointly with the Registrar. We established a Planning Unit which provided the basis for University plans, but also supported the running of the resource centre system. There is a conundrum at the heart of a devolved system: how do we ensure that the sum of departmental plans add up to the University's plan? We sought to address this in two ways: first, there was an annual competition for development funds; and, second, there was a light-touch review, annually, of departmental plans through the Finance Director. We also had a pretty firm 'no bailing out' rule for departments that went into deficit. The loss had to be made up in the following year. (There was the occasional exception of course – for example, if there was a loss of income beyond the control of the department – and any such issue was resolved by a combination of restructuring and investment.)

To make this system work, we had to have the management capacity across a devolved system. I had immersed myself in the management literature over a number of years and I took it on myself to run regular 'management development' seminars for a variety of audiences. Part of the message was, as noted: 'We are not a business, but we have to be business-like'; and that applied to resource centres as well as to the University as a whole.

I settled into a working routine. My life consisted largely of meetings of various kinds with much of weekends taken up by reading and prep for the coming week; typically two or three dinners a week, so stamina was needed, and I was lucky with that. I kept myself reasonably fit.[11] The flow of meetings included Senate, Council, Academic Development Committee, Planning and Resources Committee, and General Purposes Committee. I abandoned the traditional Monday morning meeting and established an informal VCs Strategy Group which met on Thursdays.[12] Each of the committees had pre-meetings and I often had pre-pre-meetings on agendas and papers. I sought to keep the formal machine moving with informal meetings – around once a term – with Council, Heads of Departments, and the three main unions – AUT, Unite, and LUU: wine in the early evening for the first two, sandwich lunches in my office for the other three. All were 'off the record' to facilitate frank discussion – something the LUU executive objected to at first – 'We are a democratic body, nothing is off the record' – but in practice they quickly adjusted to the value of it.

I was pretty well supported though it was a while before I achieved a good private office. I had a driver for all my weekday business.[13] I had to be in London pretty frequently and if I stayed (sometimes with Sarah), this was at the newly opened and refurbished Langham Hilton courtesy of a deal through American Express. I managed to maintain this for 13 years through frequent user discounts keeping the price just about defendable. It had a huge advantage over most London hotels as being relatively sound-proofed between rooms.

I can try and add some colour to this by tweaking my memory into life by looking at Annual Reports, documents such as Corporate Plans and my twice-yearly speeches to meeting of the University Court.[14] Unsurprisingly, these give a positive account of progress but I also have records from the early years of my own 'priorities' running agendas, which showed a pretty massive workload though structured to delegation. However, a lot of delegation meant briefing people on what had to be done, and this wasn't always well received, for example, in relation to departments.[15] I went to speak to staff meetings in departments where large cuts were needed or where mergers were proposed and was sometimes received with hostility. In at least one such meeting, a member of staff walked out audibly saying: 'I can't listen to any more of this rubbish'.[16] In a later year, in the case of the formation of a Business School from four departments – the School to be in the new Western Campus – I had to say in a meeting of the staff of all four departments, who really didn't want to merge, that if they didn't agree, the Western Campus site would be allocated elsewhere. All in all, Year 1 was a kind of honeymoon year while in Year 2, many staff recognised that the changes really were taking place and this bred the hostility. I recall having a conversation with my wife about the shortest time we could leave the University with some kind of honour, and we thought 'three years'. I guess what then happened was that quite a lot of the objectors chose to take early retirement and we found ourselves appointing new Heads of Department who understood and supported what had to be done. And so by the start of Year 3, everything settled down, though there was still a massive amount of work to be done.

There were constant changes in government policy on universities – on funding, on research priorities, on the rate of growth in student numbers. On the last of these, we did well by accelerating growth early so that when the government announced a pause, we were committed to continue to grow at a rapid rate and, at the time, the financial penalties for doing this were weak, in fact, the 'excess' growth was always funded, albeit with a one-year lag. Research was always the top priority. The growth in student numbers was a double win: we provided more access for students (including widening access) while at the same time, the increase in income enabled staff recruitment – to new Chairs, and to research fellowships, in particular – and hence to increased research capability. For a number of years, this was a virtuous circle.

The growth curve was continually upwards through the 1990s. This was, of course, mainly driven by the staff of the University in its Schools, Departments, and inter-disciplinary Centres. This was supported by capital development: Weetwood, Clarence Dock, Biology, Boyle Library, the Business School on the Western Campus, Astbury Centre for Biophysics.[17] The official opening of the last of these produced an entertaining connection to an earlier life. I attended as a guest; another guest was John Walker, who had recently been awarded the Nobel Prize for Chemistry. I introduced myself to him. He looked me up and down and said: 'I know you: I canvassed for you in Oxford in 1964!'

There were some bonuses from these developments which helped to accelerate the University's development. New Departments and Schools were established: a School of Health, including nursing (in the refurbished Baines Wing), new academic appointments – adding 2000 students, and 200 staff; Communications Studies, Environmental, European, International Schools or Departments; a Business School on the redeveloped Grammar School site. At the request of HEFCE, we took over Bretton Hall, a Higher Education College outside Wakefield – mainly concerned with teacher training and creative arts. We took the teacher training into the university School of Education and developed it as the University's Faculty of Creative Arts. It seemed like a great idea, was moderately successful, but was wound down by my successor and the site was sold!

We introduced work-based learning part-time degrees. There was some opposition to these. The Business School didn't want to run it – they wanted to concentrate on improving their research rating. So, I established an Institute for Corporate Development, an Institute for Life-long Learning, together with a new Faculty of Work-Based Learning, to ensure that the appropriate regulations could be put in place.[18] I was also anxious to introduce work-based learning and continuing professional development (CPD) for non-academic staff in the University. I came to an arrangement with the City and Guilds Institute to accredit and establish courses up to graduate level and also set up a fund to pay the fees for any course that lower-paid members of staff chose to do – whether swimming, football coaching, or French. The cost around £100k p.a., but the courses were very popular and actually won us an award from the Unite Union.

I was never a good fund-raiser and certainly spent too little time on it. However, three examples are worth citing. I had a message that a Mrs Mary Keyworth, who lived in Jersey, wished to make a donation to the University in memory of her husband who had graduated in Colour Chemistry in 1922 and became a successful businessman. David Holdcroft and I visited her in Jersey, meeting her in her hotel with her solicitor on a dreary winter day.[19] We were the only guests for lunch. David and I had no idea what to expect or what she wanted to support – so we had a shopping list, priced around the £100,000 mark. It was all very amicable, and at the end of lunch she took out her cheque book and signed a cheque for £2M – I think, rather to the consternation of her solicitor! This enabled us to support a new initiative in engineering and, most importantly, to help to fund a major part of the Western Campus development – with the main building named as the Maurice and Mary Keyworth Building. We visited her in Jersey to thank her, and we did persuade her to visit the University – something she very much enjoyed.

A second example was a donation by Dame Kathleen Raven to fund a Chair in Nursing, to support what she would have called 'real nursing'. She took a keen personal interest and we were able to establish the Kathleen Raven Chair.

A third example was the donation of around £1.5M by Robert Ogden to support what became Ogden Scholarships. Robert was seeking to invest in a scheme that supported South Yorkshire mining villages (following the closure of the mines).[20] We decided that the only way forward was through scholarships, but that they had to be awarded at 16 to keep children in school. We awarded 40 a year over about ten years – aiming at pupils who were academically capable but from very poor backgrounds. It was very successful with a high proportion of students achieving university places (where we continued their scholarships). David Blunkett, then Secretary of State for Education, took a keep interest and they became the core idea for education maintenance awards.[21]

Finally, a very different kind of fund-raising and set of donations. I learned from a newspaper report over New Year of 1997 of two sisters, a 16-year-old and an 18-year-old, who had lost two parents between Christmas and the New Year. The latter was a Leeds first-year student. I saw her at the beginning of term and she told me that she was going to leave, to return home to look after her sister who would otherwise be taken into care. Then, to cut a long story short: I wrote to around 20 people, some known to me, some not but very well known and thought by me to be 'charitable', and I asked for donations of between £5000 and £10,000. We very quickly raised £100,000, set up a Trust Fund with the help of as local solicitor acting pro bono. The house where the younger sister lived was heavily mortgaged. The Trust bought it. We bought the older one a car so she could get home easily and frequently. And as a stroke of luck, a teacher from the younger one's school lived next door and we managed to convince Social Services that this provided enough 'care'. Both have graduated, have good and interesting jobs, and are now married with children. It was a privilege to be able to rescue them from a tragic situation.

This chapter has been about driving a large organisation forward on multiple dimensions, a community the size of a town,. But it is worth concluding with some colour. When I was asked – and am still asked – what it was like to be a Vice-Chancellor, I usually respond with the Dickens' quote – the first lines of *A Tale of Two Cities*: 'It was the best of times and the worst of times' – quoted earlier. Relations with the community are difficult. It is not easy to maintain friendships. My wife certainly lost some friends because they were using her to get to me to persuade me indirectly to deliver something they wanted. But also there were supportive good friends. At the other extreme, there was the professor who would ring me if I happened to be in my office after, say, 6, when I would pick up the phone myself. The calls were abusive and threatening. There was the German who besieged me with e-mails claiming that I was his father. But the bulk of the experience was at the other end of the spectrum: it was a privilege to have the opportunity to meet such a variety of people – from within the University, in the city, nationally, and internationally.

There was a great variety of University events and occasions – some we were responsible for, often we were guests. For our 'own' events, my wife, Sarah, took on some substantial responsibilities and all credit to her that we became rather good at organising them. I should also insert something in brackets: to get this right, University Catering has to be right, and after perhaps three attempts, with some internal, some external systems, we finally took it back inside and appointed one of our Hall of Residence Managers, Beverley Kenny, as Director of Catering. This was very successful and a huge help to Sarah and myself – as well as to the University as a whole and she was still in post over two decades later but has now retired.

In the University, we entertained with buffet suppers at the Lodge. There were, twice a term, Senate dinners – black tie, members of Senate and their guests. We even maintained the tradition of a large Lodge garden party – for one year: it was held in late June but the weather was foggy and freezing! There was a regular supply of named public lectures – always at 5 p.m. and followed by a reception and dinner. Guest speakers included Wole Soyinka, Alan Bullock, Mark Richmond, and Merlyn Rees. There were University sermons, one year notably by the then Archbishop of Canterbury; occasionally reading lessons or speaking at funerals or memorial services. There was the annual visit of the Clothworkers' Company – serious donors to the University – a three-day visit demanding two formal dinners, one hosted by the University, one by the Master. There were one-off visits: in 1995, we had three Heads of State in the space of a couple of months: Mary Robinson, then President of Ireland, and the Presidents of Mongolia and Iceland.

Notable, and tricky and difficult occasions, were Chancellor's visits – until 1999, the Duchess of Kent; after 2000, Melvyn Bragg – by this time much pleasure and fewer problems. These visits often coincided with degree ceremonies, particularly those at which honorary degrees were conferred. We had a distinguished cast on these occasions, notably with Melvyn's pulling power. Each such occasion demanded a formal lunch and a formal dinner. We even had one ceremony, for Dame Lydia Dunn, in Hong Kong, attended by the Duchess. The most spectacular ceremonies were for Melvyn Bragg's inauguration in 2000 and the University's Centenary in 2004 – both occasions masterminded by Sarah.

At the city level, there were bridges to be built. Jon Trickett, the Labour Leader of the Council was reputed as saying that he would not set foot in the university 'because it was an irrelevant ivory tower'. We very quickly achieved a *modus operandi* and worked well together. I was a member of the Leeds Initiative and I chaired an *ad hoc* Leeds Schools Commission for him. Sarah and I were entertained at High Sheriff's lunches and Lord Lieutenant's dinners – and duly reciprocated with Lodge dinners. More informally, we had private off-the-record dinners with Steven Oliver, then Vicar of Leeds and his wife, and Keith Helliwell, the Chief Constable of West Yorkshire, and his wife. We came to know the business community well – much through Arnold Ziff and his sons Edward and Michael – and all their families. Other regular contacts included Victor Watson (Chairman of Waddingtons, makers of the board game Monopoly, among many other things), Clive Leach (then Chairman of Yorkshire Television), Ken Morrison (Founder and Chairman of Morrisons supermarkets) and, through Chris Price, VC of Leeds Met, Leslie Silver (Chairman of Kaylon Paints, Leeds United, and Leeds Met Governing Body). I spoke at the Queens Hotel Friday night dinners – accountants, lawyers, and so on – usually as a warm-up act, or worse, following, distinguished and brilliant speakers like Michael Heseltine and Laurie Taylor. There was a cultural network – Jude Kelly (West Yorkshire Playhouse), Ernest Hall (Halifax Peace Centre), and Jonathan Silver (Salts Mill).

I was engaged in University business at the national level – CVCP, later UUK, the Russell Group. I had a four-year term as a member of ESRC Council. I found I could open doors – two examples being inviting myself to meet Bill Stewart, then Government Chief Scientific Adviser (which led to subsequent meetings) and Richard Sykes, then Chief Executive of Glaxo (who arranged some visits to Glaxo labs for me). Sarah and I were drawn into the national establishment in various ways: a State Banquet in 1992, dinners hosted by the American Ambassador, Raymond Seitz, and the then Lord Mayor of London, Sir Brian Jennings. John Holroyd, then the Number 10 Appointments Secretary, visited Leeds regularly and this led to me being appointed, rather oddly, as Chair of the Appointing Committee for the next Archbishop of York – a nomination that was made for a five-year term immediately after a new Archbishop had been appointed. (Fortunately, that Archbishop was still in post at the end of my five-year term so I was never 'activated'.) I chaired a review of NHS complaints' procedures for Virginia Bottomley, then Secretary of State for Health – leading to the publication of *Being Heard* (Department of Health, 1994), a title chosen (not for the first such time) by Sarah.

On the international stage, I was more limited (unlike many of my VC colleagues). One achievement came out of the setting-up of White Rose – a collaboration between Leeds, Sheffield, and York Universities– driven by the three Vice-Chancellors – myself, Gareth Roberts, and Ron Cooke – all good friends. It became very successful to the point where another VC friend, Howard Newby, from Southampton University, wanted to join. There was no way in which we could deem Southampton to be in Yorkshire, but we decided to go international and to include Southampton on that basis. We engaged a corresponding number of US universities, led by Graham Spanier, the President of Penn State, and set up the Worldwide Universities Network – WUN This led to regular trips to Washington for WUN meetings, often for only 24 hours.

Much of this was work, much of it offering its own pleasure; but we had real pleasures too. We had never been very good at holidays, but we got into the habit of holidaying in Tuscany and Umbria in the Autumn – pleasure, until one year I went down with pneumonia which put us off returning for a while. Martin Clarke took a box at Elland Road for GMAP marketing purposes and I once watched Leeds United beat Manchester United there. Robert Ogden regularly invited Sarah and myself to racing at Cheltenham and York, and to his villa in Cap Ferat. All rather spoiling.

All of this was about the growth of the University, driving more or less relentlessly to provide access to students and the resources for development, the critical part of the job. There was probably one test at the end of (almost) 13 years – 15 if the PVC period is included: the University student numbers grew by almost 200% to 33,000 and research income by 300%. And one of the great pleasures as I walked round the campus was to see (mainly) smiling students. We had a good reputation on many fronts. I was personally rewarded, both in academic and honours terms – a Royal Geographical Society Royal Medal in 1992, election as a Fellow of the British Academy in 1994, a knighthood in 2001, Fellowship of the Royal Society (later, in 2006) and a clutch of honorary degrees.

A3.4 London

A3.4.1 DfES

I was scheduled to 'retire' at the end of September 2004 at the age of 65. Leaving Leeds was slightly accelerated as serendipity again kicked in. It must have been late 2002 when a job was advertised – Director-General of Higher Education in the Department for Education and Skills (DfES) – and Sarah had suggested that it might be the kind of thing I would be interested in. I remarked on the impossibility of this as the Civil Service retirement age was 60. Several months later, in the Spring of 2003, I was approached by David Normington, the Permanent Secretary of DfES, and asked if I would be interested. David was anxious to appoint someone with senior HE experience and in the previous recruiting round had focused on the PVC level – and failed to appoint. They were now looking at retired or about-to-retire VCs. I expressed interest, I raised the question of my age, which he explored and thought it could be 'managed'; and I had a conversation with him in London. Nothing then happened for several months and I assumed any such opportunity had disappeared. In September, *en route* to a Cotswolds holiday, I took a call from David at a motorway service station: with apologies, if I was still interested, they would like to interview me the following Tuesday, and there was a short list of one! We took a day out of our holiday to return to London and I was duly interviewed and appointed. It couldn't be announced immediately as the Prime Minister had to sign it off because of my age! Of course, they then wanted me to start immediately. I eventually negotiated the 1st of February as a starting date – to be half-time until the end of June, and then full-time – this on the basis that Sarah and I thought we ought to see out the University Centenary celebrations. I started to attend meetings ahead of my formal start date and then did two jobs for five months.

This was the third time I had been a civil servant but the first time I had been in some sense a 'real' one as distinct from a 'scientist' and a 'mathematical adviser'. It was perhaps slightly odd that I moved from being a chief executive to having someone to report to – the Permanent Secretary (PS), David Normington, and in another sense, the Secretary of State and the Minister for HE. Formally, the ministers were in charge and the PS chaired a Board made up of four Directors-General, and the Directors of Finance, HR and Technology.[22] The next layer were the Directors – two for HE, Ruth Thompson and Mike Hipkins – and then the Deputy Directors – Rachel Green and Martin Williams for HE – which made up the 'senior' civil service. I had expected to have a staff of, say, 20, focused on policy; I found I had a staff of around 250. More of that later. The 'reporting to' was very light touch. David and I had a regular catch-up meeting – fortnightly, monthly? Otherwise, I was left to get on with things. I met ministers frequently, never with David in attendance.

I was lucky with the ministers I worked with: first, Charles Clarke and Alan Johnson; then Ruth Kelly and Kim Howells (with an overlap to Bill Rammell), and Alan Johnson (who returned from his first Cabinet post at Department for Work and Pensions to become Secretary of State), and Bill Rammell. Charles was very sharp, clear-sighted, and a good decision-taker, but also very easy to talk to. He liked a good discussion. Alan was also very sharp and a delight to work with. Ruth was always said to be over-promoted but I liked her and enjoyed working with her. It was slightly odd to have a Secretary of State who was not much more than half my age.[23] Kim was both capable and very laid back! Bill was a bit more difficult – protective of his position – for example, letting it be known that he was not happy for me to have meetings with the Secretary of State without his being there. (I handled this with Ruth by ensuring that I always went on university visits with her which gave me chunks of time sitting in the back of the car.) And, finally, Alan Johnson again – much cited as 'the best Prime Minister we never had'!

The Board was excellent. David was a relaxed Chair and very open in reporting what was going on in the centre of government – giving us all, in effect, a front-row seat. Peter H was DG, Schools, and later became Head of the Scottish Civil Service. Tom was DG, Childrens' Services, active, always in rolled-up shirt sleeves – later, unusually, knighted as a DG. Janice was a former Principal of an FE college and I very much enjoyed working with her – she left to go to New Zealand where she could be a Chief Executive again. Michael Stevenson became a good friend and was the basis of me working with him at Cisco later.

I commuted to London, staying in the Langham, first on a very part-time basis up to February and then half-time up to June. At that point, Sarah found us a very nice flat to rent in Devonshire Place Mews, just off Marylebone High Street. Virtually all of our possessions left Leeds in removal vans to storage. In some sense, it felt like living as a student again. It was enjoyable, not as pressured as being a Vice-Chancellor.

I realised I had to transform myself pretty quickly into being a civil servant and not presenting myself as a former VC who knew everything about HE. I was well supported – an excellent private office, in policy terms and in learning the rules and conventions. I had copies circulated to me of 'submissions' to ministers with comments in margins labelled 'DN'. I thought it remarkable that David Normington, 'DN', was able to add so many comments. It was then explained to me that 'DN' meant 'drafting note'! There was quite a lot of that – taken in good part by my colleagues who brought me into the fold and ignored my outsider status.

I found a document – a PowerPoint presentation, dated April 2004 – which offered my account of 'HE – objectives, challenges and delivery' – so I must have been in pretty good shape by then in terms of thinking things through. I had 'six areas for development': learning and teaching; widening access; research; links to the economy and communities; effective system delivery; and student support. (In relation to the last of these, I should note that I hadn't realised until I arrived that I was responsible for the Student Loans Company!) The challenge, of course, was that delivery had to be through the universities. We could promote objectives, tweak the finances, and write an annual letter of advice to the funding council (HEFCE) and the Student Loans Company (SLC). We sought to increase student numbers to work towards the 50% participation target that had been announced by the Prime Minister in an off-the-cuff speech and at the same time widen access. We had to deal with the introduction of student fees – the Bill had its Second Reading in the Commons in January and was passed by five votes.[24] We promoted lifelong learning and CPD. On research, the policy was to build on present foundations. I had to accept the RAE which I had been publicly against as being too conservative in times past – I think that was the only policy on which I had to swallow hard! There had been a report by Richard Lambert – then Editor of the *Financial Times*, I think – on the role of universities in regional development and, more broadly in knowledge transfer. I was very happy to argue for more applied research, particularly in the newer universities but I fear that too many wanted to attempt to mimic the older ones.

Working life was dominated by meetings – I even had a diary secretary. Many were with ministers for policy discussions, often with other civil servants, many in attendance for meetings with outsiders. I had an introductory 1–1 with

Alan Johnson – 1–1s were relatively unusual, nearly always a private secretary was present – about which I can remember two things. He began by saying that he had been making inquiries about me and there was one thing he didn't understand: 'You appear to have no enemies!' More seriously, he had obviously been lobbied about the importance of research in relation to teaching and he asked me whether a research base was as essential as was argued. The lobbying had clearly come from research-based universities and I had argued its value in the past – but 'essential'? I thought and said: 'Think of the very best schools and their excellent teaching – that should be possible in HE.' He smiled and I sensed he was reassured.

One early example of Charles's quick-wittedness came from a question he was asked in the Commons about why the Department didn't have a Chief Science Advisor – a CSA. He replied that was until now the case, but the Department had just appointed Alan Wilson and he would function as the CSA! I never knew whether this was off-the-cuff but it was good for me because it embedded me in the CSA community and their Wednesday morning breakfast meetings. I met, and worked with, Frank Kelly for the first time – he was CSA at Transport, and Dave King who was the Government Chief Science Advisor (GCSA). I watched Charles chair many meetings, sometimes long and with many people present. He never took a note during the meeting but would always produce a clear and lengthy summing up at the end – which says a huge amount for both his memory and his clarity of thought. He was prepared to discuss difficult issues and explore a range of possible solutions. Post-qualification admissions (PQA) was an interesting one. The 'fairness' lobby wanted to do it; everyone else – schools, universities, exam boards – argued that it was impossible. Charles said in one meeting that if we obviously couldn't do it, we should simply drop it. I rather unwisely asked if I could 'have one last go', and he agreed. This plummeted me into endless meetings, including large public consultations – I recall one in the Connaught Rooms, next to the Freemasons Hall – but I failed. Elements of it are now in place via a souped-up clearing during admissions. He could also be cross and frustrated at times: children in care, poor access to HE for children from poorer families, and it is perhaps not a surprise that more recently he edited a book titled *The Too Difficult Box*!

A few months in (for me), there was a reshuffle and Alan Johnson was promoted to the Cabinet and DWP. He was summoned to Downing Street for this to happen, and Charles had obviously been forewarned. Notwithstanding that he was in the middle of a meeting with Alison Richards, VC of Cambridge, he organised an immediate party and champagne to welcome him back – and a rather bemused Alison found that she had lost most of her meeting. Kim Howells, a long-standing Minister of State who had moved around many Departments, took over the HE role from Alan. Not long afterwards, Charles himself was promoted to the Home Office and Ruth Kelly arrived. I have two particular memories of working with Ruth, both on the edge of farce, the second more serious than the first. Ruth sat for a Bolton constituency and one November day, the University there had a ceremony for the conferment of (or celebration of) their university title. Ruth was to make the key speech at the ceremony in the afternoon and speak at a grand dinner in the evening which was held in Bolton Town Hall. On the day, I was delegated to do the speech at the ceremony as Ruth had to answer questions in the Commons – I was no doubt second-best but acceptable. Ruth had promised to be there for the dinner but there was no sign of her. Speeches, as I recall, were to be at the beginning. The soup course was served, Ruth then arrived and almost immediately was invited to speak. She started and after two minutes, the fire alarm went off and we all had to troop outside to a foggy cold night. There was no time to retrieve coats and, outside, I offered Ruth my jacket. She declined, smiling, and said that this would give her a chance to talk to her constituents, and she started to circulate.

The second occasion was about the funding of the Open University (OU) which saw itself as perennially underfunded because of the low fees charged for part-time students. Betty Boothroyd was the Chancellor and arranged a meeting with Ruth, along with Joel Barnett and another peer. I attended. Lady Boothroyd launched into a major attack on the Department and threatened motions in the House of Lords. Ruth looked increasingly flustered. I intervened and said: 'Why don't I go up to Milton Keynes and explore the situation in more detail?' A very relieved Ruth said: 'Yes, Alan can go to Milton Keynes' and the meeting drew to a close. The interesting bit was the visit to Milton Keynes and its aftermath which has continued ever since. I travelled with a young civil servant, Helen Brooks, and as our taxi entered the campus – which looked like a 'normal' university campus, I said to Helen, tongue in cheek: 'Where are the students?' At lunch with the senior management, I suggested to them that they might recruit 10,000 full-time students and at the capital cost (which others would pay for) of building some student accommodation, their financial problems would be solved and they could develop a new kind of very exciting university – teach their students with their OU distance-learning materials and focus staff time on a very superior tutorial and seminar system. One of the PVCs present said, 'But that isn't our mission, and another said, 'And you should be aware that there is a proposal to build a University of Milton Keynes'! I made no progress. I should probably have pressed the idea harder in the Department. Years later, the financial troubles of the OU have continued, recently leading to the resignation of the VC. There is now an active development of MK:U – the Milton Keynes University – and the OU have declined to be a partner. The lead partner university is Cranfield.

There was yet another government reshuffle and Alan Johnson returned from DWP as Secretary of State. This led to one (no doubt, one of many) new development. There was ongoing concern about the 50% target which I think was due to be achieved in something like 2010. Alan asked me to estimate when the target would actually be achieved at the present rate of progress. I set my analysts on to this and their best guess was 2020. I reported back to Alan who found this alarming. The target itself was measured in a very odd way as the percentage of 18–30-year-olds who 'had some experience of HE' – presumably the Department seeking to minimise its risk at the time the Prime Minister announced the target. This led me to propose a solution to Alan which was 'out of the box' but potentially solved two problems at the same time: to develop a programme of co-funded work-based degrees which would be expanded at a rate that would bring the achievement of the target back to 2010. He accepted with enthusiasm.

Another minister I worked with was Andrew Adonis. He was made a peer and given his first ministerial appointment as Parliamentary Secretary in the Department with a Schools brief, include schools science. My working with him came about in a very unusual way. With my university research brief, I worked quite closely with David Sainsbury, then Minister for Science. He became very concerned about what he saw as failures in schools science – declining numbers of A-level students in subjects like maths and physics – the start of the focus on STEM? He approached the Chancellor and suggested that the Treasury should conduct an externally-led review. This led to alarm among our ministers and the upshot was that there should be an internal review with one of David Sainsbury's civil servants on the group. I was nominated as the Chair as someone 'internal' who was 'acceptable' to David. The group was pretty hostile and defensive at first but settled down to some exploration and creative thinking. The Department's progression statistics were very good and it quickly emerged that the probability of moving on to science A-Levels from GCSE was very much higher for students who had taken three different science subjects at GCSE – physics, chemistry, and biology – rather than the single subject 'General Science'. We made a recommendation that all schools should be required to offer three subjects, and if they couldn't, they should make arrangements with a neighbouring school that could for their pupils who wanted this option. Our civil servants declared this to be impossible but Andrew backed it and it was implemented. Whether it has survived, I don't know.

The second idea, more out of left field, was intended to deal with the shortage of physics teachers. It was argued that the vacancies for graduate physics teachers could not be filled even if every physics graduate for something like the next ten years went into teaching. What could be done? Out of left field again: there was a relative surplus of biology teachers. Bribe them – that is offer significant support of some kind – to spend a year retraining as a physics teacher. We launched the scheme, I think with some success, but whether it continues – there is still a shortage of physics teachers, I rather doubt.

There was a host of meetings outside the Department. Other government departments: with Dave King, GCSA, who was responsible for the other half of the research dual support budget as well as the convener of CSA meetings; Sally Davies as CSA/Director of Research in the Department of Health who was trying to rescue her research budget from within the NHS.[25] There were intergovernmental meetings, for example, there was a European Commission group of Directors-General of HE which met once a year in whichever country held the EU presidency. My first meeting was in Luxembourg, the second in the UK. Charles (I think) decreed that the HE meeting should be outside London and so we met in Manchester for a two-day meeting, including excursions. The most interesting suggestion for the latter was Holy Cross College in Bury. This was a Catholic Sixth Form College and I did wonder what it had to do with HE. It turned out that Liverpool Hope University had rented some space for evening courses in HE, expecting to attract, say, 50 students. In fact, they took on a large number, partly to meet the demand for trained nursing assistants in the NHS – it was win-win all round.

I was an 'observer' on the HEFCE Board but the Chair always explicitly treated me as a member. I had a good working relationship with Howard Newby, then the Chief Executive, and we met regularly. I met with the various university lobby groups – the Russell Group, the 94 Group, and the Royal Society Committee on Physics Education. I believe there was even an 'unaligned group', though that may have been after my time. I made regular university visits, mainly to non-Russell Group universities on the grounds that I knew them very well anyway. I found much enterprise. Indeed, I recall a day in Liverpool where I visited Liverpool Edge Hill University in the morning and the University of Liverpool in the afternoon. I found real creativity in the former and a bit of complacency in the latter.

I was originally appointed on a two-year contract to establish the new HE Directorate. (David Normington said to me that he had done this because otherwise the DfES was more like a Department of Schools!) This was then extended for a year, round about the end of my first year, as I remember it. However, I then left slightly early, at the end of September in 2006 to become Master of Corpus Christi College, Cambridge. I thought this was a good move at the time. It would offer me a new academic base and because I was 'only' 67, I could be given a seven-year contract. How wrong I was!

It is always interesting to see what happens when one leaves a job – recall the selling of Bretton Hall after I left Leeds. In the DfES case, I can recall two examples. First, I had always defended the funding of support for people taking second degrees – whether for conversion purposes or otherwise. The funding was under threat year by year as increases were sought from a fixed budget for other purposes. Soon after I left, this support vanished. The second example was about terminology. I had successfully persuaded our ministers throughout my three years not to use the phrase 'best, or top, universities' on the grounds that those not deemed to be in this category were often excellent and doing creative things (and vice versa!). The minute I left, this crept back into use again!

A3.4.2 Cambridge

My move to the mastership of a Cambridge college was a serious mistake on my part. It was unpleasant, and the detail is best omitted. I was relieved to be 'rescued' by UCL!

A3.4.3 UCL, and more

I took up my job as Professor of Urban and Regional Systems at CASA in University College London (UCL) on 1 August 2007. The London flat now turned out to be invaluable. My UCL base was 20 minutes' walk away; and we eventually moved into our rather fine Norfolk house and had a country retreat – albeit a longer drive away than we would have liked.

I was employed on a 50% basis which left me free to do other things. There were quite a few of these, probably too many. I had been elected as a Fellow of the Royal Society the previous year and that produced two immediate commitments. It was traditional for new Fellows to be appointed to one of the Section Committees to recommend the election of new Fellows, and I was appointed to Section 10. Second, I was invited to chair SCORE by Martyn Rees, then President of the Royal Society.

The Centre for Advanced Spatial Analysis (CASA), at that time, was a small interdisciplinary research centre located in a basement in Tavistock Street – technically shared between Geography and the Bartlett Faculty of the Built Environment. A year or two in, after a fall-out with Geography, CASA became a department within the Bartlett Faculty. The Head was Mike Batty. He was the only member of staff – the rest were mainly externally funded researchers or PhD students. (Mike was a brilliant writer of research proposals!) I sat in a tiny area of the open plan with my first research student, Joel Dearden, sitting behind me. That made for a fruitful and active collaboration.[26] I joined some other projects of Mike's as a co-investigator (CoI) but it was a relatively gentle pace with probably my more pressured time taken up with outside commitments. It also allowed me to finish a book I had been working on for years, *Knowledge Power* (Wilson, 2010a). That year, or thereabouts, was a turning point both for CASA and for me.

I had always thought that small research centres couldn't survive without an income from teaching. I finally won an argument that we should start a Master's course. This started well and became very successful and allowed us to recruit new academic staff as lecturers. I did quite a lot of teaching which I enjoyed – a modelling course, and a more general one based on *Knowledge Power*. On the personal front, I was successful in being awarded a large five-year EPSRC grant to work on 'global dynamics' – migration, trade, security, and development aid – and I put a team together of six post docs and five PhD students. I had CoIs in five UCL departments. This took a serious amount of time and was both interesting and fruitful. It linked me to collaborators, including Francesca Medda who became a good friend and a co-researcher on some new projects. (She introduced me to Turing's work on evolving structures among other things.) The Global Dynamics project produced a good number of papers and two books. Indeed, it was a good time for me for writing and editing – I produced 11 books of various kinds in my CASA time. I converted my PowerPoint slides from my modelling course into Word and then into a book: *The Science of Cities and Regions* (Wilson, 2012); I edited a book with Francesca Pagliara, and I edited a five-volume history of urban modelling as well as the two Global Dynamics books. I co-authored a book with Joel on urban dynamics, and another with Francesca and colleagues on trade (Medda et al., 2017).

All in all, this was a good and productive time, though there were tensions in CASA which peaked every now and again, leaving me in a mediating role. I had occasional conversations with Malcolm Grant – having agreed to stay outside any role in university management – though I also did bits of work with David Price and the research directorate. In CASA terms, this takes me to the beginning of 2014 when I started looking around for something new. But that was partly driven by my series of roles outside CASA and this takes me back to the Autumn of 2007.

My starting date with CASA coincided with working with Michael Stevenson as a consultant for Cisco. While my role was essentially HE, it was overtaken in the early weeks by the aftermath of Hurricane Katrina in New Orleans. The Cisco philanthropic arm had committed $40M to help restore the school education system in New Orleans where they had a small team overseeing their investment. Michael, with his broad education role, was given the job of overseeing this. He must have been overcommitted and so a large chunk of that role was devolved to me. This involved a number of trips to New Orleans (and to other locations where team meetings were taking place: Greensborough and Atlanta). It was a fascinating experience. Most of the teachers in New Orleans had left after Katrina and the system was being rebuilt from scratch. The Cisco funding enabled it to be high tech, deploying one of the 'virtual school' systems available in the USA. I also used the visits to explore Cisco colleges – there was one in Baton Rouge – which Michael and I thought could be expanded as part of Cisco's potential HE role. I thought there was tremendous potential for a Cisco University and I designed one – but it never came off!

A longer-term commitment came through my appointment as Chair of the Arts and Humanities Research Council (AHRC) in December 2007. It was a drawn-out process, reminiscent of the DfES. I was first head-hunted and then interviewed by a panel chaired by Keith O'Nions, then DG in Business, Innovation and Skills (BIS) (as it then was) – I think, in September. I heard nothing until December and assumed it had disappeared and someone else had been appointed but not announced. When Keith rang me, I assumed that someone else had been offered it and then turned it down, but Keith said firmly that this was not the case. I assumed I hadn't got the job because I knew there was, in my book, a much stronger candidate: Stewart Sutherland. I knew of this because on the day I was interviewed at 1, Victoria Street, when I arrived and was given a badge at reception, I could see the names of two other candidate on the pile – and as I was taken upstairs, I met Stewart coming out of the interview room! Not carefully handled! When I was phoned and offered the job, and accepted, I was told that the Minister, John Denham, wanted to announce it at a meeting a few days hence, and I had to be there. To my horror, I saw Stewart in the audience and wondered what I should say. In fact, it says everything about his character that he came over to me, congratulated me, and said: 'If it wasn't going to be me, I'm very glad it was you!' However, he also told me that it was only that morning that he had been phoned and told that he hadn't got it. Appalling! A good thing about the process was that it was a Ministerial appointment and I hope it removed any bad taste that may have been lying around about my exit from Cambridge. Those recommending and making the appointment would have been fully aware of the circumstances.

AHRC was an interesting challenge. It had only recently become a fully-fledged Council from being a 'Board'. Its strategy seemed to be weak and there was the usual tension with the community who believed that its role was simply to run open calls and to make sure that many of the awards facilitated the writing up of monographs. It was located in Bristol and it was two or three years before it relocated to Swindon alongside the other Research Councils in Polaris House. This period also coincided with the controversial 'impact' agenda and an early task was to publish a paper on our view of impact which was both sensible and satisfied the competing views of the government (represented by BIS) and the academic research community. BIS was represented on the group doing this work, which I chaired, by Graeme Reid very helpfully. He later became a Professor of Science Policy at UCL.

In my early CASA years, I did a small amount of work for Oakleigh Consulting, mainly working with one of their partners (and MD?), Phil Hawkey. We did one job for SOAS on internal restructuring and strategy and a more substantial one for the University of Newport through a period (around 2011) when the Welsh Government was seeking to reduce the number of universities in Wales through mergers. In the end, when all else failed, we had to support a merger with the University of Glamorgan, albeit at the price of the new university having a new name: The University of South Wales.

In 2009, Alan Langlands, then Chief Executive of Higher Education Funding Council for England (HEFCE), asked to see me. He asked for my help in chairing a group to review JISC, the oddly named Joint Information Systems Committee which had special funding from HEFCE. Its objective was to develop IT systems to support the sector as a whole – the most successful of which was the Joint Academic Network (JANET). It quickly seemed to me in practice that it was acting as a mini research council for university directors of IT and for Chief Librarians. What it was not doing was starting from the key agenda of universities – teaching, research, and wider engagement, and working from there. For the first meeting of the group, I drafted a structure for what the final report might look like – as a way of specifying our future work programme – but picking up the point about strategy. The group thought this was good, and the HEFCE representative, at the end of the meeting, said that he had never sat on a group before which had such a clear idea of its final outcome in its first meeting. I then undertook the task of having 1–1 conversations with senior managers. To my surprise, there turned out to be 12 of these, not very strongly connected, sometimes in more or less independent divisions. A very time-consuming but illuminating process. We made some radical recommendations which were all accepted and implemented by a new Chief Executive. I had one potentially difficult conversation in Edinburgh with Tim O'Shea, the University Principal, who was the Chair of the JISC Board, to explain our recommendations. To my surprise, over a good lunch in his Vice-Chancellor's office, he accepted it all with equanimity.

A different kind of ex-CASA engagement came from meeting with Carl Gombrich in 2011. He had the responsibility of building what amounted to an in-house liberal arts (and science) college within UCL – something that was fundamentally interdisciplinary. He had somehow discovered my *Knowledge Power* book and sought my help. This led to me lecturing to his first-year students – a class of around 80 – on a 'flipped' basis: for each lecture, they had to watch a recording in advance and then the 'lecture' itself was purely Q and A. I was very sceptical at first but it seemed to work and I certainly enjoyed it. Carl became a good friend and I have enjoyed working with him.

Year by year, new roles continued to kick in – two significantly substantial. In 2012, I was approached by Bernard Silverman (whom I had come to know through the Royal Society and was then CSA at the Home Office) to work with him to revive, and to chair, the Home Office Science Advisory Council (HOSAC). The brief of the Council was to be 'critical friend' and adviser to Home Office Science and Technology. This was quite a substantial operation with its own research establishment, the Centre for Applied Science and Technology (CAST), on two secure sites outside London. Bernard was responsible for the whole operation, though in the later stages, the CSA role was more limited to science and policy and operations were run separately. The Council itself had a core of members who were chairs of Home Office Committees (though it had no responsibility or oversight of these, but at least it established connections) along with a number of mainly academic members. We held seminars, had working groups – for example, on the costs of cyber crime, and we did some deep dives – for example, on science and technology (s and t) support for OSCT – the Office for Security and Counter-Terrorism. Particular members were available to advise on specific topics ranging from the police funding formula via operational research (OR) to ethics. We visited CAST and were consulted on, and encouraged by, its merger with the Defence Science and Technology Laboratory (DSTL), which broadened its base considerably. A personal advantage for me was that I was security-cleared to the developed vetting (DV) level which turned out to be helpful in a later phase of my life.

As Chair of HOSAC, I also sat on Defence Science Advisory Council (DSAC), the Ministry of Defence equivalent. It seemed to me to have a rather scrappy agenda. There was a core of long-standing members but the most senior people often didn't turn up – never a good sign. HOSAC was entirely within the Home Office with unpaid members while DSAC was an NDPB and its members were paid. As an NDPB, it had to have a Triennial Review – part of the government's policy of deciding whether quangos should continue or not. By some means unknown to me, in 2013, I was deputed to carry out this review. I did this on the basis of a series of 'structured interviews' over three or four months both with policy-makers and particularly, the higher ranks of the military – in many ways, the main customers of DSAC. I thought that having to talk to me would be a bind but it turned out that even the most senior people seemed to welcome the opportunity to speak to an outsider. By combining intelligence from these conversations, I built a good knowledge of the MoD –

valuable in itself, as I started knowing little – as the foundation for evaluating DSAC. I produced a series of detailed recommendations but with one overriding one: the need to have a 'big picture' perspective as the basis for, in consultation with customers, determining ongoing priorities – distinguishing the short run from the longer run and being strategic in doing this.

The second substantial role was to chair the Lead Expert Group of the Government Office for Science Foresight project 'The future of cities'. I took this on in May 2013 and the time commitment led me to retire from chairing AHRC at the end of the year, two years early, after six years. This ran through to December 2015. The origins of this typified the London networking which produced so many of these opportunities for me. I met Mark Walport at a British Academy pre-dinner reception where we both happened to have arrived early. He had just been appointed as GCSA and started chatting about a new Foresight project he was to start – on cities. We started to have a long chat about it and he promised to stay in touch. I was then visited by increasingly senior civil servants seeking further advice and, in retrospect, it was clear that I was being 'interviewed'. My appointment followed.

The group was duly appointed – an eclectic mix of very bright people with varying views on the future of cities. We met regularly and at a very early stage, we identified a set of topics which provided a structure for our work: living in cities (people); the economy of cities; sustainability; urban form; infrastructure; and governance. We were supported by an excellent civil service team led by Eleri Jones – who became a key working partner and a good friend – and a number of young researchers and administrators. We had been given a 50-year time horizon on the basis that this would lift us clear of immediate 'politics' – 'up to a point' as it turned out. Mark had argued at the outset that we couldn't do this without visiting cities. I was very nervous about the time commitment but he turned out to be exactly right. We visited over 20 cities between us, roughly evenly split, and occasionally both of us being there. There was much enthusiasm for the project and in a number of cases, local Foresight projects were established with seedcorn funding from us. The best examples were Newcastle and Milton Keynes, of which more below.

We commissioned essays and produced working papers, all of which are now on the Future of Cities website (https://www.gov.uk/government/uploads/system/uploads/attachment_data/file/520963/GS-16-6-future-of-cities-an-overview-of-the-evidence.pdf). We established a City Visions Network to bring the 20 cities together – and I think I am right, that having persuaded Peter Hall to come to one of these and asking him to say something informally for five minutes (after he had failed to produce a promised presentation), he then gave us a masterly off-the-cuff account of what we should be thinking about. Sadly, a few months later, he died. We ran workshops – including one which brought together 14 Whitehall departments, each of which had some interest and responsibilities in relation to 'cities'. The enthusiasm with which we were met in cities around the country was not matched here: colleagues were reluctant to escape from their silos! We also held four public meetings around the country –

Cambridge, Manchester, Glasgow, and Bristol, as I remember. Each produced audiences of between 100 and 200 and produced real and lively public discussion – and some good new ideas.

A key to our work was in articulating future 'scenarios' as forecasting for 50 years ahead was clearly impossible. It was, however, very realistic to predict substantial population growth which was pretty uncomfortable for government thinking about the resources that would be needed to sustain effective urban growth in the future. Our final products are on the website – with four final reports and all the working papers and essays which between them represent a formidable resource for anyone who has to think about the future of cities. The four final reports were:

1 The future of cities: imperatives and challenges.
2 Foresighting for cities: a manual, available at: https://www.gov.uk/government/uploads/system/uploads/attachment_data/file/516443/gs-16-5-future-cities-foresight-for-cities.pdf.
3 The science of cities: research priorities, available at: https://www.gov.uk/government/uploads/system/uploads/attachment_data/file/516407/gs-16-6-future-cities-science-of-cities.pdf.
4 Summary of Evidence.

We didn't solve any problems but I think we were pretty good at articulating the challenges, and how to approach these. Insofar as we had recommendations, our top one was that all the challenges are interdependent and must be tackled on this basis – a strong argument for restructuring government agencies to drive cities' policies outside silos.

The two cities that were most effective in developing their own foresight projects were Newcastle and Milton Keynes. The Newcastle project was outstandingly led by Mark Twdyr-Jones, producing its own three scenarios, a report and a very popular exhibition. I worked in more detail with Milton Keynes. They set up an MK 2050 Commission, chaired by Peter Gregson, the VC of Cranfield, strongly supported by the Council through Geoff Snelson and Sarah Gonzales as officers and Peter Marland as the Council Leader. After an initial exploratory meeting, supported by the Foresight team, Eleri was added as a member of the Commission and I was asked to continue as an honorary adviser. They had their own workshops and presentations, and met community groups to ensure a wide range of input. Milton Keynes has been very successful but has its social challenges and was beginning to be rather 'tired'. The Commission decided to look for six big ideas that would drive the city forward. I was responsible for one of these which is now on the edge of implementation: to establish a Milton Keynes University – MK:U – to be built in the 'car park land' near the City Station. It was an interesting and exciting time and I became an MK supporter! A bonus was getting to know Peter Gregson and the MK principals well.

I did various other less time-consuming things in this period. The spin-out company set up on the basis of an Innovate UK £2.5M grant was set up and I chaired the small Board of Directors. I was a member of the Centre for Cities Board. I was involved in a trip to Vienna with Mark Walport and a small group to make a recommendation about whether the UK should rejoin the International Institute for Applied Systems Analysis (IIASA). It did, and I am now a member of the UK IIASA Committee. I became a member of the Global Challenge Research Fund Strategic Advisory Group. I did various things for the Royal Society – initially chairing the the Science Community Representing Education (SCORE), I had a year on the Council and was co-opted by Paul Nurse when he became President to be on a small Strategy Group – which in turn led me to chairing the new Nominations Committee. I chaired a joint British Academy/Royal Society working group on education research.

I was more than fully occupied. Was it all worth it? Most of it was! CASA, certainly, was very productive in writing and research terms and I enjoyed different kinds of teaching. That was the core. AHRC was challenging and important. I give top marks to the Foresight project, though it was difficult to manage at times. Eleri's role was critical in making it work and I think what we produced in the end was very good. Most of the rest of it was certainly interesting and gave me new insights on how different kinds of organisations work.

A3.4.4 The Alan Turing Institute

In December 2015, two big time commitments came to an end – an EPSRC-funded project on trade, migration, security and development aid and the Foresight project. There were ongoing tensions around CASA and I started to think that it would be good to do something new. The opportunity came to be seconded from UCL to a new research institute, the Alan Turing Institute – designated as the national institute for data science. I consulted Anthony Finkelstein, then Dean of Engineering in UCL and a Trustee of the Turing Institute, as to whether 'modelling' was part of data science, and whether I should apply to be seconded. His reply was: 'You can't have big data without big models – so go for it!' So I applied through UCL and was accepted. I had a talk with Andrew Blake, the Director of the Institute – wasn't very enthused, but decided to go ahead, perhaps more push than pull. I was to be a Faculty Fellow on 40% time. I retained 20% in UCL as the CoI on an Engineering and Physical Sciences Research Council (EPSRC) research project. Most new Fellows were scheduled to arrive in October, but the UCL 'leads' for Turing, Sofia and Patrick, suggested that I moved in July. I decided to move physically as I couldn't justify keeping my rather nice UCL/CASA office for one day a week. So I moved and found myself a desk in an un-refurbished part of what is now the research end of Turing. I started to plan an urban programme and ran a workshop in August. I suspect that my Turing colleagues – mainly from the Business Team – found it rather odd that I had turned up and was in full-time residence!

The urban analytics workshop in August was a success, though it was by no means clear where the resources were going to come from to support the research ideas that emerged. I did make some new contacts, notably Weisi Guo. However, the most significant was probably Pete Grindrod. I had met him earlier, excellent mathematician, an eye for certain kinds of applications in industry – very successful. He was also a Turing Trustee and later in the summer, he gave be an inkling of what the Board were intending to finalise in September: essentially to reorganise and appoint a CEO.

The Trustee Board was meeting in early September. Following the talks with Pete, Sarah (I think) suggested that I should talk to Anthony Finkelstein, also a Trustee, as noted. By this time, he had left UCL and was the Chief Scientific Adviser (CSA) for National Security – and difficult to get hold of. But I managed this and told him what I thought the Trustees should be doing! Without any suggestion from me, he must have contacted Howard Covington, the Chair of the Trustees, and I had an e-mail out of the blue asking for a phone call. I went through the 'agenda' again – this becoming more polished as the sequence of phone calls proceeded. I spelled this out to myself in a computer note dated 7 September – noting that the phone conversation with Howard was the previous Sunday morning (the 4th). The Board meeting must have been on the 5th or 6th, and I met Howard in the Institute after that, and we rehearsed the conversation again. I was then asked to have a phone meeting with Richard Kenway and John Aston – two Trustees who had been given some executive authority in the Institute over the summer. Roughly speaking, my pitch was: we need more executive capacity to implement the strategy, more research leaders, both foundational and domain-related, a senior management team, more nurturing of an inexperienced administration; a three-year rolling budget related to a strategic plan; a welcome for new Faculty Fellows and Research Fellows in October – they were entering a new Institute without a structure for them. Better liaison with joint venture universities (JVUs) and partners, An expanded stakeholder base, some early wins. I offered myself for an executive role to be specified – Pete and Anthony had suggested Interim CEO. A few days later, as I was about to go out to Fischers for dinner with Sarah, I received an e-mail offering me the Interim CEO job.

Andrew Blake, the Director, accepted the position gracefully, indeed, I think with some relief: someone other than him could cope with the demands of the Board! He even introduced me to an all-staff meeting as the new CEO. There were some surprises and even raised eyebrows as the announcement was made: I had been around for three months as a researcher and no one had anticipated this transition. (Slightly oddly, I had attended a Board away day on 21 September and the senior staff present began to realise why I was there – not being any other obvious reason.)

On 1 October, new Faculty Fellows and Research Fellows started to arrive, some puzzled, some determined to be enthusiastic and who became significant assets. There had been a large number of scoping workshops which had been turned into a strategy: the SIS – Science and Innovation Strategy. (I assume this had been led by Patrick and Sofia – Andrew remarked to me later that 'he didn't do strategy'.) This included a matrix which was good and survived for quite a while: the columns were the 'challenges' and the rows were the 'methods' – the foundations. I inherited some structure – a newly formed Programme Committee, chaired by Ulrike Ulman and a so-called Executive Board, mainly made up of the University Liaison Directors (ULDs), one for each of the founding universities. This wasn't really 'executive': it had management functions in the early days and most of its members saw themselves as supporting a focus on foundational research, with decision-making on funding based on a set of 'panels' – not unlike a traditional research council committee system (with all its inadequacies). The executive authority had in effect been transferred to the CEO. The ULDs dominated the Programme Committee and there were many battles and quite a lot of bad temper. At that time, the Institute had four strategic partners who had each committed to invest of the order of £10M over five years: Lloyds Register Foundation (LRF), Intel, Government Communications Headquarters (GCHQ) (representing all the security services and MoD more widely) and HSBC. Having these in place was a significant inheritance, but they were all different, they had different expectations, and their oversight was not without difficulties. They each had a Strategic Programme Director (of varying strengths) and a Programme Board with executive authority. I took over the chair of each of these to try to add momentum.

The external perception of the Institute was that it was rudderless and weak. Many academics had been to scoping workshops but had seen no follow-up. Many people who approached the Institute with data science challenges or offers of collaboration were turned away. Some time in October, I attended a book launch, for Rick Rylance, in the School of Advanced Studies in the University of London. Adrian Smith was there and took me into a corner – having a few days earlier sending me a message saying that he needed to talk to me urgently. His message that evening was that the learned societies in mathematics and statistics had a very poor view of the Institute. Partly through him, I was invited to the Council of the London Mathematical Society (LMS), I met the senior officers of the Royal Statistical Society (RSS) (including Hetan Shah) and I had a private meeting with David Hand who said, bluntly, that the Institute had no strategy. I had to set about building bridges.

Internally, I set up my own (informal) Senior Management Team (SMT): Jon Atkins (Chief Operating Officer, COO), Donna Brown (Director of Academic Engagement), Nico Guernion (Director of Partnerships), Emma Cooke (Head of Finance), Sophie McIvor (Head of Comms) – all excellent people – so whatever else, I inherited some good appointments. From April in the following the year, we added the first of a sequence of fast streamers: Jenny Stuart, followed at six-month intervals by Arne Blackman and Amit Mulji. There were other key people in that early period: Mihaela van der Schaar, Graham Cormode, Mark Girolami, and (slightly later) Mark Briers. The SMT met more or less weekly and was my source of support, guidance, and preparation for all the work that had to be done.

What follows is not a chronological account but a view through the lens of aims and achievements. There was a lot of 'thinking things through' and a sequence of papers, building on the initial SIS and especially, the 'matrix'. We managed to produce a Strategic Plan, articulating the Institute's activities in terms of research (pure and applied), training and policy. We saw the Institute as 'distributed', made up of two interacting networks– the university network and the partner network – and a key aim was to grow both. A key issue to be dealt with was the fact that all the funding was committed to appointments of Fellows and PhD students – there was little money, beyond some seedcorn funding, for 'projects'. So a key aim was to find ways of funding real projects. This led, in time and via the renaming of Faculty Fellows as Turing Fellows, to a new model for Fellowships: there would be more seedcorn support, but new Fellows would also commit themselves both to collaborating across universities and to bidding for research council funding. It was only towards the end of the second year that this was achieved. A related aim was to expand our reach within universities beyond initial Fellow appointments, Projects could take place with the hub in London, in universities, in Turing Innovations Ltd (TIL) or through organisations deemed to be delivery partners. Looking ahead, the possible sources of future funding for a project-driven distributed Institute were: the core (through EPSRC); UKRI through the Strategic Priorities Fund (which kicked in formally in my last six months as CEO – the SPF) along with the Industrial Strategy Challenge Fund (ISCF) and IS sector deals – both under the control of UKRI; all the research councils through projects and new Turing Fellowship (TF) model; universities; charities such as the Cystic Fibrosis Trust and the British Heart Foundation; and partners – the four founders plus more recent examples such as UCH, Accenture, HDR UK, and others. All of this was captured in slides for presentations, with examples, particularly of challenges.

There were some fundamental transformations here, not least listing 'challenges' ahead of methods. There were significant battles in what became a long-running war, for example, through prolonged discussions in the Programme Committee and the Executive Board. Fortunately, the Trustee Board was nearly always supportive – though even in that case, there were long discussions on expanding the university network – 'criteria for acceptance, how many?' – and about TIL – 'will it compete with our university business organisations?'. And where the Board was ultimately supportive, we were held back on developing TIL, and at the time of writing still are.

We succeeded on most fronts, albeit imperfectly in places. One of the biggest achievements was the expansion of the universities' network – adding eight new university partners – all paying the £1M annual subscription. Nearly all involved meetings with Vice-Chancellors. All had to be convinced that they would somehow not be second-class. This last point involved inventing a University Partners Board to get as near as possible to Trustee Board membership – this being impossible – partly because of the terms of the joint venture agreement (JVA), partly because in any case, it wouldn't scale. The new TF model – project focused – was successfully launched – with the new universities full of enthusiasm – and this in itself impacted on the other five. We had very successful comms and events teams – Turing Lectures were very successful and could fill a 250-seat auditorium easily. I gave lots of presentations, some internally (including a Turing Lecture), mostly external.[27] Many colleagues contributed to this and it all enormously increased the Institute's public perception and profile.

As my diary shows, I was very thinly spread. A colleague listed the meetings recorded in my diary over my two years as CEO – and they numbered something like 400. I had a brilliant PA, Jackie El Nemer, and that helped, not least in providing the core of a good working environment. Looking back, it was difficult in the first year to maintain focus – there were too many relationships to develop and nurture. The JVUs were a starting point: UCL was especially difficult because of a major fall-out, just before my time, which had led to Patrick and Sofia leaving the Institute. Warwick was edgy, relieved by having Graham Cormode as the ULD. Oxford had a crazy model – with the subscription being shared across five departments, each wanting to see a 'return' on their 'investment'. Edinburgh and Cambridge were at least friendly – and in the former case, there was the prospect of serious engagement through a City Deal (though this did not materialise). The engagement was mainly through their ULDs: David Pym (UCL), Jared Tanner (Oxford), and Chris Williams (Edinburgh) could be almost guaranteed to oppose any development in the Executive Board or Programme Committee and to stir things up in their universities. Zoubin Gharamani (Cambridge) and Graham Cormode (Warwick) were the opposite – excellent! The relationships with senior managers were generally good. I repaired the relationship with UCL, had a conversation with Ian Walmsley, PVC at Oxford, about their 'model' but made no progress. I had little contact with the Warwick management. Edinburgh and Cambridge were fine. The JVUs, of course, had their nominated Trustees and relations in that case were good, though Pete (Oxford) was capable of being eccentric and outspoken while being supportive. Needless to say, all of this took a lot of time, including university visits of various kinds, such as from the ATI 'Committee', groups of Fellows and researchers to 'Town Hall' meetings.

The process of expanding the university network took most of my two years but was ultimately successful. It involved meetings with most of the Vice-Chancellors, sometimes PVCs. We had originally planned a second tier of universities on the basis that new members would not want to commit themselves to the £1M p.a. subscription. However, it became clear that this was not the case and we abandoned the 'second tier' idea for the time being.

Other key points of contact included government departments – the Department for Business, Energy & Industrial Strategy (BEIS), Health, the Home Office, the Ministry of Justice, the Department for Culture, Media and Sport, the Department for Environment, Food and Rural Affairs (DEFRA), mostly through civil servants, occasionally ministers – Greg Clarke, David Prior, and Matt Hancock for example. Data science and, increasingly, AI, were seen as critical to the Industrial Strategy – indeed, AI was one of its four planks.

Wendy Hall and Jerome Pesenti were commissioned by BEIS to write a report on AI. We were able to stay close to this, not least through Arne Blackman, our fast streamer, working with the supporting civil servants. There was a hint that there could be a recommendation to establish a National Institute for AI. This came to a head at a small dinner in Lancaster House, chaired by Greg Clarke, including David Prior as the Minister for the Industrial Strategy, Wendy Hall and Jerome Pesenti,[28] and a handful of outsiders, including me. I managed to steer the argument away from a separate AI Institute by changing our subtitle from 'National Institute for Data Science' to 'National Institute for Data Science and AI'. (I had to concede 'AI' should come first but later we realised that the acronym would then be 'AIDS' and we quietly dropped it.) The links through Chief Scientific Advisers was important – not least through Mark Walport as the GCSA. These included Chris Whitty and Sally Davies (Chief Medical Officer) at Health, Bernard Silverman and then John Aston at the Home Office, Ian Boyd at DEFRA and Phil Blythe at Transport – but the links were not as strong, Mark excepted, as they should have been.

We needed to connect to all the research councils since they all had data science and AI interests. EPSRC was our 'parent', our source of government funding – and Neil Viner was an excellent Trustee and Phil Nelson, the CEO, and Tom Rodden, his deputy, were good supporters. ESRC sponsored a £3M fellowship and PhD programme. The Science and Technology Facilities Council (STFC), initially through the Diamond Light Source at Harwell hub drew us into our 'data science for science' theme. We had lesser contacts in the first instance with the Natural Environment Research Council (NERC), the Medical Research Council (MRC), the Biology and Biochemical Sciences Research Council (BBSRC) – but growing links with AHRC.

The learned societies were important. We had good links with the Royal Society, partly through Julie Maxton, a good friend who was a Turing Trustee, and through their 'data' initiative led by Natasha McCarthy; some with the British Academy; more with the Royal Statistical Society and the Operational Research Society; I probably neglected the Royal Academy of Engineering, but perhaps links were maintained by others.

The final group demanding meetings was that of actual or potential external partners. Progress with the original four strategic partners was different in each case. The most successful was (and is) the Lloyds Register Foundation (LRF) through the leadership of Mark Girolami as Programme Director. The one led by GCHQ had contractual difficulties in the early days but again very effective leadership has kicked in through Mark Briers. HSBC was problematic. The Programme Director resigned; there were many management changes in HSBC. It now seems to be in good order. Intel has proved difficult, again mainly through management changes in the company. There were other developments, notably Accenture. A potential big one is the Toyota Motor Foundation: complicated negotiations led to a £600k grant with the potential for £10M to follow. Health has already been mentioned (British Heart Foundation, University College Hospital (UCH), Health Data Research UK), and this included meetings chaired by Jeremy Farmer, CEO at Wellcome, to try to find systematic ways of releasing NHS data. I had many meetings with the National Infrastructure Commission, aiming at a UK digital twin of which a UK urban model would be a key part – essentially the argument was won – but there was no funding![29] A particularly interesting possibility, which arose from when we entertained a delegation from the New Zealand Government in 2017, is the possibility of a Turing hub in New Zealand. This led to me visiting New Zealand in June 2018 – in the end, only some small joint projects were generated.

All of this is something of a shopping list but it does illustrate the range of meetings that I was committed to – not least because in building new relationship-s for a new Institute, people really want to meet the CEO – so it was difficult to delegate in the first instance.

Through the two years, I managed to maintain the practice of running a personal research programme, in this case, mainly through working with others. This generated a number of research publications.[30] The most important came from a conversation with Mark Girolami after I had heard him give a seminar. (My ability to attend seminars diminished rapidly as the CEO job expanded.) I recognised the possibility of using his maths skills to solve one of my long-standing problems. He introduced us to a research student, Louis Ellam, who could work on it, and an Imperial colleague, Greg Pavliotis, an expert in statistical mechanics. This team solved the problem and it produced a paper which was published in *Proceedings A* of the Royal Society. I worked with Weisi Guo, adding spatial interaction models and dynamics to his topological analysis of conflict networks. There were remnants of UCL collaborative research which appear in the list. A different project was on the 'future of libraries'. It originally stemmed from a Mark Walport suggestion – that Turing and the British Library together should be able to do something on this. It was finally launched with Flora Roumpani as the researcher, funded by the Library,[31] located in Turing. For the longer term, my most important collaborator may be Mihaela van der Schaar. She introduced me to the idea of what I came to call 'learning machines' (though I then discovered later that this was a term in common use!). The development of the work also further illustrated the opportunities from serendipity in Turing. I gave a breakfast talk on Turing to a group of CEOs and company chairs. At the end, I was approached by someone who said that she didn't want to talk about her company but about the Cystic Fibrosis Trust of which she was a Trustee, I think, the Chair. To cut the longer story short, I introduced her to Mihaela who, with her team, demonstrated the power of her research with a Cystic Fibrosis Trust pilot with real and excellent data. She and I will pursue this, and I think it offers a new approach to urban modelling as well as to other fields beyond health.

Throughout the period, I had a number of external commitments which had been taken on long before (in most cases) I took on the Turing CEO role. Needless to say, with my new job, I was too thinly spread and in most cases, I couldn't offer what I was supposed to be offering and where possible, I started to withdraw. I was still committed for a day a week to UCL as CoI on an

EPSRC project – the Urban Dynamics Lab. This was devolved across UCL and not working collaboratively or well. This led me to resign from UCL in August 2018 even through this project had two or three years to run. I was Chair of the Home Office Science Advisory Council and could manage this on a minimalist basis but and resigned from that in the Spring of 2019. I was a member of the Strategic Advisory Group for the Global Challenge Research Fund – and a poor attender – a Board member of Centre for Cities, which I admire and support but from which I have had to resign for non-attendance at meetings. I have been associated with various reviews, including what turned into a three-year project on education research for the British Academy and the Royal Society. I chaired the Board of Prospective Labs Ltd, a UCL spin-out. And, more recently, possibly foolishly, I took on the chairmanship of a group to guide the development of MK:U – a university in Milton Keynes but after one meeting, had to resign because of the pressure of other work. There are longer stories behind most of these cases.

Looking forward: half-way through my first year as CEO at Turing, I was asked to stay on for a second. I agreed but on the basis that the Board would then proceed with the process of appointing a permanent CEO. This led to Adrian Smith being appointed early in 2018 to take up the post in September. It was agreed that I should stay on, couldn't really think of a title but settled for Director, Special Projects. Much of my last six months as CEO was dominated by what became my biggest 'special project' for the future.

From April 2017, Mark Walport moved from being GCSA to CEO-designate of UKRI and this formally came into operation in April 2018, now responsible for all seven research councils, Innovate UK, Research England and much of the Industrial Strategy funding. Budgets were allocated to each of these elements but a substantial chunk of an overall increase retained for a Strategic Priorities Fund (SPF), aimed at supporting large multidisciplinary cross-council projects which at least in part would support government strategy. Research Councils were invited to bid – not the universities – in relation to their top priorities. I, on behalf of the Institute, was involved in two runners: one became top priority for AHRC, one for EPSRC.

The AHRC project stemmed from a visit Mark Walport made to Lausanne where he saw a demonstration of the Venice Time Machine: 'Why didn't we have one of those?' We worked on a new idea for several months ahead of SPF being announced, and then, when it materialised, we realised we had a good candidate. It became 'Living with machines' (LWM), a computer-data-driven history of the Industrial Revolution – promising both new findings, particularly from data linking, and a new way of doing history. Andrew Thompson and I put the idea together, initially working with Barbara McGillivray, a Turing Research Fellow, and then taking on Ruth Ahnert as the PI. We added more historians: Emma Griffin (University of East Anglia) and Jon Lawrence (Exeter) as well as a British Library team (Mia Ridge and Adam Farquar). When the time came to assemble it for an SPF bid, AHRC were ready to make it top priority.

In the EPSRC case, the Council wanted to support an AI project as top priority and I worked on this with them. I took five of the Turing's eight themes, added a methods theme, and put a bid together. I included 'urban analytics' as half a theme and Mihaela's work, combined with my drive on learning machines, as a substantial component of a health theme. I also argued for a learning machines element for a Ministry of Justice project within our Criminal Justice theme. It took a massive amount of time to build this between April and the submission date in June. These were unusual projects: in the LWM case, it was analogous to a responsive model bid with named participants but on a much larger basis; in the AI case, I was named as the Director, responsible to a Management Board and ultimately, to EPSRC.

The upshot was an £9.2M LWM bid and a £40M AI one. Both were approved by the UKRI Board in early July. At the end of July, I presented to the UKRI Investment Committee on behalf of EPSRC only to find they wanted more detail and I had to return at the end of August with a better business plan. I did this on the basis of a pre-circulated 65-page document, and this time it was accepted. It then had to have ministerial approval from both BEIS and the Treasury. There was then a further hiatus: we could not announce it until a Minister announced it, and this was not done until early December. Nonetheless, we had started making appointments from 1 November. (The Investment Committee stage was not needed for the LWM project as its size was below a threshold which required that.)

As I prepared to move on from the CEO role, I signed a new two-year contract with Turing on a three-day week basis, from 1 September 2018, directing the large new project, potentially over five years. This became known as the 'AI for Science and Government' project (ASG). In August, I allowed myself to be pushed – by a combination of Julie Maxton, Colette Bowe and Tim Gardam – into being the Executive Chair – for a day a week on an 18-month contract – of the new Ada Lovelace Institute. Needless to say, this has taken more than a day a week in its start-up period. We finally managed to appoint an excellent Director, Carly Kind, and she has successfully fully launched the Institute and in effect changed my job from 'Executive Chair' to 'Chair'! I was succeeded at the end of my contract by Wendy Hall.

How to summarise what has been achieved in my two years as CEO at Turing (and what hasn't been achieved!)? Much time, in effect, has been invested in keeping the peace while changing the culture – successfully – at least up to a point. If we can take (potential) income as a measure of purposeful activity, the new university partners add £8M p.a. and the SPF projects (together) wound £10M p.a., hence more than doubling the Institute's annual income in the two-year period. The new Turing Fellow model could, I estimated, add another £30M p.a. of research activity. If the industry/public sector partner side can add more, then it means that the Institute is in sight of an annual income of around, say, £75M p.a. within another two or three years. (This latter needs the TIL problem to be solved.) We will have successfully shifted to a project focus, we have a good publications record – so some of Andrew's model worked! We have an excellent public profile, helped by the addition of the AI brief. There was much more that I would have liked to do!

Around the end of my two-year contract extension, I decided that I did not want to continue with ASG management. By this time we were employing around 100 researchers and PhD students and so I handed over to John Rowe as Chair and Ben MacArthur as Director. I reduced my commitment to one day per week. I retained a couple of specific projects, one in ASG, one in LWM and a small research team. I finally ended my Turing contract in March 2023. I continued my research on a pro-bono basis, and this continues at the time of writing.

A3.5 Norfolk and London

A3.5.1 To Norfolk

In March 2020, the COVID-19 pandemic took off and my working life changed on another dimension. My wife and I switched from having London as our main base to our house in Norfolk which provided much more space for working at home. Work then progressed through Zoom and Teams and for well over a year, I had researchers working for me whom I only met virtually. By early 2022, we moved to a position where we spent a week every month or so in London and that revived in-person work meetings. Opportunities then turned up for two new jobs, each for one day per week.

A3.5.2 The Institute for Finance and Technology in UCL

The first, from January 2022 was as Director of Research at the relatively new Institute for Finance and Technology in UCL. I was recruited to support my former colleague Francesca Medda who was the Director of the Institute to help in the development of a research strategy. It was interesting to be involved in a new field and I learned a lot about the workings of the finance industry in areas like private equity. However, I decided that 'finance' was not a field I wanted to be heavily involved in and I left the Institute (with a strategy in place but no good means of implementing it) at the end of March 2023. This also coincided with the end of my Turing contract.

A3.5.3 The London Interdisciplinary School

The second new opportunity kicked in at the beginning of 2023, supporting my former UCL colleague Carl Combrich, the Academic Director of a new and enterprising small private university, the London Interdisciplinary School (LIS). This fitted well with my interests, notably with my book *Being Interdisciplinary* (Wilson, 2023) which had been published in the previous year. This was congenial – a very bright faculty, good to work with, and an interesting challenge to establish something seriously new in HE. I was formally Director of Research but as I settled in, I took on wider roles ranging from teaching, enjoyable as always, to advising on management challenges. I did devise a new research strategy but as was the case with IFT, there were no resources to implement it. I ended my contract with LIS in September 2024 as I didn't want to commit myself to what had become a rather routine academic role.

A3.5.4 End games

Leaving LIS left me formally unemployed for the first time in over 60 years. I have continued with a serious research project on 'the physiology of cities', working with Guy Solomon, now a Lecturer in Sheffield, who was part of my ASG/LUM team; and I continue to work on this book on 'leadership and management'. I am an Honorary Fellow and Professor in UCL, and an Honorary Fellow of the Alan Turing Institute. These provide academic bases, for example, for publishing and a small amount of teaching. I have had a small consulting contract with Turing, a committee role with the Royal Society, and some informal collaboration and mentoring roles with friends and colleagues.

Notes

1 Later Sir Christopher; and see Foster and Beesley (1963).
2 See Lakshmanan and Hansen (1965), an important innovation in retail modelling.
3 SRC: the Science Research Council.
4 SSRC: the Social Science Research Council until Keith Joseph insisted on the 'science' being removed, and it became the ESRC.
5 My own research is charted in my publications. In the 1980s, there were five books, two single-authored, two co-authored and one edited; and 94 papers. See Annex A2.5 for a list of key publications.
6 Sadly, Giorgio died in the mid-1980s and I recall visiting him in Milan shortly before he died. I am still in touch with his widow, Giovanna and their two sons, Davide and Stefano. Sylvana had a stroke which has left her out of action. Giovanni died in 2016. Demographics kicks in from time to time.
7 ULIS was the University umbrella company for both consulting and for spinning out.
8 MVA stood for Martin Voorhees Associates, a UK subsidiary of Alan Voorhees' US company.
9 Sally Macgill and her daughter sadly died in the Thai tsunami.
10 Brian Jewell was Director of Medical Development, later, Dean.
11 One day I jogged down to Woodhouse Moor to do two or three circuits – about one mile round – when I passed two teenage girls and heard one say to the other: 'I hope I can still run round the park when I'm his age!'
12 From Year 2, this was in effect the senior management team though it was never formally established as that: four PVCs, Registrar, Bursar (later Finance Director), HR Director.
13 Bill, Andy, Bobby Collins …
14 The University Court is a large representative body of University stakeholders which meets twice a year. It has few formal responsibilities, though it does approve the appointment of the Vice-Chancellor!
15 Chemistry, Textiles, the Medical School …
16 In the case of Chemistry, I had to say (in seeking to 'lose' 10 posts) that while I supported a policy of 'no compulsory redundancies', I had never said anything about

compulsory transfers. This turned out to be enough to stimulate half a dozen early retirements shortly afterwards.

17 I have referred a couple of times to 'the Western Campus'. This was on the site of the former Leeds Grammar School and an interesting set of circumstances created this opportunity. We speculated on developing the Boddington Hall site, and because the present use was university sports fields, we had to be in a position to replace them; we bought two farms in North Leeds for this purpose but we never proceeded to seek planning permission. When the Head of the Grammar School wanted to move, we sold the Leeds School one of these sites, thus facilitating our taking over the old Grammar School site as the Western Campus.

18 Later, all of this machinery was in fact absorbed into the Business School – the Christensen argument kicks in here: some *post-hoc* rationalisation on my part.

19 This was the second attempt. The first time, we flew to Heathrow only to find that all flights to Jersey were cancelled because of fog.

20 An early business for Robert was doing the surface work on all the coalfields and he wanted to put something back into these communities.

21 It was perhaps not a coincidence the Robert and I were knighted in the same Honours list: Birthday 2001.

22 Peter Housden, Tom Jeffrey, Janice Shiner, myself, Peter Makeham, Susan Thomas, and Michael Stevenson.

23 There were times when I found myself being protective.

24 I was in the Gallery for the debate. Charles opened and Alan wound up. There was a lively celebration on the Terrace afterwards.

25 She succeeded!

26 We combined all our research into a book: Dearden and Wilson (2015).

27 Presentations – my diary lists around 25 presentations of a formal kind per annum through this period.

28 Hall and Pesenti (2017).

29 See National Infrastructure Commission (2018).

30 Guo et al. (2017); Ellam et al. (2018).

31 See Roumpani (2019).

Bibliography

Alexander, C. (1964) *Notes on the synthesis of form*, Harvard University Press, Cambridge, MA.

Alpaydin, E. (2016) *Machine learning*, MIT Press, Cambridge, MA.

Andersson, C. (2005) *Urban evolution*, Department of Physical Resource Theory, Chalmers University of Technology, Gothenburg.

Arthur, W. B. (1988) Urban systems and historical path dependence, in Ausubel, J. H. and Herman, R. (eds) *Cities and their vital systems: Infrastructure, past, present and future*, National Academy Press, Washington, DC.

Arthur, W. B. (2009) *The nature of technology*, The Free Press, New York.

Arts and Humanities Research Council (2009) *Leading the world: The economic impact of UK arts and humanities research*, AHRC, Swindon.

Ashby, W. R. (1956) *An introduction to cybernetics*, Chapman and Hall, London.

Baghai, M., Coley, S., and White, D. (1999) *The alchemy of growth*, Perseus Publications, Cambridge, MA.

Barber, M. (2015) *How to run a government*, Penguin, Harmondsworth.

Batty, M. and Milton, R. (2021) A new framework for very large-scale urban modelling, *Urban Studies*, doi:10.1177.0042098020982252.

Baudains, P. and Wilson, A. (2016) Conflict modelling: Spatial interaction as threat, in Wilson, A. (ed.) *Global dynamics*, Wiley, Chichester, pp. 145–158.

Becher, T. (1989) *Academic tribes and territories*, Open University Press, Milton Keynes.

Beer, S. (1972) *Brain of the firm*, John Wiley & Sons, Chichester.

Beer, S. (1994) *Designing freedom*, John Wiley & Sons, Chichester.

Birkin, M., Clarke, G. P., Clarke, M., and Wilson, A. G. (1996) *Intelligent GIS: Location decisions and strategic planning*, Geoinformation International, Cambridge.

Boyce, D. and Williams, H. (2015) *Forecasting urban travel*, Edward Elgar, London.

British Academy (2008) *Punching our weight: The humanities and social sciences in public policy making*, British Academy, London.

Caro, R. (2021) *Working*, Vintage, London.

Christensen, C. M. (1997) *The innovator's dilemma*, Harper Business, New York.

Cisco (2007) *Equipping every learner for the 21st century*, Cisco Systems Inc, San Jose, CA.

Clarke, G. P. (ed.) (1996) *Microsimulation for urban and regional policy analysis*, Pion, London.

Clarke, G. P., Clarke, M., and Wilson, A. G. (1986) Re-examining old problems with new methods: Portbury re-visited, *Environment and Planning, C*, 4, 353–374.

Clarke, G. P. and Wilson, A. G. (1987a) Performance indicators and model-based planning I: The indicator movement and the possibilities for urban planning, *Sistemi Urbani*, 2, 79–123.

Clarke, G. P. and Wilson, A. G. (1987b) Performance indicators and model-based planning II: Model-based approaches, *Sistemi Urbani*, 9, 138–165.

Clarke, M. (2020) *How geography changed the world, and my small part in it*, Sweet Design Ltd, Bristol.

Coyle, D. (2025) *The measure of progress: Counting what really matters*, Princeton University Press, Princeton, NJ.

Davies, D. (2024) *The unaccountability machine: Why big systems make terrible decisions – and how the world lost its mind*, Profile Books Ltd, London.

Davies, T., Fry, H., Wilson, A. G., and Bishop, S. R. (2013) A mathematical model of the London riots and their policing, *Nature Scientific Reports, 3*, 1303. doi:10.1038/srep01303.

Dearden, J. and Wilson, A. G. (2015) *Explorations in urban and regional dynamics*, Routledge, Abingdon.

Defence Scientific Advisory Council (2014) Triennial review report, 24 March, Ministry of Defence, London.

Department of Health (1994) *Being heard: The report of a review committee on NHS complaints procedures*, Department of Health, London.

Department of Health (1995) *Acting on complaints*, Department of Health, London.

Department of Levelling Up, Housing and Communities (2022) *Levelling up*, HMSO, London.

Department of Trade and Industry (1999) *Biotechnology clusters*, HMSO, London.

Dixon, T. and Tewdwr-Jones, M. (2021) *Urban futures*, University of Bristol Press, Bristol.

Education Policy Institute (2021) Analysis paper: Preliminary research findings on education recovery, Education Policy Institute, London. Available at: https://epi.org.uk/publications-and-research/analysis-paper-preliminary-research-findings-on-education-recovery/.

Ellam, L., Girolami, M., Pavliotis, G., and Wilson, A. (2018) Stochastic modelling of urban structure, *Proceedings of the Royal Society A*, 474, 20170700, http://dx.doi:10.1098/rspa.2017.0700.

Foster, C. D. and Beesley, M. E. (1963) Estimating the social benefit of constructing an underground railway in London, *Journal of the Royal Statistical Society, A*, 126, 46–92.

Freedman. S. (2024) *Failed state: Why nothing works and how we fix it*, Macmillan, London.

Glass, N. M. (1996) *Management masterclass: A practical guide to the new realities of business*, Nicholas Brealey, London.

Gould, P. (1972) Pedagogic review, *Annals of the Association of American Geographers*, 62 (4), 689–700.

Government Office for Science (2013) Future of cities project report. Available at: https://www.gov.uk/government/uploads/system/uploads/attachment_data/file/520963/GS-16-6-future-of-cities-an-overview-of-the-evidence.pdf.

Guo, W., Gleditsch, K., and Wilson, A. (2019) Retool AI to forecast and limit wars, *Nature*, 562, 331–333.

Guo, W., Mosquera Donate, G., Law, S., Johnson, S. M., Liakata, M., and Wilson, A. (2017) Urban analytics: Multiplexed and dynamic community networks, paper presented at Advances in Data Science conference, Manchester, May.

Hall, W. and Pesenti, J. (2017) *Growing the artificial intelligence industry in the UK*, DCMS and BEIS, London.

Harris, B. and Wilson, A. G. (1978) Equilibrium values and dynamics of attractiveness terms in production-constrained spatial-interaction models, *Environment and Planning, A*, 10, 371–388.

Harris, R., Sleight, P., and Webber, R. (2005) *Geodemographics, GIS and neighbourhood targeting*, Wiley, Chichester.

Hicks, C. (2021) Experience: I was orphaned at Christmas – and saved by kind strangers, *The Guardian*, 17 December.

Hotelling, H. (1929) Stability in competition, *Economic Journal*, 39, 41–57.

Huber, H., Spiekermann, K., and Wegener, M. (2011) Cities and climate change: A simulation model of the Ruhr Area 2050, in *Proceedings, REAL CORP 2011*. Essen. Available at: programm.corp.at/cdrom2011/en/proceedings.html.

Jacobs, J. (1970) *The economy of cities*, Jonathan Cape, London.

Jordan, M. I. (2019) Artificial intelligence: The revolution hasn't happened yet, *Harvard Data Science Review*, 7 (1), doi:10.1162/99608f92.f06c6e6.

Lakshmanan, T. R. and Hansen, W. G. (1965) A retail market potential model, *Journal of the American Institute of Planners*, 31, 134–143.

Layard, R. and Glaister, S. (1994) *Cost-benefit analysis*, Cambridge University Press, Cambridge.

Leeds Schools Commission (1993) *The new partnership: Quality, governance, choice and resources*, Leeds City Council, Leeds.

Leontief, W. (1967) *Input-output analysis*, Oxford University Press, Oxford.

Lotka, A. J. (1925) *The elements of physical biology*, Williams and Wilkins, Baltimore, MD.

Lowry, I. S. (1964) *A model of metropolis*, RM-4035-RC, The Rand Corporation, Santa Monica, CA.

Marchione, E., Johnson, S. D., and Wilson, A. (2016) Agent-based models of piracy, in Wilson, A. (ed.) *Geo-mathematical modelling*, Wiley, Chichester, pp. 217–236.

Marchione, E. and Wilson, A. (2016) Spatial interaction as threat: Modelling maritime policy, in Wilson, A. (ed.) *Global dynamics*, Wiley, Chichester, pp. 187–194.

Marris, R. (1964) *The economic theory of managerial capitalism*, Palgrave Macmillan, London.

McKinsey and Company (2007) How the world's best school systems come out on top, McKinsey and Company, London.

Medda, F. R., Caravelli, F., Caschili, S., and Wilson, A. (2017) *Collaborative approach to trade: Enhancing connectivity in sea- and land-locked countries*, Springer, Heidelberg.

Miller, R. E. and Blair, P. D. (2022) *Input-output analysis: Foundations and extensions*, 3rd edn, Cambridge University Press, Cambridge.

Ministry of Transport (1966) Portbury: Reasons for the Minister's decision not to authorise the construction of a new dock at Portbury, Bristol, HMSO, London.

Mintzberg, H. (1989) *Structure in fives: Designing effective organisations*, Prentice-Hall, Englewood Cliffs, NJ.

Mintzberg, H. and Quinn, J. B. (1992) *The strategy process*, Prentice-Hall, Englewood Cliff, NJ.

National Infrastructure Commission (2018) *Data for the public good*, The Alan Turing Institute, London.

National Science Learning Centre (2008) The STEM framework, University of York, York.

O'Neil, O. (2002) A question of trust, Reith Lectures, BBC, London.

Palsson, B. O. (2006) *Systems biology: Properties of reconstructed networks*, Cambridge University Press, Cambridge.

Pontzen, A. (2023) *The universe in a box*, Jonathan Cape, London.

Rees, P. H. and Wilson, A. G. (1976) *Spatial population analysis*, Edward Arnold, London.

Rittel, H. W. J. and Webber, M. M. (1973) Dilemmas in a general theory of planning, *Policy Sciences*, 4, 155–169.

Roumpani, F. (2019) The role of procedural cities in the future of planning: An integrated method, PhD thesis, University College London.

Royal Society (2019) *Harnessing education research*, British Academy and the Royal Society, London.

Schintler, L. A. (2023) Alan Wilson: A renaissance man in regional science, in Batey, P. and Plane, D. (eds) *Great minds in regional science*, vol. 2, Springer Nature, Cham, Switzerland, pp. 249–267.

Schlecty, P. C. (2005) *Creating great schools: Six critical systems at the heart of educational innovation*, Jossey-Bass, San Francisco, CA.

Sen, A. (1999) *Commodities and capabilities*, Oxford University Press, Oxford.

Singleton, A. D., Spielman, S. E., and Folch, D. C. (2018) *Urban analytics*, Sage, London.

Spooner, F., Abrams, J, Morrissey, K., Shaddick, J., Matty, M., Milton, R. Dennett, A., Lomax, N., Malleson, N., Nelissen, N., Coleman, A., Nur, J., Greig, R., Shenton, C., and Birkin, M. (2021) A dynamic microsimulation model for epidemics, *Social Science and Medicine*, 291. www.sciencedirect.com/science/article/pii/S.

Tanton, R. and Edwards, K. L. (eds) (2013) *Spatial microsimulation: A reference guide for users*, Springer, Heidelberg.

Turing, A. M. (1952) The chemical basis of morphogensis, *Philosophical Transactions of the Royal Society of London, Series B*, 237, 37–72.

Volterra, V. (1938) Population growth, equilibria and extinction under specified breeding conditions: A development and extension of the theory of the logistic curve, *Human Biology*, 10.

Weaver, W. (1948) Science and complexity, *American Scientist*, 36, 536–544.

Weaver, W. (1958) A quarter century in the natural sciences, in *Annual Report*, The Rockefeller Foundation, New York, pp. 7–122.

Webber, R. and Burrows, R. (2018) *The predictive postcode? The geodemographic classification of British society*, Sage, London.

Williams, H. C. W. L. (1977) On the formation of travel demand models and economic evaluation measures of user benefit, *Environment and Planning, A*, 9, 285–344.

Wilson, A. G. (1967) A statistical theory of spatial distribution models, *Transportation Research*, 1, 253–269.

Wilson, A. G. (1970) *Entropy in urban and regional modelling*, Pion, London.

Wilson, A. G. (1972) Understanding the city of the future. *University of Leeds Review*, 15, 135–166.

Wilson, A. G. (1974) *Urban and regional models in geography and planning*, John Wiley & Sons, Chichester.

Wilson, A. G. (2000) The widening access debate: Student flows to universities and associated performance indicators, *Environment and Planning, A*, 32, 2019–2031.

Wilson, A. G. (2010a) *Knowledge power: Interdisciplinary education for a complex world*, Routledge, Abingdon.

Wilson, A. G. (2010b) Knowledge power: Ambition and reach in a re-invented university, in Munck, R. and Mohrman, K. (eds) *Re-inventing the university*, Glasnevin Publishing, Dublin, pp. 29–36.

Wilson, A. G. (2010c) Entropy in urban and regional modelling: Retrospect and prospect, *Geographical Analysis*, 42, 364–394.

Wilson, A. G. (2012) *The science of cities and regions: Lectures on mathematical model design*, Springer, London.

Wilson, A. G. (ed.) (2013) *Urban modelling: Critical concepts in urban studies*, 5 vols, Routledge, Abingdon.

Wilson, A. G. (ed.) (2016a) *Global dynamics: Approaches from complexity science*, John Wiley, Chichester.

Wilson, A. G. (ed.) (2016b) *Approaches to geo-mathematical modelling: New tools for complexity science*, John Wiley, Chichester.

Wilson, A. G. (2016c) New roles for urban models: Planning for the long term, *Regional Studies, Regional Science*, 3 (1), 48–57, doi:10.1080/21681376.2015.1109474.

Wilson, A. G. (2018) Research and innovation in an ecosystem, *FST Journal*, 22, 9–10.

Wilson, A. G. (2020) Epidemic models with geography: A new perspective on r-numbers, ArXiv, 2005.07673 [physics.soc-ph], doi:10.48550/arXiv.2005.07673.

Wilson, A. G. (2021) Entropy in urban and regional modelling, in Reggiani, A., Schintler, L. A., and Czamanski, S. (eds) *Handbook on entropy, complexity and spatial dynamics: A rebirth of theory*, Edward Elgar, Cheltenham, pp. 20–31.

Wilson, A. G. (2022) *Being interdisciplinary: Adventures in urban science and beyond*, UCL Press, London.

Wilson, A. G., Hawkins, A. F., Hill, G. J., and Wagon, D. J. (1969) Calibrating and testing the SELENEC transport model, *Regional Studies*, 3, 337–350.

Wilson, A. G. and Oulton, M. J. (1983) The corner-shop to supermarket transition in retailing: The beginnings of empirical evidence, *Environment and Planning, A*, 15, 265–274.

Wilson, A. G. and Pownall, C. M. (1976) A new representation of the urban system for modelling and for the study of micro-level interdependence, *Area*, 8, 256–264.

Wilson, A. G. and Senior M. L. (1974) Some relationships between entropy maximising models, mathematical programming models and their duals, *Journal of Regional Science*, 14, 207–215.

Wilson, A. G. (1963) Direct measurement of ≅− and ≅°C lifetimes, *Physical Review Letters*, March.

Index

accessibilities 81
account ability 53
accounts 87; open 42
Ada Lovelace Institute 154
Adams, J. 64
Adonis, A. 138
Ahnert, R. 153
AHRC 141–142, 153
AI 90–92; for science and government 154–155
Alan Turing Institute 23, 67, 146–155
AlphaGo 91
analytics 87–101
Ashby, J. 114
Ashby, R. 3
Aston, Sir John 147, 151
Atkins, J. 148

Barber, M. 52, 61, 68
Barnard, J. 119
Barnett, Lord 66, 137
Batty, M. 101, 140
Beaumont, J. 120
Beer, S. 3, 53
Beesley, M. 109
Bertuglia, S. 121
big picture 3
biotech 17–18
Birkin, M. 118, 121
Blackman, A. 151
Blunkett, David 64, 130
Blythe, P. 151
Boothroyd, Baroness 66–67, 137
Bottomley, Virginia 132
Bowe, Dame Colette 154
Boyd, Sir Ian 151
Bragg, Lord (Melvyn) 131–2
Briers, M. 148
British Academy 146
Brown, D. 148
budgets 42
Burren, J. 106

Cabinet Office 79
Cairncross, Sir Alec 118
Canada 109
Canterbury, Archbishop of 131
capability framework 77
Caro, R. A. 41–49
CASA 140; *see also* UCL
Castle, Barbara 112
Centre for Environmental Studies (CES) 114–115
CEO role 29, 41, 49 91
CERN 105–106
challenges, future 70–86; grand 85–86
Channell Tunnell 118
ChatGPT 90–91
Chilver, Lord 114–115
Christensen, C. 48, 62, 68, 71
Cisco 44, 141; formula 9, 32–33, 71–72
cities, Centre for 146; future of group 15–16,36, 144–145; levelling-up 75–79; planning 99
Clarke, Charles 134, 136
Clarke, Graham 118, 120
Clarke, Greg 151
Clarke, Martin 118–119, 133; *see also* GMAP Ltd
Clothworkers Company 66, 131
Coelho, J. 120
Collins, Sir Kevan 80
complexity, types of 88
Cooke, E. 148
Cormode, G. 148
cosmology 88–89
cost-benefit analysis (CBA) 96, 113

COVID-19 71, 155
Covington, H. 147
Cowan, P. 113–114, 118
Coyle, Dame Diane 96
Cranfield University 67, 137
Cresti, M. 106
Cripps, E. 115
Croutchley, R. 120
Cullingworth, B. 114
Cystic Fibrosis Trust 152

data science 90–92
Davies, D. 53
Davies, Dame Sally 138, 151
Dearden, J. 140
Deep Mind 91
defence 24, 57–58; DSAC 36, 67, 143–144
delivery 51–69
demographics 95
devolution 30, 48
DFES 9, 33–35. 133–139; big strategic questions 34–35; CSA role 35, 135; PQA 136
disruptive technologies 48
Donnison, D. 115, 118

Eastern M. 106
economics 96–97
ecosystems 5
education 8–11, 31–35, 53–54, 62–67, 71–74; how financial management can change the culture 45–46; research 38, 146, 153
Ellam, L. 152
employment, personal 102–104
engineering 96; control 99
entropy-maximising models 97
Environment and Planning 114, 120
EPSRC 68, 140

Farmer, Sir Jeremy 152
Farquar, A. 153
finance 3–4, 41–49
Finkelstein, Sir Anthony 147
Forte, P. 120
Foster, Sir Christopher 108–109, 111–115
Freeman Fox Wilbur Smith Ltd 112

Gardam, T. 154
GDP 76
geography 97–98
Girolami, M. 148, 151
GMAP Ltd 48, 58, 120–123
Gombrich, C. 143, 155
Gonzales, S. 145
government 11–16, 55–58, 66–67; funding 46–47; funding of research 19–23, 33–36; joined-up 35–36, 75–83; *see also* cities
Grant, Sir Malcolm 141
Gregson, Sir Peter 145
Griffin, E. 153
Grindrod, P. 147
Guernion, N. 148
Guo, W. 152

Haag, G. 121
Haggett, P. 113, 115
Haight, F. 113
Hall, P. 114
Hall, W. 151, 154
Hansen, W. 109
Harris, B. 109–111, 119, 121
Harrison, A. J. 108
Harvey, S. 120
Harwell 105–106
Hawkey, P. 142
Head, R. 123
health 57; Dewsbury Health Authority, 120; NHS Com plaints Process 132
HEFCE 9, 139, 142
Helliwell, Sir Keith 132
Hicks, C. 45
Holroyd, J. 132
HOSAC, 143
Hotelling, H. 98
Howells, K. 134

image processing 91
index of multiple deprivation 76
industry 16–18, 36–37, 58, 67, 83; classification 92
information system 3
Innovate UK 23
integration 61–69
interaction 87; spatial 109–111
interdependence 3, 88; chains 77
interdisciplinarity 3, 64, 99
initial conditions 89
Into the woods, 2
Irwin, S. 120

JISC 9, 35, 54–55, 142
Johnson, Alan 34–35, 134, 136
Jones, E. 144–146

Kelly, F. 136
Kelly, R. 66, 134, 137
Kenny, B. 131
Kent, Duchess of 131

Kenway, R. 147
Keyworth, M 43–44, 65, 130
Kind, C. 154
King, Sir David 136–138
Kirkby, M. 118
knowledge, requisite 98–99

Labour Party 106–108
Lakshmanan, T. G. 109
Langlands, Sir Alan 142
Lawrence, J. 153
leaders, what do leaders and managers do? 2
Lee, D. 123, 125
Leeds Grammar School 65
Leeds Schools Commission 66
Leeds 115–133; University of 31–32, 115–133: Bretton Hall; events 131; Chancellor's visits; Geography 116–121; GMAP Ltd 121–123; Pro-Vice-Chancellor 123–125; Vice-Chancellor 125–133
Legal and General 79
Leigh, C. 119
Leonardi, G. 119, 121
Liverpool Hope University 139
levelling-up 75–79; investment in education 82
life-long learning 33
Llewllyn-Davies, Lord 114
Lombardo, S. 121
London 111–115, 133–156; Greater London Council 113; *see also* DFES, UCL, The Alan Turing Institute 155–156
London Interdisciplinary School 155–156
Lotka, A. J. 97
Lowry I.S. (Jack) 109
Lynch, M. 91

McDonald, A. 120
Macgill, S. 64, 118, 126
McGillivray, B. 153
McIvor, S. 148
Mackett, R. 120
maintenance and development 31, 51
making things work 3–4, 61–69, 85–86
March, L. 114
marketing 47, 72
Marland, P. 145
Martin, B. 112
Massey, D. 114
Mathematical Adviser 112; Mathematical Advisory Unit (MAU) 112–113
Maxton, Dame Julie 154
Medda, F. 140, 155
Meyerson, M. 114
Mintzberg, H. 48, 51, 62, 71
Milton Keynes 36, 66–67, 137, 145
Milton, R. 101
models 3, 87–101; entropy-maximising 109–111; prey-predator, 98; competition-for-resources 98; and phase transitions, 98; and simulation 88–89; transport 109–111
Mulvey, J. 106

Nelson, P. 151
Nemer, el J. 150
Newby, Sir Howard 139
New Orleans 141
Newcastle 36, 145
New Zealand 152
NHS: data, 152; *see also* health
Norfolk 155
Normington, Sir David 133–135, 139
Nurse, Sir Paul 146

Oakleigh Consulting 142
Occelli, S. 121
Ogden, Sir Robert 44, 130, 133; scholarships 44
Oliver, S. 132
Open University 66–67, 105–111, 137
Oulton, M. 121
Oxford 105–111; University, Institute of Economics and Statistics, 108–111

PAD 5; for universities 10
Pagliara, F. 140
Pahl, R. 114
pandemics 24
Parkes, Sir Edward 123, 125
Pavliotis, G. 152
Pennsylvania, University of 119
Pesenti, J. 151
philanthropy 43–45
pillars, the four 3–5, 30–31; *see also* SSFS
politics 98
Pontzen, A. 88–89, 91
Portbury 12, 47, 112–113
Poston, T. 121
Pownall, C. 120
Price, C. 132
problem solving 3
Prospective Labs Ltd 23, 153
protein folding 91
Pro-Vice-Chancellor; *see* Leeds
publications, key personal 104

Quarmby, D. 112

radical change 70–86
Rabino, G. 121
Rammell, W. 134
Raven, K. 44, 130
Rees, P. 118–119
regions, three capabilities needed 33
requisite variety 3, 99; knowledge 98
research 19–23, 37–38, 48, 59, 67, 83–85, 99; assessment exercise (RAE) 66, translational 33
reserves 42
resource centres 65, 127
retail 17, 48, 100
Richardson, T. 107
Ridge, M. 152
Ridley, A. 112
Rihll, T. 121
Roberts, Colonel Alan 123–124
Rodden, T. 151
Roumpani, F. 152
Royal Society 146; Nominations Committee 146

Sainsbury, Lord 138
scales 87
Schaar, van der M. 148, 152
scholarships, *see* Ogden
schools science 9, 138
SDG (UN) 77
security 24
Seitz, R. 132
SELNEC (South East Lancashire North East Cheshire) 112
Sen, A. 77
Senior, M. 118
Silver, L. 132
Silverman, Sir Bernard 143, 151
simulation 88–89; as a new way of doing science 89
Smith, Sir Adrian 153
Snelson, G. 145
social inclusion 24
Solomon, G. 156
Spanier, G. 133
Spence, R. 112
Stevenson, M. 44, 141
Stewart, Sir William 132
Stibbs, A. 107
STM 5; for universities 10
strategy 3–4,29–38, 64; big strategic questions 34
strategy building tool, Baghai, Coley and White (BCW) 37, 47
structures 3–4, 51–69
superconcepts 3, 90, 99
supermarkets 100–101
sustainability 23–24
Swingler, S. 112
Sykes, Sir Richard 132
systems 3, 5–28, 87–101, 93–95

Tadei, R. 121
Teach First 80
technology 24, 96–97
teaching hospital, university 33
Thompson, A. 153
Torino, Politecnico di 119
transport: engineering 16–17; Ministry of 111–114
Transportation Research 113
Treasury, H. M. 79
Tressider J. 112
Trickett, J. 66, 132

unaccountability 53
underspend 42
United States, tour of 109
universities 31–33, 53–54, 62–66, 71–74; estate 65
University College London (UCL) 113, 139–146; Institute of Finance and Technology 155

Viner, N. 151
Volterra, V. 98
Voorhees, A. 109

Waggon, D. 112
Walkinshaw, W. 105
Walport, Sir Mark 36, 144, 151–153
Walsh, J. 123, 125
Watson, D. 123
Weaver, W. 88; types of system 88
Webber, M. 114
what works 61–69
White Rose Ltd 64, 132
Whitty, Sir Christopher 151
Wilkinson, C. 106
Williams H.C.W.L. 118
Willmott, P. 114
Working life: a personal memoir 105–156
World-wide Universities Network 64, 133
work-based learning 129

York, Archbishop of 131

Ziff, A. 132